16-14

The gradual passage from intuitive thinking, still tied to the information of the senses, towards operational thinking, which forms the basis of reasoning itself, may be studied in the light of the particularly simple examples which are found in the areas of movement and speed.

Through a series of brilliantly simple experiments, Piaget describes how the child forms his notions of movement and speed—concepts which relate especially to the child's comprehension of mathematics and general science.

"The unique contribution of Jean Piaget seems to me to be in the sensitive and imaginative way in which he has explored the inner world of the child's thought; the child's way of understanding the world, the social order and himself; and the long process of development from the infantile to the adult way of thinking. The observation of games and free play; the experimental method; and above all the method of the clinical interview permit the development of a systematic psychological framework for the understanding of the child, and of the dynamics of his growth towards adult ways of thinking."

—Gardner Murphy

THE CHILD'S CONCEPTION OF MOVEMENT AND SPEED

Jean Piaget

Translated from the French by

G. E. T. Holloway
and
M. J. Mackenzie

BALLANTINE BOOKS • NEW YORK
An Intext Publisher

Translated from the French *Les Notions de Mouvement et de Vitesse chez l'Enfant* Presses Universitaires de France 1946

English translation © 1970 by Routledge and Kegan Paul

Library of Congress Catalog Card Number: 70-84025

SBN 345-02372-2-165

This edition published by arrangement with Basic Books, Inc.

First Printing: November, 1971

Printed in the United States of America

Cover photograph by Morgan Kane

BALLANTINE BOOKS, INC.
101 Fifth Avenue, New York, N. Y. 10003

89331

Contents

List of Collaborators

Mlle *Barbara von Albertini* Senior Assistant at l'Institut J. J. Rousseau (Chapter Three).

Mlle *Madeleine Blanchet* Teacher in Geneva (Chapter Eleven).

Mlle *Esther Bussman* Senior Assistant at l'Institut J. J. Rousseau, Assistant at the Berne Institute of Applied Psychology (Chapters Two and Three).

M. and Mme. *Claude Ferrière* Diploma students at l'Institut J. J. Rousseau (Chapter Four).

Mme. *Olga Frank* Diploma student at l'Institut J. J. Rousseau (Chapter Ten).

M. *J. Frei* Teacher in Geneva (Chapter Eight).

Mlle *Monique Lagier* Teacher in Geneva (Chapter Eleven).

Mlle *Madeleine Martin* Diploma student at l'Institut J. J. Rousseau (Chapter Three).

M. *A. Mauris* Teacher in Geneva (Chapter Eight).

Mlle *Madeleine Reymond* Senior Assistant at l'Institut J. J. Rousseau, Assistant to The Vaud Educational Health Service at Lausanne (Chapters Six and Seven).

Preface

These studies of the child's conception of movement and speed are a sequel to those recently published on the formation of the concept of time, with which they are closely bound up by the very fact that these three basic concepts are interdependent.

But is it not overrating them to devote an entire work solely to the notions of movement and speed in a child's mental development? In fact we are very well aware of this, and the primary object of this foreword must be to justify ourselves to the reader. Our only excuse is the still surprisingly unrefined state of the knowledge we have of children's intellectual growth. While botanists have catalogued all the world's plants, and zoologists have counted the hairs upon every little animal, and that at each stage of their growth, the science of child development i.e. the embryology of the human spirit itself in effect, continues to be confined to general studies, upon which teaching techniques and therapy etc. can be based only in the most empirical fashion.

Now the concepts of movement and speed especially touch upon the fields of mathematics and general science teaching, in which it would be of great value to know precisely the way in which these concepts develop; in other words, their psychological as well as their logical build-up.

But there is still more. The most fruitful use of psychology will not be found purely by seeking an immediate application. The gradual passage from intuitive thinking, still tied to the information of the senses, towards operational thinking, which forms the basis of reasoning itself, may be studied in the light of the particularly simple examples which are to be found in the fields of movement and speed. It is this general position that we shall take up in the present work, and this is what justifies its size. Indeed when wishing to consider such questions, it is only by examining the facts step by step that one can hope to avoid indulging in mere verbal abstractions when one comes to making a synthesis.

In this work (as in previous works on the child's conception of number, quantity and time) we shall take the term 'operations', in a limited and well-defined sense, to mean actions or transformations at once reversible and capable of forming systematic wholes. We have tried to show that prior to the formation of mathematical 'groups', which always imply the occurrence of a metrical or at the least an extensive quantity, logical operations already form systems, which are likewise reversible and capable of synthesis (simple relations between the part and the whole), at the level of intensive quantity, though far less rich, which we have called 'groupings'. Such are the mechanisms which we shall find at the root of the first operational ideas of movement and speed, and that as a precondition of their subsequent mathematization.

We shall use the term intuition, or intuitive thinking, in an equally limited sense, and narrower than that of the mathematician in particular—for us it will mean preoperational thinking, i.e. thinking which relies only on perceptual configuration or on tentative empirical activity and is as yet unready for 'grouping' or 'groups'. It is necessary, therefore, to speak here of 'image-using intuition', or even 'perceptual intuition' as opposed to rational intuition, but for brevity we shall confine ourselves to talking of intuition alone.

Thus, the essential problem which we shall study in relation to movement and speed is the passage from image-using or perceptual intuition to the forming of operational systems. We were earlier leading up to the study of a child's conception of movement through the analysis of his attempts to explain movement in nature and assign a cause to it. We laid stress on the child's animism in this respect, attaching as he does a consciousness and a purpose to moving things, and above all, on his finalism and his dynamism: all movement tends towards a goal and implies an inherent vital or creative power. Hence a number of curious analogies with Aristotle's physics, in particular the hypothetical need for two motive forces, one internal and the other external, to explain a movement like that of clouds or river water, and above all, a very systematic diagram of 'environmental reaction' attributing the motion of missiles to the responsive action of the displaced air.

These facts will not be returned to in the present work, but it is useful to recall them, to illuminate the operational development of the conception of movement and speed. In fact, it is through this teleology, always more or less coloured with animism, that one understands the important place given by children's intuition to the 'point of arrival' of the movement and consequently to 'overtaking' in the reckoning of speed. The ideas of order and 'placing' which play, as we shall see, a fundamental rôle in the formation of these concepts are to be explained in this respect, as sharing in physics which are imbued with finalism and the idea of the proper place, and where purely qualitative or intensive operations long precede mathematical or extensive operations. But, to reiterate, our emphasis will be exclusively on this operational aspect of development.

PART 1

Successive Order or Placing

The two chapters which form this first part are devoted to the study of the order of succession, linear or recurring in cycles, by way of introduction to the analysis of change of location itself. The idea of movement implies in fact the idea of order first of all, in both mathematics and psychology: viewed fundamentally, a change of position is of necessity related to a system of positions, i.e. to be precise, positions conforming to a particular order. That is why we shall begin the analysis of the development of the conceptions of movement and speed with the evolution of the idea of order. But as we are not examining the child's relation to geometry, but solely his relation to movement, we shall here choose as examples of succession not points on a static line, but objects transported by one and the same movement whether linear or cyclic. From the point of view of operations of order or disposition this comes to the same thing, and from the psychological point of view, there will be the benefit of placing these operations in an intuitive context of movement from the outset.

CHAPTER ONE

The Problem of Alternative Directions of Travel

Let us consider three elements A, B and C, such that A precedes B, and B precedes C, during a movement from right to left A←B←C. We achieve this in three different ways: Technique 1. Three beads, A=red, B=black, and C=blue are threaded on a small piece of wire; this is then placed within one's half-closed hand with the two ends of the wire projecting, then the beads are made to reappear on the other side in the same order ABC, then to retrace their path in inverse order CBA etc. Technique 2. Three small wooden balls A=red, B=brown and C=yellow are placed in a chute made of cardboard in the order ABC and are guided with A leading, into a tunnel occupying the central part of the slide to emerge in the same order or to return in inverse order. Technique 3. Three little wooden dolls A=blue, B=green, and C=yellow, are strung on a wire and pass in the same order of A←B←C behind a screen. The following questions are asked systematically, although giving way to free conversation in so far as may be profitable, depending on the child's reactions.

Q 1. In what order will the objects emerge at the other side of the hand, tunnel or screen?

Q 2. In what order will the objects reappear, on travelling through the tunnel (or passing behind the screen) in the opposite direction?
Note: The child draws the objects with suitably coloured pencils in the direct order (either after or before Q 1). so as to serve as a reminder. To solve Q 2. then, he has

3

only to look at his paper and read off the colours in reverse order. In this way the problem of reasoning is quite
separate from memory.

Q. 3. When the first two questions are solved (and if they
are not at the first trial, the experiment is repeated until the
child is sure of the answer), one then presents Q 3 and 4.
(Q 3 applies only to the Technique 2). The objects are
inserted in the direct order ABC into the tunnel, after
which the child is asked to change places and sit at the
other side of the table. If in his starting position the
movement took place from right to left, it will now appear
from left to right in the subject's new position: he is then
asked in what order the balls will emerge on the right
hand side and he should realize that this will be the direct
order though he himself has changed his place in relation
to the tunnel and so the balls seem to retrace their path. In
other words the child must judge their order of progress
from the starting point of the balls and not according to
the left and the right of the tunnel. This question involves the two ways in which the child may judge the
direction of travel when faced with the same objective
order.

Q 4. The three objects are put back, in view of the child,
in the order ABC, whether within the hand or into the
tunnel or behind the screen, and a rotary movement 180°
is described either with the hand and the wire jointly
(Technique 1), or with the cardboard tunnel (Technique
2) or by the wire alone (Technique 3). Care is taken that
the movement is fully visible, describing what is being
done[1] and drawing attention, in Technique 1 and 3 to the
ends of the wire visible in the process of turning on itself.
This semi-rotation completed, one asks in what order the
objects will emerge, in the same place as that where in Q 1
they came out in the direct order. This Q 4, thus bears,
like Q 2 on the inverse order, but owing to the rotation of

---

[1] The semi-rotation is made on the horizontal or on the vertical
plane.

the apparatus, and no longer to a simple sending back as in Q 2.

Q 5. Same question as 4 but with two successive semi-rotations (in the same direction), either in two moves, 180° + 180°, or in one move: 360°.

Q 6. Same questions for a random number of semi-rotations, either uneven (=emerging in inverse order) or even (=emerging in direct order).

Q 7. If up till now the child has not spontaneously thought that the middle object B could come out in first place, in any of the preceding situations, the question is then put as follows. A random number of semi-rotations is described (about 10 but without counting) and one asks which object 'might emerge first? Could it be A? or C? or B?' Each time one asks why, or why not, and in the case of an affirmative for B, 'How could that happen?' (it should be stated that the tunnel in Technique 2 is of a diameter hardly greater than the balls, to avoid any leap frogging).

Finally, the same Q 1 to 7 may be asked in relation to four or five objects, and not merely to three.

The following stages were observed among the responses made by about fifty children between 4 and 8 years of age. In stage I the child is able to answer Q 1 (which is without doubt the case from the second year on) but not Q 2, i.e. simple inverse order. In the course of stage II, Q 2 is solved, but not 3 to 5, at least not at the first attempt; during the second half of this stage (sub-stage IIB), by contrast, Q 3 and 4 produce an immediate reply while 5 and 6 as yet only produce wavering attempts. During a third stage, finally, Q 1 to 5 are solved at once and soon after lead to a generalization in the form of a solution to Q 6. As for Q 7 which is concerned with the central object, at the start of stage I, the child spontaneously allows that B could come out first or last as well as staying between A and C; towards the end of this stage he is seldom inclined to think of such a transformation himself, but it is enough for the question to be asked in the form already observed, for him to accept it without more being said. From stage II on he thinks it impossible for the order to be broken in the case of three objects, B staying in the middle in both directions of travel; for five elements, however, it still happens in the course of this stage that objects not at either end may spontaneously be thought capable of coming out first.

1. The first stage: Path retraced without inverting the order and displacement of middle object

This first stage ends on average towards 5 years of age but it is not unusual for examples to be found up to 5½ years. Here are some examples.

AN (4 years). Technique 2. Which will come first out of the tunnel? The red one (A). And then? The brown one (B) and the yellow (C). (dem). And now they are coming back, which one will come out first? The red one, the brown, and the yellow one. Look! (dem). Oh, no, it's the yellow, then the brown and the red. Why? Because coming back it's the yellow one. Fine. And now, look, I'm turning the tunnel, (Q 4). Which will be first this time? The red, then the brown, then the yellow one. Look! (dem). It's the yellow one. Why? Because I didn't know. We'll start again. It will be the yellow one. (dem). Why? Don't know.

Right then, look: I am going to turn it twice, you see, one, two. Which will come first now? The brown one (B). Why? Because you turned it two times. But why is it the brown one first if it's turned twice? . . . (dem). Look! The red one! (A). Why? Don't know. And now I'm going to turn it three times, look. This will be? The yellow one, no, the brown! Why? Because you did it three times. (dem). Well? Oh, the yellow one! Why? Don't know. And now? (Five to six half turns). The brown one (B). Why? Because you turned it lots of times. Can the balls in the tunnel jump over each other? No. Why? The hole is too little. Good. And where is the brown one? In the middle. Then which is going to come out first? The brown one. Look! Oh, dear no, it's the yellow one. What does it mean when the brown one is in the middle? That it is behind the red one and behind the yellow one. Fine. Now look (several turns). Which will be first? *It's the yellow one*. And now? (several more turns). *The red*. And now (rep.)? *The yellow*. And now (rep.)? *And now it's the brown one!* Why? *Because you turned it I don't know how many times!* Look! Oh, no, still not that one.

Technique 3. Can these little fellows hop over each other? *No, because there's a wire*. Right; then which one will be first out there? (Q 1). *The blue (A)*. And after that? *The green (B) and the yellow (C)*. Is that right? (dem). *Yes*. And now, coming back? *The yellow one* (dem). And if I turn the wire this way? (Q 4). *The blue one*. (dem). Oh, no, *it's the yellow one because you turned the wire round*. And now, if I turn it twice? *The blue one*. And if I turn three times? *The blue* (dem). *No, the yellow one*. And if I turn it four times? *That will be the green one (B) first*. Why? *Because the green one (B) is after the blue one (A)*. (dem). Is that right? *No, it's the blue*. And now? (turning some more) *The green one!* (B).

Ros (4; 6). Technique 2. Which one will come out first? *The red one (A)*. And then? *The brown (B) and yellow (C) ones*. Now you see? (dem). The journey's over. They're going back into the tunnel and will come out this side. Which will be first? *The red (A)*. Why? *Because there it is* (pointing to the first in direct order) *and Look!* (dem). That's not right. Why? . . . And now? (first direction). *The red* (dem). Yes. And this way? (back)? *The yellow*. (dem). Yes. And now I am going to turn the tunnel. (Q 4). Which will be first? *The red one*. Look! (dem). No, the yellow. Once more (going back to the starting point). *The red one*. (dem). No, again it's the yellow. Why? *Because it always goes this way* (pointing to the pathway travelled). And why is the red one last? *Because it stayed back there*.

Technique 3. Which? *Blue (A) then green (B) then yellow (C)*. And coming back? *Blue, green, yellow* (going to dem). No, yellow, green, blue. Look, now, I'm turning it. (Q 4). Which will be out first? *Blue*. (dem). Right? *No*. Why not? *Because it's behind the yellow one. The bit of wire turned round*. (New try). *Yellow*. (dem). Yes. Why? *Because it turned the other way*. And after it? *Green*. Why? *Because that's behind the yellow one*. (turning several times) Which will be first? *Blue (A) or yellow (C) or green (B)*. Can the green one be first? *Yes*. How would it do that? . . . (turning five or six times). Which do you think? *Green*. What's that? . . . Look (showing the wire stem and the three

dolls). *It can't.* Why? *Because of the wire.* And now (turning
more than ten times)? *The green one this time!* Why? *It
turned.* Was it at the front? *In the middle.* And if you turn
it, can that one come first? *Yes.* Look! *No.* And this time
(five more turns). Can the green one be first? *Yes.*

JAC (4; 8). Technique 2. Direct order, correct. Inverse order:
first, confusion with direct order; then correction by experience and three correct answers in a row. Could the black
come first (B)? *It probably could.* (Return to direct order
and child moves to other side of table: Q 3). *That will be
the yellow one* (C). Why? *That's the way it goes* (judging
from left to right without taking into account that the tunnel's opening, for balls travelling in inverse order, is no longer
on the right. Look! (dem). *No, the red one* (A). And now
(rep)? *The red one* (dem). Right. And now? (same) *Yellow*
(C). Look! (dem). *No red again.* Look, now, I'm turning
it. (Q 4). *Red* (then points out alternately the three colours).
With five colours, direct order successful, but again not in
the case of inverse order.

FRAN (4; 10). Technique 2. Direct order: right. Inverse
order: expects direct order again. *Red* (A) *then brown* (B)
and yellow (C). (dem). Is that right? *No, because the red
one came out first here* (far left) *and there* (to the right) *it
came down another way.* Look again. (direct order). *Red.*
And now (inverse order). *Yellow.* That's right. Now I am
going to turn the tunnel round. (4). Which will come out
first? *Red, because it's there* (showing left end of tunnel).
Right? (dem). *No, because it was turned round.* (another
try) *Yellow* (correct). And now I'm turning it twice. *Yellow.*
Look. Is that right? *No, because it got turned the other way.*
How many times did I turn it for red? *Twice.* And when I
turned it once? *Yellow.* And if I turn three times? *The yellow
one again.* And four times? (dem). *The brown* (B). Why?
Because it turned four times. Look! (dem). *Oh, no, red
again!*
   Technique 3. Direct order correct and inverse order at first
confused with direct. And if I turn the wire (Q 4)? *Blue* (A).
Look. *Oh, no, yellow* (C). Why? And if I turn it twice
(doing it but concealing result)? *Green* (B). Why? *Because
it was turned twice.* Where was it? *After the blue one, in the
middle.* And if I turn it twice, it will come first? *Yes, because
of it turning twice.* But how will it come first? *You make it*

move in front of the blue one. What has it got right through its middle? A wire. Then it's easy for it to hop across the blue one? No. Then if I turn it twice, which will come first? Green!

DER (5; 6) begins (Technique 2) by thinking that inverse order will be the same as direct order. Look! (dem). No, it's changed now. Why? Because when they came back, they didn't turn round. So it's yellow (C). (Another try correct). Look now! I'm turning the tunnel round (Q 4). Red (A) then brown (B) then yellow (C). Is that right? (dem). Oh, no, it's yellow! But over there (= on the right before the half turn) it was yellow last and now it's yellow first over there (= on the right after the half turn). How did it change? What do you think? Oh, its because you turned the box round (= the tunnel) (Another try: right). Good. Now then I'll turn it several times. Which might be first? I think it will be red now because it was yellow before. (compensation!) And now look! They're the same as before. (ABC). I turn it twice. Which is first? It will be brown! (Confidently). Why? Because you did it twice. Why? Before that it was behind the red one and in front of the yellow one: in the middle. How can it get to one end if it's in the middle? Maybe this is the way it could happen: brown starts off in the middle and after that brown is at one end. Look! (dem). Oh, no, its' red. Again (dem). Yellow! Once more! (dem.) Red! Again! (dem). Yellow Again! (dem). Red! And now, one more time? It will be yellow. And why is it never brown? Because the brown one can't turn round and come out at this side. And now I'm turning it lots of times (seven to eight). Which one will be out first? Yellow (C) or else red (A) or else brown (B)!

Technique 3. Same commencement with confusion of inverse and direct order. Then Q 4: It will be blue (A) because coming this way (= from the left) it's blue. Look! (dem). Oh, no, it's changed because you turned it. On subsequent tries he forecasts by turns A or C. Why not green (B)? Because you'd have to take away the other ones. I'm going to turn it a bit faster. Which one first? Green (B). Why? Because you did it that way!

These responses in stage I are of some interest in connection with the psychology of the intuition of order, and for the study of the relation between intuition and operation.

We note first of all that all the subjects interviewed, from 4 years upwards, are able to solve Q 1, i.e. they have awareness of direct order and its conservation during a lateral movement: they are sure that three balls unable to overtake one another, and three mannikins or three beads strung on a wire will be in the same order at the other end of a tunnel or cardboard screen. That this awareness is due, in part at least, to experience is obvious. An infant a few months old not yet possessed of the outlines of the conservation of the object would not, under the conditions we have just described, be able to foresee conservation of order. But once the invariability of objects, and the relations of cause and effect preventing them from travelling over one another out of one position into another inside the tunnel or along the wire are recognized, the conservation of order during a direct journey ('outwards') is plain sailing for the child and fits intuitive evidence with three objects.

In contrast—and a very characteristic thing about preoperational intuition—from the beginning—the subjects in this stage I do not manage to deduce the order of the objects on the return journey to be the inverse of their order on the outward journey. Lasting for a longer or a shorter time according to the subjects, their mistake then consists in accepting that when the objects have moved off in the order ABC they can come back only in that same order, as though it were some sort of stroll during which the participants follow one another without ever changing places. It is obvious that no serious difficulty should prevent the child from visualizing their returning in the order CBA, the first one now last and vice versa, since experience might already have given the child numerous examples of these reversals. Moreover, it should be enough for the child to look more closely at the cardboard tunnel, or the fixing of the mannikins, to see that on the way back the objects cannot resume direct order, since they cannot change places with one another; we stress in each interview the impossibility of overtaking and passing. Then why does the child not think of inverse order, preferring to keep direct order which, on reflection, would imply conditions impossible to fulfil with our apparatus? It is clearly, and this is the sole interest of these early replies to Q 2 that at this purely intuitive level, reasoning consists simply in retracing, by the act of representation, events just as they were perceived, instead of imagining an alteration or inversion. In the case of the order coming back, nothing would seem easier than to effect intuitively a 'mental experiment' describing the process in detail. That is what the subject seems to do as soon as experience in reality has put him in contact with inverse order. 'When they came back,' says Der for example, (after actually observing the return journey) 'they did not turn round; so it's yellow (C) first'. Or again 'It came down another way'. (Fran) etc. But the important point is exactly this, that the subject cannot manage to see this simple inversion before the actual experience and has to wait for the latter in order to imagine their return in inverse order. In other words, he is not yet able to anticipate intuitively this return in reverse, but only to recall and then to generalize it once it has been observed. In short, the subject refuses to imagine such a simple inversion because he is loath to attempt at all an act of representation other than a simple copy, and prefers therefore, from inertia, to preserve the perceptual figure ABC just as it is.

With Q 3 and 4 things change and the error observed is no longer due to this kind of mental sluggishness, but to a more stubborn and systematic difficulty. Q 3 presents no great interest in this stage because it implies the solving of Q 2, which happens only after two or three repetitions the experience of the return journey. Nevertheless, once this training is acquired one notes the following suggestive fact. (Jac): the child having learned, thanks to repeated observations, that object A always emerges from the left end of the tunnel and object C from the right end, does not reverse these results when he moves to the other side of the table, and now, seeing the former on his right expects object C to emerge. In other words, he does not reason in terms of direction of travel in relation to the tunnel, but in terms of a static indication of which he simply records the *absolute* position relative to his own body. It is precisely both this lack of understanding of relative direction of travel, and this recourse to reference to *absolute* position which we find in the responses to Q 4 and 6.

Q 4 gives rise, in fact, to answers of a notable uniformity, which range from complete lack of understanding of the effect of the semi-rotation, to the commencement of an empirical understanding. The reason for this failure is quite clear: convinced that object A emerges first on the right hand side and object C on the left, the subject no more takes into account the half-rotation of the tunnel or wire than he did his own change of place in Q 3. He thus judges once more in terms of the *static* indication established by the location of the extremity upon his right, and not in terms of the direction of travel, reversed by the semi-rotation of the line formed by the objects ABC or ABCDE. When the question is first given (with, of course, the child looking on while the tunnel or wire is turned, and only objects ABC out of sight) all subjects at this level expect that if the objects reappear on the right, the direct order ABC will plainly be maintained. But once the result of the experiment is observed, the child, while recognizing he was wrong, does not see why, or not immediately, and that is the essential difference from Q 2. It is true that the subject, taking into account what he has just seen, usually expects object C to be first again when the question is tried again. But the rest of the questioning reveals this to be purely empirical association without understanding why. It is also true that some subjects reply: 'it's because it was turned round', but this connecting of C in first place, with the half turn, which was at the same time in his sight and brought explicitly to his notice, still does not prove his understanding of the reason: e.g. Fran, who gives this answer at the first trial, (after his initial error based on absolute position: 'the red one because it's over there', i.e. on the right), thinks that on two successive half-turns it is once more object C which will lead out first. As for Der, he is astounded by what he observes, after his mistaken forecast: 'But over there (on right) it was yellow last and now over there it's yellow first (again on right)—how did it change?' To which he spontaneously answers: 'Oh, it's because you turned the box round'. He appears to understand perfectly, but subsequently he thinks that yellow (C) and red (A) will emerge by turns, irrespective of the number of half-turns. It is the same with Technique 3. To sum up then, at this stage two constant responses are observed on Q 4. First, the child expects direct order to persist despite rotation, because he estimates the order of appearance of the objects in relation to one or other extremity of the tunnel, or wire, depending on whether this extremity is upon his right or his left, not according to the direction of travel itself. Secondly, when the experiment is made and the error noted, the child does attribute the reversed order to the half-turn, but in a purely empirical way (post hoc, ergo propter hoc), and without visualizing the inversion of the objects themselves. The unforeseen appearance of object C instead of A seems to him a kind of lucky dip rather than a comprehensive result built up of the sequence of paths of travel. The proof is easy to show: it rests in the responses to Q 5 and 7.

Q 5 and 7 form in fact the natural compliment of problem 4. If the subject understands that a half-turn of 180° reverses the order, he will thereby understand that a second semi-rotation of 180° cancels out this reversal, in other words that a complete rotation of 360° does not alter the order at all. (Q 5). In fact if he thinks operationally, and not merely intuitively, he will see that a double inversion is a straightforward operation, i.e. that a double negative becomes a positive. On the other hand, if he abides by the empirical observation that a half-rotation alters the order, he cannot forecast the result of two half-rotations. Likewise Q 6 generalizes without elaboration on Q 5 and simply deals with the succession in turn of direct and inverse order.

Now the replies given during this stage to Q 5 and 6 are of great interest and reveal just how far the reactions of young children remain pre-operational. E.g. An expects after two half-turns the middle ball B will appear first; with three operatons he forecasts C or B, and when B still does not appear, he anticipates it after five or six semi-rotations. Der, seeing C leading the way after one half-turn thinks that with several rotations 'it will be red because it was yellow before', as if there should be some compensation in favour of A regardless of the number of turns! He applies this principle so thoroughly that in the case of two semi-rotations he goes on to forecast that the middle object B will take the lead. . . . In short, the subject in no way understands the relationship between the successive rotations, viz. (and this is what concerns us here) direction of travel and its reversal, which gives support to the replies to Q 3: instead of visualizing the hidden objects and imagining their sequence in one direction or the other, the child, being unable to fix upon their order according to the location, on his left or his right of the end in question (since this system is contradicted by the experiment) forecasts according to whim, manipulating frequency and compensation as if drawing lots among the objects.

This absence of any controlled mental representation, even in the way of intuitive anticipation, such as that of experiencing in fantasy, is particularly striking in Q 7. Without any prompting on the part of the experimenter, subjects of 4 to 5 years spontaneously suppose, in effect, that of three elements ABC in a straight line the median B can take precedence if the direction of travel is changed. It happens less often that the subject may expect to find B at the head, after a simple return journey, when he has noted from experience that it cannot be A. In contrast, when the tunnel or wire undergoes a semi-rotation the forecast for B is common. E.g. An expects to see B after two half-turns 'because you turned it twice'. The experiment producing A, he repeats the hypothesis B, 'because you turned it three times', and when the trial results in C, he once more expects B after n turns, 'because you turned it lots of times'. However he himself states that the balls cannot by-pass one another in the tunnel because 'the hole is too little', and that if B is in the middle it means 'it's

behind the red one (A) and behind the yellow one (C)',
hence in second place irrespective of direction of travel.
Nevertheless after some more turns and after forecasting
A and C, An. announces triumphantly, 'and now it will be
brown', 'because you turned it I don't know how many
times', as if the number of semi-rotations inevitably
changed the order round. Most significant is that after
noting 'Oh, no, still not that one', he resumes the same
hypothesis with Technique 3, even though the doll in the
centre, B, is transfixed by a metal strip in between A and
C! Ros, too, thinks it quite in order for the doll, B, to
appear first because 'it was turned round', after looking at
apparatus three and saying 'it cannot change places because of the wire'. Fran and others reason similarly. Der,
after noting his failures, seems to see it all ('you'd have to
take the others off'), but when it turns faster he returns to
his first idea 'because you turned it in that way'.

These facts, which are of great interest in the study of
the geometry of the child as well as his understanding of
movement, seem to us to involve two related conclusions,
the first concerns the nature of the relationship expressed
in 'between', and the second pre-operational intuition.

A celebrated axiom of Hilbert states that 'if B is situated between A and C, it is also between C and A'. In other
words, the relationship 'between' persists regardless of direction of travel, whether this continues to exist only in
the mind, or takes form in an actual movement. Far from
being an axiom for our subjects, this proposition begins by
being quite unrecognized by them. Later it comes to be
seen as a simple, experimental truth. Such an initial lack
of understanding, may we say right away, brings to mind
the behaviour of infants of 10 to 12 months who in order
to place a ring on a wire rod, do not slide the wire through
the hole in the ring but merely touch the wire with the
ring, as if it would encircle the former as a result of this:
experience alone teaches them the topological relationship
existing between a mass perforated by a hole, and a body
passing through the hole. In the case of the relationship
expressed by 'between' what is the significance of its conservation irrespective of direction of travel? If A, B and C

are three objects placed along the same line, B could only cease to be between A and C by moving in a second dimension; if A, B and C belong to a single surface of which no one part can move about on the same level relative to the others, B could only cease to be between A and C by moving in a third dimension; finally, if A, B and C belong to the same mass, the order of whose parts cannot be rearranged, (whether it be because of a box too narrow to allow leap-frogging, or a rod passing through rings or beads, etc.). B could only depart from its place in the middle by moving according to a fourth dimension. But, bringing this in, one knows that objects may be taken from a box without opening it, left hand gloves made into right hand gloves, etc. So there is nothing intrinsically impossible in trying like the infant to slide a rod through a ring without using the opening in it, or in changing round the order of three balls in a narrow tunnel or of three objects bored through by the same bit of wire. It is only impossible in our three-dimensional world, and therefore it is natural that it must be experience which teaches a child these different points. In the fairly common case of the ring and the rod, the experimental discovery takes place from the second year on. In the case, more remote from the child's life, of the balls in their tunnel or the beads strung on their wire rod, we must wait till the age of 5. But in all these cases, the impossibility is primarily of physical order, as indeed is the actual existence of the three dimensions themselves. In contrast, as soon as it is granted that corresponding to the direct order ABC there is the inverse order CBA, it then becomes not only impossible but contradictory to allow that B could cease to occupy its median position: in fact, as soon as inverse order is conceived operationally as simply the reversal of direct order, without any changing around of the objects in their sequence, the relationship in 'between' becomes symmetrical and expresses the invariable interval existing in relation to either order. Now, in this first stage, it has been seen that the inverse operation is, as yet, not logically constructed at all but merely discovered empirically: hence it is in the nature of things that the relationship 'between', in its relationship as an interval, shares the same pre-operational and intuitive state.

But there is more to it than this: it remains to be understood why, even lacking operations and confining himself to the use of intuitive methods, the child at this level should prefer to create such an adventurous hypothesis as an unimaginable change of place, rather than to construct a clear picture of the semi-rotation of the objects. Yet they know full well in what way their supposition lacks intelligibility, and it is not for want of calling to mind the known conditions of the apparatus that they do this. But the fact is that, not understanding the mechanism of inversion, they go on—one mystery for another—to think it equally likely that the median B can appear in first place, as that one or other of the extremes A and C should come up. The lesson to be drawn from these reactions of theirs is therefore just that—but it is highly instructive from the point of view of the development of logical thinking at a certain level of development the empirical or intuitive attitude sometimes raises such a complete barrier to operational grouping that it ends up in this bizarre and contradictory result, of unimaginable images, or intuitions incapable of being grasped intuitively. And the reason for it is simply that disconnected structures (each imagined whole being independently formed once and for all, according to the images which immediate experience has had to offer in one single field of perception) remain separated from each other by gaps impossible to bridge. In fact, if 'intuitions' remain unconnected in this way, it is precisely because the relationships between the intuitions which might succeed each other are not themselves objects of which intuition is possible, for want of being clearly recognized, whence these non-intuitive empty spaces, which it will be just the role of operations to fill by means of a system of reversible transformations. Operations will arrive at this result by using just those organizational procedures, applied to the gaps in relationships between intuitions, which intuition uses within its own area, but they will be generalized through becoming mobile and reversible.

2. The second stage: Inverse order on return journey and beginnings of invariability of the median object but no understanding of the effects of semi-rotation (sub-stage IIa) then forecasting of the first effects of this, but without generalization
(sub-stage IIb)

This second stage is therefore of the joining together of the intuitions, but without operational generalization, e.g. when going from three on to five objects, or from two to three on to a number of rotations. Here are examples of sub-stage IIa:

CHRI (5; 4). Technique 1. Look at these beads going into the tunnel. How will they come out on the other side? Red (A) first, then black (B) and blue (C) last. Good. And now I'm making them come back. So? Blue (C) first, then black (B) then red (A). Why are they the other way? Because you're coming from the other direction. Fine. Now, look: I'm sending them in as I did before, as on your drawing, then I'm going to turn the tunnel over. Which is first? Red (A). Why? Because the wire is the other way. And then? Black (B) and blue (C). Look: they're going in now and I'm turning the tunnel like that (half turn). Which will be first? Red (A). (Exp.). Is that right? No. It's blue because you made it go the other way. Let's start again (same explan.). Which first? Red (A) because the wire is this side. Look (exp.). Oh, no, blue again because it was turned the other way. (Start again). And now? Blue (correct). And now, listen: I'm going to turn it twice, not just once any more. Which first? Blue. Why? Because it was turned the other way. Look. (exp.). Oh, no red! I thought it would come out on the other side. (Several turns). Which would it be now? Red or blue. Why? Or else black. Why? Oh, no, it couldn't because it's in the middle.

Jos (5; 6). Technique 2, (Q 1). Red (A) then brown (B) then yellow (C). Right. Now they're coming back. How? Yellow (C) then brown (B) then red (A). Why? Because they're coming back. Now they're going into the tunnel— but it's a funny one: I'm going to turn it upside down. Which will be first here? I don't know (looking a long time). Red. Why? . . . (dem). Yellow! Why? . . . (start again).

And now? *Yellow*. Why? *Because you turned it round*. Right.
Now I'm going to turn it twice in a row. Which will it be?
Yellow. (dem). Is that right? *Red*. Why? . . .

BER (5; 8). Technique 2. Simple return correct. One half
turn. *Red* (A). Why? *Because that's first*. Look. (exp.). *Yellow*. Why? *I don't know* (start again). *Yellow*. Why? *Because it was turned round*. (start again). Could it be the
brown one? *No, that's in the middle*.

Technique 3. Simple return correct. One semi-rotation.
Yellow (C). Very good. Why? *Because it's first*. Fine. Now
I'm making it come back. Which first? *Blue* (A) *then green*
(B) *and yellow* (C). Very good. Now I'll turn it twice.
Which first? *I think it will be yellow* (C). Why? *Because
you turned it twice*. Look. Oh, no, blue (A). Why? . . .

WIL (6; 0). Technique 1. Simple return correct. One half-
turn. *Yellow* (C) *because it's on the other side*. (right). Fine.
Once more *Yellow* (right). Good. Now I'll turn it twice
(complete rotation). Which first? *Black* (middle one!). Why?
No, yellow (C) *or blue* (A) *or black* (B). Look, I'll put
them as they were at first and turn them once (semi-rotation). Which? *Blue* (A). (Has forgotten correct answer at
beginning). Look. No, yellow. And now (two turns)? *Yellow*.
Look. No, blue. And now (three turns)? *Blue*. Sure? *No.
Could it be yellow? Yes*. And black (B)? *Yes that as well*.
And turning five times? . . . Black will always stay in the
middle? *No*.

PIL (6; 0). Technique 2. Direct order successful—and if they
come back? *Brown* (E) *then green* (D) *then red* (C) *then
blue* (B) *and yellow* (A). Very good. Why? *It's because they
turned around*. Could red (C) come out first? *It could never
be red* (C); *that's behind the blue* (B) *and behind yellow*
(A). Now we'll start again, but you go round to the other
side of the table (Q 3). Which one will be first out? *Green*
(D). Why? *It will turn around*. (Exp.). Look, yellow!
Watch. We'll start again, but I'll turn the tunnel round
(180°). Which? *This time it will be blue* (B) *because you
turned the thing around and it turned around too*. (Exp.).
Oh, no, brown (E). And now (360°)? *Yellow* (A) *or brown*
(E). Just those two? *Might be red* (C) *because you turned it
last*. Q 6: Total failure.

LAN (6; 6). Technique 2. Return journey. *Red (A) no, yellow (C). Why? Because red (A) is over here.* (Replace balls. Semi-rotation). *Red (A) then brown (B)—then yellow (C). Look.* (exp.). *It's wrong, I thought that it would be red because it was on this side.* And why is it yellow? *Because you turned it round.* Now I'm turning it twice *Red (A)* (correct). Why? *Because the thing was on its side.* And if I turn it once more? *Red, because this is its side . . . No, yellow!* (Returning to a single semi-rotation). *Red* (wrong). Lan does not indicate brown (B) at all.

WAG (7; 3). Technique 2. Return journey: *Yellow (C). First because it was last before and they can't get mixed up.* (Half turn). *Red (A). Look.* (exp.). *Yellow (C). Why? Because you changed the balls, you turned it round.* (360°). *Red.* (three half-turns). *Red. Look! No, yellow, because if you turn it four times it's red. And brown (B)?* (he smiles).

Technique 3. Return and semi-rotation correct. Twelve turns. Is the green one still in the middle? *No.* Why? *Yes, it's still there because you turned it round and you can't take it out.*

MAR (7; 6). Technique 2. Return: correct. Semi-rotation: *Red (A). Look! No, yellow.* Why? *Because you turned it round* (two half-turns). *Yellow, no, it's red.* (three times) *Red. Look! No, yellow* (four times?) *Red.* (random number). *Could be either red or yellow. Not brown (B)? No, because it's in the middle.*

It is interesting to compare these many intermediate reactions with the initial intuitions of stage I and with the foreshadowing of operations of sub-stage IIb.

The only general progress to be noted is the correct forecast of return order (Q2) and this applies to five objects as well as three. But one may wonder whether this discovery is still intuitive, or already operational, in other words whether it is a case of a return journey known only by experience, or of a reversibility that cannot be otherwise. Now, in order to understand inversion it is enough for the subject to imagine, by an intuitive anticipation or theoretical representation, the return of three people walking in single file who cannot overtake or change places with each other. This is what Chri says, (it's back to front 'because they're coming from the other direction') and especially Wag: 'Yellow is first because it was the last one and they can't get mixed up together'. It is true that operational reasoning would not state anything else, regarding Q 2 on its own, but the difference between operations and articulated intuitions, is that the former give rise to generalizations, while the latter are restricted to the small area within which their association was brought about, without any generalization to other problems. Now, from this point of view, it is very characteristic that the discovery of inversion does not forthwith bring about the solution of Q 3 to 5, success in answering them comes but gradually.

Q 7, first of all (invariability of the median position) is the one most rapidly solved as a result of the understanding of inversion: in fact, if direct order and inverse order are only conceivable in the absence of any leap-frogging, the intermediate objects can only remain as they are. But it is in fact extremely interesting to observe that the answer to Q 2 (inversion) does not always produce at the outset the answer to Q 7. When there are only three objects, the latter answer is generally found, but Wil (6; 0) who at once solves the question on inversion and even the one on semi-rotation, expects in the case of rotation through 360° to see the median object appear first. So too, Chri, upon a number of rotations, allows the possibility of the median preceding (though less likely than those at the end), then corrects himself. On the other hand when there are five objects, the understanding of inversion, in itself more difficult, brings about the idea that the intermediate elements (which now number three) will never take the lead. Eg. Pil (6; 0) while foreseeing quite correctly the reversed order of the five balls ('since they turned round about') and while refusing to allow that the median can appear first during this return journey, settles on D the penultimate object when he goes round to the other side of the table (Q 3), and on B, the second object, during semi-rotation, and on either of the extremes or the middle object in the case of a complete rotation: his mental experience of the return journey thus rests in a state of articulated intuition and in no wise at the level of an operation since none of the three intermediate positions is conceived as invariably by fact of being intermediary. Thus we may conclude that the answer to Q 7 (invariability of the intermediate objects), when found at this sub-stage IIa, is no more than the result of an articulated intuition, (in the same way as inversion itself), which is based on the image of the apparatus as making leap-frogging impossible: 'because you turned it (=because you only turned it) and you can't take it out', says Wag speaking of the middle object. If it were already a question of operations properly so-called, the answers to Q 2 and 7 together would in effect bring about without elaboration the solution of Q 3 up to 7.

Examination of the answers given in sub-stage IIa, to Q 3 to 7, shows sufficiently what is wanting in these responses to lead to grouped operations. When the child, leaving out any sort of semi-rotation of the apparatus, has moved to the other side of the table (Q 3) we note at once that he cannot reverse left and right hand and cannot understand that object A will lead out on his left (see Pil). Moreover, on the first semi-rotation (Q4) the subject cannot foresee the inversion of the order (it is this absence of initial prediction which distinguishes sub-stages IIa and IIb: only Wil is an exception, but as he does not solve Q 7, he belongs, as yet, clearly on the level of IIa). But the child, having observed that with one semi-rotation the order is reversed, at once takes this experience into account (except at the commencement of the stage) and thus expects that if we put everything back in its place and repeat one semi-rotation, then inversion will appear again (Ber and others even carry over this result from Technique 2 and Technique 3). Only, although the subjects in sub-stage IIa are able in this way to take this experiment into account when repeated as before, are still so far from understanding the effect thus observed that they are even unable to generalize from what they have just learned from the first semi-rotation on to those that follow. It is in this way that Chri, Jos, and Ber in the case of two semi-rotations (Q 5) settle for the same result as upon one half-turn, as though the number of half-turns had no importance and the mere fact of moving the tunnel or rod round about would ensure the appearance of the last element (C) in first place. Moreover, Lan, Wag and Mar, who successfully solve this Q 5, and so invert in the case of two semi-rotations the reversed order they observed upon one half-turn (but without foreseeing this initial inversion before the experiment)—are already lost when it comes to three semi-rotations. It is only after observing the result of one, two and three half-turns that Wag and Mar (the two most advanced subjects) begin to have an inkling that the order changes with each new half-turn, so announcing the reactions of sub-stage IIb. Hence it is clear that in the course of sub-stage IIa, Q 3 to 5 are solved only under pressure of a succession of experiences and without as yet any grouping of the transformations being brought into play.

The criterion of the existence of operations would then be their grouping, and it would be in the absence of this grouping (in the absence therefore of the solution to Q 3 to 5) that we should consider the correct replies given to Q 2 to 7, as being intuitive and not yet operational. But isn't this begging the question, and could we not concede that inversion of order, and preservation of the intermediate elements, are already operations, merely easier than the rest and only awaiting the appearance of these last, in order to result in grouping? And above all could we not say that rotations have nothing to do with relationships of order, and that the relationships in question in the case of problems 1, (direct order), 2, (inverse order) and 7, (relationship 'between') are enough to constitute an autonomous grouping, that of 'position', earlier than that of 'change of position'?

These questions may be answered in two ways. Logically, it is clear that relationships of order imply a direction of travel, and that change of location likewise implies this, both relative to the system of positions in a series serving as points of reference, so much so that the two kinds of grouping are indissociable. (See Conclusions 1 and 2).

Psychologically on the other hand it is essential, in establishing whether a subject is capable of inverting any kind of relationships of order, to have him change his place or to change the location of the objects in their series, according to the arrangement of Q 3, and 4 to 6, for in order to forecast a sequence of outward and return journeys upon the model of Q 1 and 2, the subject can content himself with anticipating the arrival of the outermost objects in terms of left-right or front-back, and this with automatic regularity: when Lan, e.g. foresees the appearance of object (C) upon the return journey (Q2) he says quite simply 'because (A) belongs to this side here' thus each object has once and for all 'it's side', which dispenses with any reasoning. It is therefore only on Q 3 to 7 that one can establish whether there actually is operational inversion.

It is nonetheless true that articulated intuition, which allows Q 2 and 7 to be solved, does act as transition between the early, static intuitions, and operations themselves, in the following manner. At first the child can succeed in imagining intuitively only certain exceptional situations, corresponding to what he has previously perceived as a function of his actions (in contradistinction to the sensori-motor level, where the subject does not actively imagine anything, but where that which he perceives immediately sets off motor programmes prolonging the perception). These exceptional situations then constitute so many intuitive images acting as internalized models for actions, but there are gaps between these from the point of view of thinking, since the actions linking them remain impossible to imagine. This is the level of stage I, in the course of which the subject certainly intuits object B between A and C, then object B before or after A (or C), but without managing or even trying to visualize how B changes places with A or C in this way. Then comes an effort to bridge these gaps in intuitive representation, which consists in anticipating or reconstructing intuitively the action itself which might lead from one image to another. It is this sort of mental experience which constitutes articulated intuition, more mobile than the static intuition of the first simple perceptual reconstructions. It is in this way that the subject in stage II imagines the return journey of objects ABC in the inverse order CBA and above all how he discovers little by little (and not immediately) the impossibility of B's changing places with A or C. But these articulated intuitions are not yet operations because the subject cannot manage to generalize nor, what comes to the same thing, to regulate them; they are still only adaptations or diffusions of the original islands of intuition, and thus they will remain in their pre-operational state so long as they cannot be 'grouped' in stable and reversible operational wholes.

Subjects at sub-stage IIb, without arriving at a complete solution (Q 5 and 6 together), manage however to anticipate the order, when they themselves change places (Q 3) or upon one semi-rotation of the apparatus (Q 4) and even, at the end of this stage, upon two half-turns (Q 5).

Sul (5; 6). Technique 2 with three objects: return journey correct. And if I turn it like that (Q 4)? *It will be yellow (C) then brown (B) then red (A). Why yellow first? Because you turned the tunnel round.* Look. (exp.). Correct. And now I'll turn it twice (from the starting point again). What first? *Yellow, because . . . I don't know.* Look: I turn it once (very slowly) and again once (same). Which? *Red, because that was first in the beginning, and you turned the tunnel twice round.* And three times? *I don't know.* Once? *Yellow.* Twice? *Red* (turning each time in sight of the child, but not showing the result). Three times? *Yellow.* Four? *Red.* Five? *Yellow.* Six? *Red.* Good. Now listen: if I turn two times? *Red.* Four times (turning the tunnel still in sight of the child)? *Yellow.* Six times? *Red.* Eight times? *Red.* Ten times? *Yellow.* And if I go on, will the brown one (B) ever be first one out? *No, because that's in the middle.*

Bru (5; 7). Technique 2 with five objects. Return journey (Q 1) correct. Could red (C) come out first? *No, that's not possible: it would be too far away, it's in the middle!* (Child changes place to the other side of table). And there (on child's right) which comes out first? *Yellow* (A) (correct). And if I turn this (180°)? *Brown* (E) *because you turned it round.* And when I turn the tunnel could another one, e.g.

blue (B) or green (D) come out first? *No, only yellow* (A)
or brown (E), *the rest are in the middle. Look.* (360°).
Brown (E). *Once more* (very slowly, he watches closely)?
Yellow (A). *Look.* (exp.). *Correct. And now three half-
turns? . . . Can you tell which will be first? No. It depends.
What does it depend on? One time it's brown* (E) *and one
time it's yellow* (A) *which comes out first, but you can't tell
beforehand which one it will be.*

Jac (6; 10). Technique 1 (three objects). *Return journey
correct. And if I turn it* (180°)? *It will be blue* (C) *because
that one's in front, now that you've turned the rod. Two
times? Red* (A) *because it's first when you turn twice. Why?
Because it was last the time before. And three times? Red*
(A) *or blue* (C). *Which? Don't know. And black* (B)?
*No, because it's in the middle. But can't it come to the
front? No, because you'd have to take the beads off the wire
to change places. Then three times? Blue* (C). *And five
times? Red* (A) etc.

Quel (6 years). Technique 2 (three objects). *Correct return journey because yellow* (C) *was last: now it's the first
one.* (180°) *Yellow* (C) *then brown* (B) *then red* (A).
And two times? Red (A) *then brown* (B) *and yellow* (C).
*Why red first? It's red first because it was yellow the last
time. Three times? Yellow. Why? Because it was red last
time. Now four times? Yellow. Look.* (exp.). *Oh, no, red, because it was yellow last time. Five times?* (Thinks). *Red, yellow, red, yellow, red; it's the red one! Very good. Now I'm
turning it three times* (from initial position). *Red. Look.*
(exp.). *No, yellow. Four times? Yellow* (wrong). *Could it
ever be brown* (B)? *No, because that one's in the middle.*

Lep (6; 8). Technique 2 (five objects). *Direct and inverse
order correct: Could red* (C) *ever be first? No, because it's
brown* (E) *first, red can't take its place. Come round here.*
(Q 3). *Which will be first here? Yellow* (right). *And if I
turn it* (180° horizontal). *Brown* (E). *And like this* (180°
vertical)? *The same. How do you know which comes first?
I watch you, and first you turn it this way and then that. And
like this* (360°)? *Yellow* (A), *its the same thing again. And
now* (three times etc.)? *I don't know.* Even after going back
to the beginning and counting Lep does not discover the

rule. On the other hand he never predicts the emergence of any of the three intermediate objects.

PIA (7 years). Technique 1. Return correct. 180° *Yellow* (C) *because before it was the blue one* (A). Two turns. (360°)? *Blue or yellow. Look.* (1 + 1 slowly)? *Blue* (A) *because it starts off first and if you turn this once it's yellow* (C) *and if turn it again it's blue* (A) *once more.* Four times? *Blue* (A) *because it's blue, yellow, blue, then yellow and blue again.* Five times? (He works it out again). *Yellow.* Six times? *Blue.* Three times? *Blue* (wrong). Eleven times? *Blue* (wrong). And black (B)? *Ne because that's always in the middle: it can't get out because of the others beside it.*

OD (7; 6). Technique 2, same beginning. (Q 4-6): One time? *Yellow* (C). Two times? *Red* (A). Three times? *Yellow.* Four? *Red.* Five? *Yellow.* Six? *Red.* Twenty-five? *Yellow.* Forty? *Red.* Forty-eight? *Yellow.* Fifty-two? *Red.* Fifty-eight? *Yellow.* Once? *Yellow.* Twice? *Red.* Four? *Yellow.* Six? *Red.* Eight times? *Yellow.*

It is of some theoretical interest (and might possibly become diagnostic) to note the constant regularity with which the child progresses in solving Q 4 to 6. Indeed one recalls that in the course of sub-stage IIa the subject who cannot solve Q 4 (one half-turn) by anticipation subsequently concedes, having learned from experience, that the order changes with the rotations, but he does not solve from the start Q 5 as such, not yet understanding that two half-turns are equal to a single one. Then, when he solves it, he again fails in Q 5, thinking now that three half-turns are equal to only two: from zero to one half-turn, from one to two, and finally two to three, we thus already observe three successive steps in the course of sub-stage IIa. Now this development continues in IIb as follows. First of all, the child becomes able to solve spontaneously and by anticipation Q 4: one half-turn (vertically or horizontally) reverses the order. In correlation with this innovation, Q 3, is also solved (conservation of order upon observer changing place) and so to Q 7 (invariability of median positions). Likewise—and this is extremely interesting—when Q 4 (one half-turn) has once been solved spontane-

ously, Q 5 (two half-turns) is as well: the reversal of
inverse order becomes once more direct order ('it's blue
that started off first, says Pia: 'if you turn this, it's yellow,
and if you turn it once more it's blue again'). It is only in
the case of five objects that hesitation persists (see Bru).
There is then yet another step, marked by the simultaneous solution to Q 4 and 5 since within sub-stage IIa, Q 4
is solved only after the experiment, and when the solution
has once been observed empirically it does not lead directly to that of Q 5 but only with a time-lag. Now, once this
step is reached, the upward climb begins to go forward
again. First, in the case of three half-turns, the least
advanced subjects of sub-stage IIb do not have an immediate solution (Sul, Bru and Jac), while the most advanced
of them answer correctly right away. Only, they do not
succeed in finding the order corresponding to three half
turns except when the question about these follows immediately after the questions relating to one and two half-
turns (e.g. Quel and Pia). Some children are found to be,
as it were, exhausted after three half-turns and fail on
four, even when questioned after each half-turn (e.g.
Quel) and some are successful only when one proceeds in
correct order. Finally, among these latter cases, distinction
must be made between those who with five, six, seven ...
half-turns easily discover the alternating order (the most
advanced, Od etc.) and those who are finished after 'n'
half-turns, this number increasing gradually, therefore,
with their development, just as has been seen in the advance to four.

Consequently what distinguishes sub-stage IIb, the ver-
satility of whose upper range we have just observed, is
that even subjects who can invert the order of the object
upon each new half-turn, when the questions are asked
following the series of whole numbers (1, 2, 3 ... 'n'
half-turns), are lost as soon as one jumps from one number to any other number, once past the level of three or
four half-turns, or upon counting backwards (see Jac, Sul,
Pia and even Od especially at the end of his interview).

These then are the facts. One can see that they confirm
the pattern sketched out earlier of the passage from intui-

tive to operational thinking. The problem is in fact to explain at the same time the failures which persist in sub-stage IIb and the discovery characterizing this stage: the discovery at the same time, of inverted order upon one half-turn, and of the inversion of this inversion, in other words the return to direct order, upon one complete rotation. Now this double acquisition most certainly already verges on operations since it fits the two criteria of operational thinking, that of conceiving the operation of inversion (here inversion of order) and that of following through to an accurate 'composition' (inversion of the inversion). But on the other hand it is not entirely operational since it does not lead to an immediate generalization of the solution which has been found, neither is the 'composition' of the inversions jumping from one number of half-turns to any other yet possible for the subject who has to follow the succession of whole numbers in actual fact (and not just in imagination). We are therefore faced with the upper limit of 'articulated intuition', as also, by this very fact, with the lowest limit of operations as such. In other words after having succeeded, from sub-stage IIa, in imagining the return of the objects in the inverse direction (Q 2) the invariability of the median objects (Q 7), the subject manages by a simple refinement of these articulated intuitions to make the experiment, mentally, of inverting the order by semi-rotation (Q 4). That this inductive inversion, when resulting from an anticipation in the imagination and no longer from observation of the experiment, should immediately give rise to a correct anticipation for two half-turns, is quite natural since in sub-stage IIa, when inversion is observed after the event in the case of one half turn, the most advanced subjects are already drawing from this the double inversion for two half-turns. But since the child, upon each half-turn, endeavours to follow the inversions in every detail in his thoughts he only gradually manages accurately to forecast the result of three, four, five half-turns. Once this game of visualizing the objects in alternation is set in train, he finally discovers (and this forms the ceiling of sub-stage IIb) that upon each half-turn the order changes once more. Only, the fact that up to this upper limit the subject continues to rely on visualizing intuitively and therefore needs to imagine one by one the direct and indirect order of the objects upon each new half-turn, is proved because he is lost when a jump is made from one number of half-turns to any other, instead of keeping to the sequences of whole numbers.

What is the operational mechanism upon which the subjects of this level are verging without ever fully attaining? It may be understood by seeing exactly what they lack in order to generalize the solution found during orderly progression. Operations, one might say, are nothing other than articulated intuitions rendered adaptable and completely reversible since they are emptied of their visual content and survive as pure 'intention'—taken in the sense fixed by Buhler in his celebrated analysis of thinking without imagery (Bewusztheit) (i.e. awareness). In other words, operations will come into being in their pure state when there is sufficient schematization. Thus instead of demanding actual representation, each inversion will be conceived of as a potential representation, like an outline for an experiment which could be performed but which it is not useful to follow to the letter, even in the form of performing it mentally. So one understands why the criterion of operations is 'composition' or 'calculation': detached from their representational content, operational schemes may no longer be based on the actual fact alone, even as imagined through a succession of reproductive or anticipatory intuitions, and will now only serve as a basis for deductions by resting on each other interdependently and this is just what 'composition' consists of. But by the very fact that it frees itself from the bonds of intuition, this composition becomes endlessly fruitful and allows of any combination whatsoever of potential representations: whence the forecasting of the results of 'n' half-turns independently of the order followed in choosing these numbers. We are now about to see in stage III that operations therefore consist of the generalization of actions performed, through mental experiment or through articulated intuitions, and generalizing these by replacing their

experienced intuitive content by a ruling which verges on
final and coherent 'grouping', (but indefinite in its construction) of all possible actions.

3. The third stage: Operational solving of Q 1 to 7 inclusive

Some examples of entirely correct answers follow, allowing us to complete this analysis.,

Gɪʟ (6; 6). Technique 2: Q 1 to 4 answered correctly. And
if I turn this twice? It's red (A) first, because you turned it
once and then a second time: that makes it the same side as
at first. And three times? Yellow (C). Four? Red (A) because you turned it four times. It's easy. You don't know how
I work it out. I can see through the cardboard (really he
moves his lips and works it out as he goes along). Six times?
(But without actually turning it). In any case it will not be
brown (B) first because it cannot change. Well? (he works
it out in a low voice). Red (A) and five times? Yellow.

Lᴀᴍ (7; 4). Technique 2: Starting off the same. And if I
turn it twice? Red (A) because you turned it twice. (Ten,
twelve turns, very fast). Could it be brown (B)? No because
it is in the middle of the other two. And if I turn it all day on
a motor? It's always in the middle. And three times? Once
yellow, twice red, three times yellow. And five times? Yellow.
Six times? Red. Twelve times? Red. Fifteen? Yellow. Eleven
times? Yellow. What do we call numbers, 2, 4, 6, 8? Don't
know.

Aʟ (7; 2). One to eight turns (in order) correct. And if I
turn it once? Yellow (C). Five times? Yellow. Seven? Yellow.
Four? Red (A). Six? Red. Eight? Red. Twelve? Red. Fifteen? Yellow. Seventeen? Yellow. Twenty? Red.

Technique 3: correct with 1, 2, 5, 8, 13, 25 and 40 times.
What do we call numbers 2, 4, 6, 8 ?—Even numbers.
Thus we see that these subjects manage to forecast the
order of the objects with any number of semi-rotations
and whatever the order of the chosen numbers. Moreover,

they quickly abstract from these forecasts the law according to which direct order corresponds to even numbers and inverse order to odd numbers of semi-rotations.

The problem which arises at the culmination of this development is therefore to understand how the subject comes to deduce all the transformations in question, while each of them, without exception, has necessitated the occurrence of the experiment during previous stages before they were understood. It is this question of experiment and deduction, or generally of those structures which are inherent in the subjects, and the pressure of things outside, which faces us as a consequence from the beginning of this study of movement and speed, since it already crops up in relation to the idea of order.

If experience is necessary to get a clear idea of each new acquisition, the activity of the intelligence is equally necessary granted that deduction is finally possible. So we will at once set aside the classical solutions of associational empiricism and a priori rationalism as both being unilateral or, if one prefers, as refuting each other because they are necessarily complementary. Phenomenology is undoubtedly right in underlining the radical interdependence of subject and objects, and from the same point of view, the theory of form in so far as it establishes the functional totality which respectively frees the organism from its environment, the perceptor from the field of perception, or the structuring intelligence and the structured objects. But epistemological phenomenology and psychological gestaltism remain idle doctrines when from this initial verification they conclude the non-construction of operational schemes and the permanence of the laws of organization, instead of seeing in the progressive adjustment of mental assimilation and accommodation to external objects an infinitely subtle constructive force.

In actual fact the relationship which exists between the activity of the subject and the experience is in no way permanent because neither the schematization of assimilation nor contacts with things are laid down once and for all, and this relationship is transformed from one stage to another in such a way that the general solution of the problem can only be sought in terms of this development itself, i.e. of the progressive equilibration of this interaction. This is precisely what we would like to bring out from the preceding facts, particularly in the case of the grouping of relationships of order.

Moreover the question may be put in two complementary ways: either in the explanation of complete experience, or the forecasting of experiences to follow, or of the reconstruction of earlier experiences (actual or potential). From the first of these points of view, it is clear that the same empirical observation (e.g. inverse order found when the objects retrace their path or when the apparatus is rotated through 180°) will give rise to quite a different construction according to the way it is understood and that this understanding is transformed in terms of the mental stages already traversed: this commonplace fact alone is enough to attest the existence of an intellectual assimilation distinct from structurations where the subject would remain passive. Whether this regulates the actual perception of the facts or whether there be active assimilation of this perception, is not our business to discuss here. But from the point of view of understanding the perceived facts, as such, it is clear that from stage I to stage II, i.e. from simple intuition to operational intelligence by way of articulated intuitions, neither the activity of the subject nor the effect produced by the facts of the experience remain identical and this is the respect in which the relationship between the two changes its character. From the point of view of forecasting, on the other hand, according to whether the subject does not anticipate or reconstruct anything (stage I) or whether he anticipates and reconstructs by imagining the experiment though not realized in action (stage II) or whether he calculates by means of operational composition (stage III) the two factors and their relationship equally change their character in a continuous way.

From this dual point of view, one may interpret the foregoing results as follows. In the course of stage I, the experiment is only observed without being understood and gives rise to no foresight exceeding the simple reproduction of this static and limited observation. Now by this very fact, the activity of the subject, without being non-existent reduces itself to a simple centring of intuition on the given fact, which is allotted exceptional emphasis precisely by virtue of the fact that it is not related to any other earlier or subsequent fact. Thus it is that, observing inverse order CBA with one half-turn, the subject forecasts this likewise for two half-turns etc. In stage II, the action of the experience is prolonged beyond the observed fact, because it furnishes the content of the gradual reconstructions and anticipations which mark the successive advances of this period (IIa and IIb). But this is because intuition, diffused in relation to the facts presented, gives rise to a regulating activity which permits an extension of the subject's power of representation up to variable limits, but gradually expanding as a result of this very diffusion. In the third stage, finally, the experience is expanded indefinitely in constant accord with a power of 'composition' which marks the liberation of the activity of the subject. Only, and this point is fundamental, deduction does not succeed in embracing the experience in this way except by going beyond it and constructing a schematization having the double qualities of complete reversibility and abstract generalization which are evidence of its constructive nature.

The activity of the subject is thus marked in the beginning by a simple concentration consisting of overestimating the significance of the data of transitory intuition (stage I) then of diffusing these data to relate them to earlier and subsequent intuitions (stage II), and finally of subjecting them to operations regulated by their reversible composition (stage III). In all three cases, this activity therefore consists either of an act of relating the facts with the personal point of view (stage I) or of relating the facts with one another through progressive co-ordination of points of view (stage II) or finally of relating the actions leading to these successive points of view (stage III), while the experience is formed by the facts themselves, at the start simply phenomenological and disconnected (stage I) then related by the imagining of the intermediate events (stage II) and lastly by the totality of possible images (stage III).

But then, if the activity of the subject is confined to establishing relationships between the data of the experience, are we not driven to the following alternative: either these relationships copy those of reality and the action or operations engendering them simply duplicate the transformations of the experience itself, or else the work of reason is original but more restricted and is confined as was insisted, to an identification grappling with external diversity. Now there is no reason for considering identity alone as rational when the other operations on every grouping or group constitute an entirely rigorous reversible system: operational identity is only a product of direct and inverse operations. Is that equivalent to saying that they merely duplicate the relationships of the experiment? Definitely not ultimately, since, they then add to them complete reversibility. But in the beginning is not every operation the result of a simple action which stays empirical before becoming reversible? Is it not a simple internalization of pure experiences to go from experimental rotations with simple authentication of the result obtained, to operational rotations grouped into a deductive system?

But it is just here that the genetic point of view blocks any discussion aimed at settling, once and for all, between activity of the subject and pressure of objects outside. The truth is that, at the starting point, the co-ordination on the part of the subject and the data of the object are undifferentiated in the highest degree and that their differentiation is defined in the course of development: now corresponding to this differentiation there is a gradual mutual adjustment because if the initial individual co-ordination blocks the experience and reduces it to phenomenology, the final grouping, on the contrary, forms at one and the same time a system of deductive compositions free of internal contradictions, and a series of potential experiences fully and finally in accord with any actual experiment.

So we must say, and this at every level, that action—starting point common to image—using intuitions and operations—adds something to the actual fact, instead of merely taking from it (or, as they say, 'abstracting' from it) the elements of its own structure. Moreover, there is more in the action of 'placing' one object following another than just reading off a simple order of succession: there is a modification of reality by the subject. This transformation is at first distorting in so far as it is incomplete because confined to the subject and his actions of the moment, but as it is diffused and adjusts to each potential modification of reality it adds to the latter the taking into account of earlier and subsequent states and consequently a mobility and reversibility which it does not intrinsically possess and which the subject alone has power to confer upon it.

In this respect the rôle of experience in the construction of mathematical relationships is, therefore, of a very special nature and one which often escapes the attention of psychologists and epistemologists: experiments of order (number, space) are experiments the subject really makes on himself, i.e. on his own actions and not on the objects, as such, to which his actions simply are applied. That is why these actions once co-ordinated into coherent 'groupings' may at a given moment dispense with any experiment and give rise to an internal and purely deductive composition, which would be inexplicable if the initial experience had consisted of extracting the knowledge from the objects themselves. But before this co-ordination is possible and composition of actions as such is translated into a 'grouping' and hence becomes operational, it goes without saying that actions require experiences in order to co-ordinate themselves and consequently require objects to serve as a basis for these experiences. This is the explanation of the fact that the concept of order, with all the differentiation we have just studied, has an origin at once experimental but not empirical, since it results from experiments the subject makes on his own actions, leading to deductions at once necessary and not a priori, it being essential to achieve the composition of these actions, this composition being gradual and not given from the outset.

CHAPTER TWO

Order of Succession Inherent in Cyclic Movements

The work on alternative directions of travel described in Chapter One called for a complementary study of cyclic order, the peculiarity of which is that if A is followed by B and B by C, C itself is followed by A in the order ABCAB. . . . The new difficulty is therefore the understanding of this periodicity in direct and inverse directions.

In order to examine this problem we show our subjects a cylinder or, better still, a prism with four or six facets, revolving around its longitudinal axis, and differently coloured on each facet; the questioning bears purely on the succession of the colours. First the cylinder or prism is shown quite openly and is turned while counting the colours with the subject. Then we put it in a cylindrical box slit by a wide longitudinal gap revealing a coloured strip of each of the facets presented in turn (but only one at a time) and revolve the prism very slowly inside the box. But, so that this arbitrary order should not make calls upon the memory and remain entirely a matter of intellectual understanding, the child has a collection of strips of coloured paper and during the first rotation of the prism he lines up four or six strips in a model series serving as a reminder and reproducing the colours observed in turn: in this way the replies to the subsequent questions will be based on the model series without any need for efforts of memory. Once the series ABCD or ABCDEF is made up, the child is asked, when the first colour A reappears, to reproduce as the second rotation proceeds, a second series A—D or A—F beneath the

first. The subject thus arranges two or three series, one
under the other, and so has from the start the chance to
observe the periodicity of the colours. We then remove
these repeated series leaving on the table only the first (the
model series) and then ask the following six questions.

Q 1. The first colour (A) belonging to the cylinder inside
the box is made to appear in the slit (this corresponds to
the first colour in the model series) and the subjects are
asked to forecast the order of the colours which would be
shown by turning the cylinder (the latter remains stationary, but the model series is naturally visible all the time).
To do this the child places bands of colours on the table in
a series similar to the model series, the latter having to be
moved a little aside to prevent the new strips of paper of
the same colours being simply placed underneath the corresponding colours.

Q 2. Once the series is made up, one asks which colours
come after the last (D or F) if you continue to turn the
cylinder. It is thus a question of arranging the periodic
series ABCDABCDAB....

Q 3. One starts from the beginning again but starting this
time with an intermediate colour (e.g. B, C or any other
than the first or last).

Q 4. We once more show the cylinder open to view and
draw the child's attention to the fact that it can be turned
in either direction. To make the child aware of inverse
rotation when the cylinder is replaced in the box, it is
useful to mount a flag on it, which projects from the box:
the direction of the flag's rotation will then indicate to the
subject the movement of the cylinder. We ask the child
besides, for greater clarity, to reproduce, while the cylinder is open to view, a model series of the succession of the
colours in the direct order. This series reconstructed, we
then ask Q 4: to find the order of the colours in inverse
direction (from D or F, with the cylinder once more in its
box).

Q 5. Continue making up the series in inverse order but continuing beyond A: so DCBADCBAD. . . .

Q 6. Same questions but starting with an intermediate colour (e.g. CBA and CBADCBA. . . .)

The reactions observed in the course of these few questions may be graded according to the same three stages we observed in Chapter One, in the development of linear order. During the first stage the order of succession of the series is not understood. During the second stage the order ABCDEF is understood, but the succession is faulty if one starts with one of the intermediate elements B to E: in particular the subject cannot then manage to continue after F according to the periodicity A ... FA ... F; the inverse order is likewise not understood, even starting with F. During the third stage lastly, the answers are correct. These stages I and II include subdivisions which we shall return to in §1 and 2.

1. The first stage: Lack of understanding of succession

It will be recalled that all the children examined in Chapter One on the question of linear order of succession were able to foresee the conservation of direct order during the passage of three or five objects behind a screen. Now it seems that in the case of cyclic order this understanding of direct order is no longer immediate. The difficulty for the subject is presented in two ways which reinforce one another continuously. On the one hand (sub-stage Ia) during the construction of the model series, the youngest subjects can scarcely manage to translate cyclic order into a linear sequence; on the other hand (sub-stage Ib) once this difficulty is overcome subjects do not succeed in foreseeing which colour will follow another, even by referring to the model series. Here are some examples of sub-stage Ia.

LIL (3; 8) as the rotation of the cylinder with four colours proceeds, places ABC following our instructions. Then D:

Lil puts it in front of A: But does (D) come before (A) or
after (C)? (Puts it according to the suggestion, after C). We
go on after D and place A, which reappears, under the first
A. Then comes B: Lil puts it before A. We put this right and
present C: Lil puts it before A in the first line. Another correction, and D appears: Lil again puts it in front of A.

We then refrain from interfering and ask the child to construct the series of colours as we go along, rotating the cylinder (in the box): Lil arrives at DBCA though the series
ABCD is before him and though no question of forecasting
has been asked it is merely a question of reading off the
colours successively observed and translating these into a
linear series. There is thus complete failure.

We start again: this time Lil manages ABC but puts D
before A, hence DABC. What is there after C here? (Turning) (Lil puts in B and D again, giving DABCBD).

CHRI (4; 6) constructs correctly, but with our help, the series
ABCDA: What comes next? Blue (B). Find it (he does).
Where will you put it? After green (A). Good. Next? (C).
And then? Red (D). Good. After that? (Puts B in front of
A and C in front of B). The subject thus seems to understand
and even to foresee the order of the colours, only the periodicity escaping him. But when six colours are used the series
constructed actually during rotation (and so without forecasting) produces FEABDC.

LUC (4; 8) likewise, after placing A and B in the form AB,
says about C, putting it first of all to the right of B (thus
ABC): You can put it here as well (between A and B). Why?
It's beside that one (B).

   Sub-stage 1b.

ANT (4; 5) constructs without difficulty three series ABCD
one under the other. One is left there, and the cylinder is put
in its box. What comes after (A)? (He puts ACBDB). With
six colours, he reproduces easly ABCDEF: What comes after
(A)? . . . (C)? I don't know. Try (He puts down AFACEB).
This line (the model) might help you? Yes, we did that
right. Then after (A)? (he places ACAEFAFC).

HEL (4; 11) copies ABCDEF. What comes after (A) and
(B)? (E) (Turning). No. After that? . . . Could this line

(model) help you? Yes. How? *There's blue* (C) *after red*
(B) *and then yellow* (D) *after* (C). Well then? (Gets on no
better).

Jos (5; 0) Gets on very well with forecasting when she places
her colours underneath those of the model line. As soon as
this is set a little to one side she forecasts ACDBCDB and
ABDFDFD.

Ren (5; 0) during rotation of four colours (cylinder still in
full view) arrives at ABCCDA then removes one (C). When
we move on to forecasting, he foresees correctly each time
looking at the model series, but places the successive colours
in order BABCDAA.

With six colours, he copies correctly the order observed in
the form ABCDEFA, but moving on to forecasting he is
lost. What comes after A if I turn it? (E). Why? *Because
it's behind it there* You are guessing, are you, or can you
really tell? Yes, *it's* (C). Look (turning). *It's* (B). And after
(B) what comes then? (E). Look (showing C, then D, then
E). And now after (E)? (A). And can that (model) give
you any help? Let's try again. After (A)? (Ren this time
copies the whole model series without paying any attention
to the cylinder). Now you must simply put your fingers on
the colour which comes next. Look, if we begin with that
(C) what comes next? *That* (B) *because it's beside* (C).

Ray (5; 3) after correctly making up the model series
ABCDA, is asked to forecast the order after A: he foresees
ABDA, then ADCB. We try to make things more concrete
by showing the prism stationary and in full view, and making
a little doll turn round it, with the model series right in front
of the child. You see, she is looking first at brown (A) then
green (B) etc., like this (model series). Now, back in the
box. What comes after brown (A)? *Green* (B). And after
(B)? *Red* (C) and after that? *Blue* (D). Good. And before
blue? *Brown* (A). And after red (C)? *Green* (B). And before red (C)? *Brown* (A). After Brown (A)? *Red* (C). And
before brown (A)? *Green* (B).

Thus we see that these subjects cannot foresee the order
of succession of the four or six elements of the cycle
(sub-stage Ib) nor even at first (sub-stage Ia) construct a

model series representing this order. How do the difficulties peculiar to cyclic order arise when they no longer exist for linear order?

The striking fact in the constructing of the model series by simply reading off the colours successively observed (and when the cylinder is still in full view nearly as much as when the colours appear through the slit) is the initial inability of the little ones to preserve the direction of travel: seeing D appear after C, Lil puts it in front of ABC which are already ranked from left to right (the mistake is repeated with B, C etc. after that). Likewise Chri, who manages in turn ABCD, fails with six colours, placing D before C, E before A, then F before E. Doubtless there still persists some element of convention in the translation of cyclic order into a linear sequence. Whether the cylinder turns on its longitudinal axis, or an observer moves round the cylinder (like Ray's doll) colours ABC ... appear one after the other in time, this temporal succession expressing the phases of the rotation (of the cylinder or the observer) in space. Now, one asks the subject to express this spatial temporal succession by a series of positions ranged from left to right in a straight line, when one could just as well do it from right to left, or by superimposing (A under B, B under C etc. or the reverse) etc., and equally the model series could be represented by a circumference of any other curves. So it is normal that the child should not at once recognize the chosen conventions and that his adaptation should include some errors. But the initial reactions of Lil and Chri provide examples of difficulties other than those relating to the understanding of the symbolism adopted: there are reversals from before and behind and mistakes concerning proximity itself. Indeed it matters little whether we represent succession in relation to left-right, or right-left, the main thing is that the order of succession which is chosen should be preserved. Now this is precisely what Lil and Chri do not grasp: the colour coming 'after' the previous one is placed indiscriminately on the left or on the right of it. So everything goes on as if for the youngest subjects, the relationships of succession expressed in 'before' and 'after' were not yet understood in the case of cyclic order, and remained undifferentiated in the form of a simple relationship of juxta-position. The reaction of Luc is perfectly typical in this respect: after correctly placing B after A, he automatically puts C after B, but next feels that one can put it equally well in the form ABC or ACB because 'it's next to (B)'. But, even more strange, this feeling for juxta-position (being 'next to') is not at first assimilable to the 'proximity' of the topologist, since at the start the subject does not trouble with the idea that there is such proximity in the model series: Lil puts D in front of ABC and Chri with six colours, hits upon the series FEABDC, in which E and A or B and D are juxtaposed although they are not neighbours in the succession of the cylinder (without returning to the inversions of order FE and DC).

We can therefore understand why, when we pass from the conception of the model series to the forecasting of the succession by the use of this model, the reactions of the most advanced subjects (sub-stage Ib) remains so inadequate: the fact is that, even more than the reproduction of an observed sequence, the anticipation based on this reproduction demands co-ordination of the relationships of proximity which keep the direction of travel constant. Now this dual synthesis is naturally more difficult in the case of an anticipatory intuition than in that of a purely perceptive or reproductive intuition: it is in this way that Ren either thinks of the direction of travel and misses on proximity, (E and C after A, E after B etc.) or else preserves proximity but not direction of travel (B after C 'because it's next to it'). Likewise Ray wavers between preservation of proximity without direction of travel (B after C) or the reverse (A before C).

But the reason for these difficulties common to reproduction and forecasting with cyclic order remains to be explained. It may be recalled (Chapter One) that the subjects of this same first stage are able to conserve a direct linear order with three or five objects, but upon semirotation of the tunnel or wire rods they do not manage either to invert the order or to maintain the relationship 'between'. The similarities between these facts and the

present observations are mutually self-explanatory. It is
clear firstly that direct linear order remains intuitive or
even perceptive in stage I since an analogous number of
objects arranged in cyclic order (abstraction made from
periodicity) can not be put in series. So we understand
why the inversion of this linear order and conservation of
the relationship 'between' remain impossible upon semi-
rotation; they both imply, in the same way as reproduction or anticipation of cyclic order itself, conditions which
go beyond perception or immediate intuition. The words
'before' and 'after' in the case of the revolving cylinder,
cannot, indeed, present the same simple significance as
that of a rectilinear movement, since there is no longer
simultaneous perception of the whole, and since the same
colours are found by rotation equally in either direction:
either then the subject strives to reconstruct proximity
which he manages by proceeding in perceptual pairs AB,
CD, etc., but losing the direction of travel, or else he
strives to preserve the latter but proximity escapes him in
this case and the relationships of interval ('between') are
dislocated. The lesson from these facts is that relationships
of order are essentially operational in nature and that even
in situations where operations seem to play no part, as in
the reproduction of a cyclic sequence of colours perceived
in order, a complex play of 'dispositions' is necessary to
co-ordinate relationships of proximity with direction of
travel.

2. The second stage: 'Rigid' series

Sub-stage IIa

There comes a moment when, whether through understanding the relationships of the colours in the model
series and those which come up in the revolving of the
cylinder, or whether by empirical observation of their
convergence, the child succeeds in forecasting or anticipating the cyclic series ABCDABCDA.

The forecasting of the series of six colours is scarcely more difficult than for the series of four (only a slight time-lag is found between the two solutions). It is most significant that as soon as the forecasting of the first colours ABCD is acquired, that the periodicity . . . DABCD ... is likewise, which clearly shows that the understanding of the latter is necessary for the forecasting of the first sequences, in contrast to linear series which children are able to conserve earlier than cyclic series. But, what is very curious and of obvious theoretical interest, in order that these forecasts may take place, one must at the start (during this stage II) begin with the initial element of the model series, i.e. A if one starts off with an intermediate term (B or C in the case of series A . . . D) the subject is lost and reacts once more as in stage I. This is sufficient to show that the formation of cyclic series in stage II is not yet operational, but remains intuitive: the cyclic series forms a 'rigid' bloc which may be spread out in one piece, and even linked with subsequent cyclic blocs, but the various constituent relationships are not yet conceived as this would involve mobile and reversible operations.

More than this, we can distinguish two levels IIa and IIb. During sub-stage IIa, subjects succeed in forecasting the cyclic series when we begin with A but fail starting from an intermediate term and also fail in general to find inverse order even starting with the last term D (or F). During sub-stage IIb, subjects manage to forecast the progressive series starting with an intermediate term, but only up to the final term, and fail to foresee the continuation of subsequent cycles. Moreover, they succeed in anticipating the series in inverse order starting with the last term but not starting from an intermediate term.

Towards the end of this sub-stage they manage this but still fail to foresee a regressive periodicity starting with any given term. Thus we see that stage II marks all the transitions between complete failure, as in stage I and complete success as in stage I. Here are some examples of sub-stage IIa.

SIM (4; 11 nearly 5; 0) foresees after A: (BCD). And after that? *Nothing*. But if I went on turning it? (A) then (BCD). (we place the cylinder at C). Do you know what would come next? (Sim again adds A and B before C then puts D on afterwards).

Look: you can turn the cylinder the other way, like this (demonstration with the object in full view). Now tell me what will come after (D) if I turn it the opposite way? (Puts down A). Look (turning). No (C). And then? (A). Look (turning). No, *it's* (B). And after (B)? *It will be* (C). We give up.

Six colours: (Forecasts correctly) ABCDEFABCDEFAB. How do you know? *I know because that's all there is* (points to the model series). (We put the cylinder at C) and after that one? (F). Could you use that to help? (model series) Yes, (puts down B in place of F, hence CB) etc.

After having another model series constructed: And if I turn it the other way, what comes after F? (D). Look (turning). (Removes D and puts down F). And after that? (Ends up with BDEF).

JEA (5; 1) same reactions with six colours. When we show him D, he forecasts series DBCEF leaving out D once more because *it's there already. I can't put another one of those down*.

AND (5; 9) constructs the model ABCD. What comes next? (ABCD). And after that? (ABCD). Now after this one (placing cylinder at C) what would come next? (CBAD). Why? *I can see from this line* (points to the model series ending in D). And after (B)? . . . After (ABCD)? (ABCD) and after (C? (CBDB). Inverse series from D: failure.

HEN (6; 2) succeeds in forecasting the cycle ABCDABCDA . . . And after red (C) what comes next? Are you able to tell? No. Guess. (CD). Right. And after blue (D)? (DBA). This is tested, corrected, and a new model series constructed. And after red (C)? (CDBA). And after green (B)? (BACD). The same responses with six colours: cyclic series reconstructed starting with A, but from C Hen forecasts CABEDF. Inverse order is a failure.

CHRI (6; 4) same reactions but when we start with C, he continues with A because *that was first as well*.

FRAN (6; 6) same reactions. Forecasts D after B with four colours. And after (C)? *Green* (B) *because it was in front of red* (C) i.e. on the cylinder. And after (B)? (A). And after (D)? (DCAB). *Why* (C)? *Because it is beside* (D). In contrast Fran is successful with inverse order when starting with D. In the case of six colours he manages the cycle from A, but fails with inverse order starting with F. As for direct order from E on, he ends up with the EFDCAB.

HUG (6; 6) is interesting because of his compositions in pairs. He is successful with the cycle ABCDABCD. But beginning with C he puts down CBDA, then CDBA. Starting from D: DCAB. And after (B)? (BACD). *Is that right?* (BCAD). With six colours same reactions. In contrast, he manages inverse order starting with F, but starting with AF he continues (AF) EDBC. For DCBA beginning with AD he goes on (in inverse order) ADCB which is correct, but he amends this wrongly after that, saying *No, that's wrong, it's* (ADBC) *because everything has to be turned around.*

These few facts are of great interest. Firstly, we can no longer say of these subjects, as we might with those in stage I, that they do not understand the questions asked: they answer quite rightly in fact the questions on forecasting starting with the beginning (A) or the end (D or F) of the model series. By contrast, even with four terms, they can no longer anticipate the sequence if we start from the intermediate terms B or C. Such a systematic response is worth a brief analysis because it attests, more than any other, the contrast between intuitive and operational thought.

For clarity let us begin with the acquisition proper to this stage II: the forecasting of direct cyclic order and its periodicity. It might seem that this discovery is insignificant since it is a question of reading off the sequences on the model series. But as we saw in the first stage this construing is not simple since it consists of the translation of cyclic into linear and vice versa, and it falls down during all of stage I because, in cyclic order each colour may be found equally to the left or the right of the starting point A. It is a question of co-ordinating the relationships of proximity while preserving a given direction of travel: it is this synthesis which is absent in stage I appearing at the beginning of stage II. But then, if it becomes possible when starting from the original colour (A), why does it remain unattainable when starting from an intermediate colour? It is plain that this time-lag between two solutions, identical from the point of view of the operations in question, proves that the synthesis under consideration is not yet operational, but that it is furnished by a simple articulated intuition: the child merely seeks to anticipate the movement of the cylinder in a particular, constant direction of travel, while he reconstructs the positions of proximity by means of the model series. But why in that case is the articulated intuition no longer adequate when we come to take the intermediate colours as starting points?

In a general way we can suppose, so far as direction of travel is concerned and especially its preservation through successive forecasts, that it is easier to follow the order ABCD or ABCDEF by proceeding from one extreme to the other of the model series rather than to start from an intermediate term, because in the latter case the attention is attracted at the same time by both of the possible directions (and so much the more so because the order of the colours on the cylinder is cyclic and not linear as in the model line). As for proximity, which is a question of reconstructing step by step while still maintaining constant the total direction of travel of the sequence, it is clear that if the latter ceases to be fixed, the former will by this very fact be mixed up. In so far as these difficulties are real, the child will moreover tend to refer back to the initial order ABCD and this recollection will further complicate the solution of the questions. In fact, while observing the successive colours of the cylinder turning in full view during the initial explanations given to the subject, just as much as during observation of the colours of the model series, the sequence of these colours acquires the character of a well integrated whole, of a *gestalt* comparable to a kind of tune whose qualities exceed those of the notes taken in isolation. It is precisely because of these perceptual qualities of a collective whole that articulated intuition succeeds in providing a possible forecast of the sequence of colours. Now, in order to foresee subsequently the order of succession starting from an intermediate term, this initial structure had to be broken up to construct another from it, which implies a relatively difficult intuitive task in contrast to the mobility of the operational methods which will later be formed. Apparently it is owing to these various interdependent factors that difficulty arises in reconstructing the order when we do not start from A: the series A ... D or A ... F are thus 'rigid' because intuitive (this rigidity not being incompatible with their articulation) and the child in this stage therefore does not surmount the level of simple image—using preoperational intuition.

In greater detail, it is easy to come across these various factors, e.g. Sim, forecasting what follows C, adds AB in front of this colour and then continues with D, thus reverting the new question back to that of the series ABCD, but with six colours he preserves the direction of travel without the proximity (C) or else the proximity without the direction of travel (CB). Jea after D puts down DBCEF as if D were equivalent to A, and he explicitly omits replacing it between C and E 'because it's already down there: I can't put it down twice'. In other words, he thus reduces the new question likewise to the earlier one. Chris does the same. And after C puts down B (proximity without direction) then AD because the model line also ends in D and A certainly has to fit in somewhere. Hen puts D after C, which seems to be a correct operation, but he adds on BA after D as if one had to complete CD by reading off the beginning of the model series going in the opposite direction. So too Fran and others.

In a word, so long as the child thinks about the bloc of the cyclic series starting with A and continuing to the final term D or F, he manages intuitively to reproduce proximity while keeping direction of travel constant, which amounts to a 'rigid' intuitive series in a single bloc, represented by the model series but, when we begin at an intermediate term he cannot break up the rigid frame

work and he then either returns to this without any more
ado, (Sim, Jea and Chris), or else he tries a new synthesis
but then he starts once more to lose the direction of travel
if he thinks of promixity or to lose the latter if he
maintains the direction of travel. The subjects of this
sub-stage IIa are thus comparable to children who can
count en *bloc* 1, 2, 3, 4, 5, 6, but only by virtue of a sort of
verbal syncretism, and who are lost if one asks them what
number comes after 3 or after 4 for want of analysis and
synthesis of an operational character.

If one grants the foregoing, one then understands from
the outset why the children at this level likewise experience a systematic difficulty in reconstructing the inverse
order of sequence. It would naturally be as easy for the
subject to proceed at the start from D to A or from F to
A, but if this order were acquired before the other it
would itself constitute a direct or initial order. Once the
order A ... D or A ... F is acquired in contrast, to
construct inverse order one must retain this initial order
AB ... and read it off in the opposite direction: it is clear
then that the difficulty is almost the same as in the case of
a new direct sequence starting with one of the intermediate elements. So only Fran and Hug, the oldest of the
subjects quoted, partially succeed in this test which broadly speaking is not successful at this level.

3. The second stage

Sub-stage IIB

The reactions of sub-stage IIb will supply a useful complement of information to the foregoing, by allowing us to
follow step by step all the transitions between the 'rigid'
series of the beginning of this stage and the operational
series of stage III, thanks to a sort of thawing and setting
in motion progressively of the intuitive structures. In the
course of this sub-stage IIb in fact we observe besides the
easy putting in sequence of A to D or A to F, a possible
sequence made between some intermediate term and the

final term D or F. But very curiously, revealing the still intuitive nature of this discovery, the subject cannot in the latter case go on correctly beyond D or F to take up the cycle ABC again, while if he starts his series from the first term A, he continues without difficulty beyond D or F! As for inverse order, we observe from the beginning of this sub-stage IIb the ability to construct the regressive series D . . A or F back to A, and beyond it, then towards the end of this sub-stage, the series proceeding from an intermediate term back to A, but without the ability to pursue this beyond A. Thus for the inverse series as for direct order there exists a time-lag between seriation from the terms at either extreme, and seriation starting from intermediate terms; moreover, we note a slight time-lag between the discovery of inverse order and the corresponding phases with regard to direct order, but this second time-lag disappears at the end of the stage and thus tends to diminish as one comes nearer the operational level.

Here first of all are some examples of straightforward cases of this sub-stage.

PIE (5; 5) rightly forecasts that after ABCD you will find the same series repeated and that after A . . . F you will again have A . . . F etc. And if I put this colour (C) here, what comes after? (CDEFBA). Why (B)? *Because it goes this way* (he follows the model line from C to F then from B to A in the inverse direction). And after that? (E). (EFD-CBA). (We construct a series EFABCD beside his). Which of these two is more correct, yours or mine? *This one* (his own). Why? *Because here it goes like that* (on the cylinder: after the order EF he points out in inverse order DCBA).

Inverse order: What comes after (F) then, if I turn it like this? (FEDCBA). And then? (FEDCBA). And after this one (C) turning the opposite way again? (CF). And then? (CEAB). Look (he observes CB). And after that? (EADC). Can this line (model) help you? *No.* Why not? *It's not the same thing. It didn't turn the same way.* And after (B)? (BCD) And if it turns in the other direction? (BEFDC).

Pie thus manages very well with inverse seriation if we begin with F and fails as soon as we start with C or B.

JOL (5; 8) same reactions with direct order: correct with A . . . FA . . . F, but fails with intermediate terms to go beyond F. We show him inverse rotation and ask (with four colours) what comes after D? (DCBA). And after that? (DCBA) And if I put (B) here? (BACD). With six colours correct after hesitation FEDCBA. And then after that? (F . . . A) again. And after (CB)? (CBFEDAF). And after (E)? (ECABDF).

STE (6; 5) puts down ABCD. And after that? (ABCD) again. And after (C)? CDBA. Likewise with six colours, forecasts A . . . FA . . . F, etc. And after (D)? (DEFCBD). Why does it finish with (D)? Because (D) is the same thing at the start and at the finish. And after (E)? (EFABDE). Is that quite right? No, it's (EFDCBA). And after (C)? (CDEFBA). And after (D)? (DEFCBA). We get him to make another model series: And if we begin with A what follows, (ABCDEF) and with (D)? (DEFBAC).

COL. (6; 6) also forecasts correctly the periodicity when we begin with A (six colours). With (C) he reverses to CDE-FBA. With E the same: EFDCBA.

MAR (6; 11) correctly forecasts A . . . DA . . . D etc. And after (C)? (CDBA) And after (A)? (ABCD) And after (C)? (CDBA). With six colours A . . . FA . . . F correct. How did you do it? *I looked along on the cylinder* (pointing to the model series, whose correspondence to the cylinder he therefore well understands). And after (D) what comes next? (DEFC). And after (E)? (EFDCAB). Look. (D) (DEF) (without hesitation). And then? (DEFBCA).

As for inverse rotation, the same phenomenon: if we start with B (four colours): BACD, and with C (six colours): CBADEF.

BAS (6; 6) is cautious and explains. After forecasting A . . . DA . . . D, he puts down after C: (CDA). And after that? *I don't know now.* How did you do it? *I looked at the cylinder* (really the model series). Does this line (model) help you? *No, that can't help me any more because I've already put down* (CDA). Now it's something else.

RIS (7; 3) starting from D (with six colours) ends correctly DEF: And then? (CDA). Why (C)? *Because it comes after it.* And after (E)? (ECDCAB). And after (D)? (DEF-BCA).

SIM (7; 7) starting with A forecasts ABCDEFABCDEF without hesitation. And after (C)? (CDEFBA). Why do you put (B) after (F)? *Because it's after brown* (C). And if I start with (E)? (EFDCBA). Could you put down (EFABCD)? *That one there* (DCBA) *is more correct.* Why? *Because it's in the right order.* What sort of order? *Because it's regular.* And that one there (ABCD) what's that one like? *That's regular too, No, it's not regular.* Why? *Because it's not the same as* (DCBA).

Likewise ROG (7; 0) prefers DEFCBA to DEFABC *because it goes in the opposite direction while for* FABC *You'd have to turn it the other way.*

CHA (7; 0) forecasts EFDCBA *because* (D) *is in front of blue* (E) and MA (7: 0) EFDCBAEFDC . . . *because it was the other way round.* (When we put the cylinder at E): (E) *and* (F) *are on the left* (instead of being on the right as in the model series) *so then* (D) *should also be the other way round towards the left.*

Here finally is an example of the most advanced responses of sub-stage IIb (thus intermediate between stages II and III), which are similar to the foregoing in respect of progressive order but mark a slight step forward from the point of view of inverse order.

DENI (6; 8) first of all forecasts the series A . . . FA . . . F *because it's the same thing here* (model series) *and there* (cylinder). (We place it at C). And after this? (CDEFBA). Could we put it (AB)? . . . . (No) . . . *because up to there* (F) *it's like the model and then it starts off again with* (BA). (We have another model series made and get him to forecast again the periodicity from A, which Deni does straight away!) And if we place the cylinder at (D)? (DEFCBA). Why do you put down (C) after (F)? *Because it starts off with* (CBA) *again.* Couldn't you put (DEFABC)? *No, because that's wrong: there on the cylinder it's not the same thing.*

Inverse series: Deni constructs without hesitation FEDC-BAFEDCBA. And if we begin here (C) turning it still in the other direction? (CBADEF). Why is (D) after (A)? *Because it goes like that* (points with his right hand towards the left between C and A and from left to right, from D to F, moving from A to D in a single stirring movement as if the rotation had as its effect the joining together of these two. And after (D)? (DCBAEF). And after (C)? (CBADEF).

The clarity of these responses leaves nothing to be desired. Contrary to the subjects of sub-stage IIa each of these eight children (and we could quote many other examples) is able when we start off in direct order with an intermediate term, to forecast the sequence up to the final D or F. Moreover, as in stage IIa, it goes without saying that if one starts with A, they forecast correctly the cyclic series in its periodicity A ... FA ... FA ... By contrast, when you start with an intermediate element they are unanimous after continuing correctly up to the final term D or F in failing with the follow-up ABC. .... In the very great majority of cases the child continues in fact by reversing the terms in the new cycle. E.g. Pie instead of constructing the series CDEFAB forecasts CDEFBA, then instead of EFABCD he forecasts EFDCBA. From Pie to Deni we find again and again this unforeseen reversal, excepting one or two irregularities. But amongst the exceptions there are some illuminating ones: so Ste who forecasts DEFCBD because D has to come at the end, and who puts down EFABDE forgetting C (the series would be correct without this omission) then upon being asked 'Is that quite right?' hastens to reverse the ending to make EFDCBA!

Now, a very curious thing, the same reaction is found again for regressive order, but then it is itself reversed. At the beginning of this sub-stage IIb inverse order is discovered when we begin with the final element F or D, but if we begin forecasts starting with an intermediate term there is failure (as was the case in the course of sub-stage IIa with direct order itself). But at the end of sub-stage IIa (the case of Deni), the child becomes capable in the case of both direct and inverse order, of correctly finishing the series up to term A if we start with an intermediate term. Only, if we ask him to carry on beyond A, he then continues by inverting the inverse order, i.e. by re-establishing direct order! This is how Deni instead of the series CBAFED forecasts CBADEF, and in place of DCBAFE forecasts DCBAEF!

The explanation of these facts may therefore be directly linked with that of the reactions of sub-stage IIa, and even simplifies it by virtue of the regular schematization assumed, in the case of these older subjects, by their intuition of 'rigid' series. The correct forecasting of cyclic order implies, we recall, a co-ordination of the relationships of proximity while keeping the direction of travel constant. Now, by the fact that in a cyclic order each term is found starting from A working from right to left and equally from left to right, the child experiences an additional difficulty in arranging the terms starting with an intermediate term, even when he manages it beginning with the initial element (A ... FA ... FA). In the course of sub-stage IIa it follows that, either the subjects reconstruct accurately their proximity but without keeping constant the direction of travel, or else preserve this direction while neglecting their proximity, or even refer back to the model series as if it could be reproduced without further ado following the intermediate term. In the course of this sub-stage IIb on the contrary the last two of these three reactions are eliminated. It is noteworthy indeed to observe that our subjects at level IIb almost invariably keep relationships of proximity constant and except, notably, for the relationship joining A to F (or A to D) when it is a question of passing from one cycle A ... F to the next, starting from an intermediate term. In contrast, when they reach F (or D) they lose the direction of travel, while they maintain it perfectly well when they start off with A! So we have here the clearest proof that the difficulty inherent in cyclic order is actually that of preserving the direction of travel, granted the fact that in either direction the same elements are to be found. It goes without saying that it is this last statement which puzzles the child for such a long time: he simply does not understand that if the same elements are to be found starting with an intermediate term, e.g. D, they will not be found in the same order; and then having finished his series up to F (e.g. DEF) he imagines that to come back to ABC he only has to turn back to D and to read off CBA on the model series, as if CBA reading from D, were the same thing as ABC reading from F!

Now we see right away that the cause of this confusion is nothing other than the 'rigid' character of the series: having before his eyes the model series when he reconstructs the fragment of series DEF, the child cannot detach his thinking from it in order to continue in the form FABC and he prefers to stick to the elements he can see preceding D (since in point of fact we do find them in either direction), but then, since he started from D to reconstruct DEF he also starts from D to reconstruct A, B, and C, whence the order CBA, because D and C are neighbours, while D and A are not.

The result is thus DEFCBA instead of DEFABC because the child remains within the rigid model series and works through it to either extremity starting from D (without seeing that he is then changing the direction of travel), instead of cutting up the series into DEF and ABC or getting outside it in his thinking.

As for the forecasting of inverse order, it follows the same pattern, but in the other direction. At the beginning inverse order is not successful, when starting from an intermediate term for the same reasons as direct order in the course of sub-stage IIa. But at the end of the stage (Deni) it is successful up to A (e.g. starting from C) but after putting down CBA the subject comes back to C and completes the remainder of his rigid series starting from this same element whence (C) DEF by a reversal of inverse order and hence a return to direct order.

This explanation by the rigid bloc quality of the model series simply translates what the subjects themselves express in their reasons: Pie, e.g. shows by a gesture, how starting from C he constructs CDEF, to add BA after, which extends D in the other direction, and states that this way of working reproduces the actual motion of the revolving cylinder: 'because it goes like this here'. In contrast, he gets lost in the inverse series because the model series 'is not the same thing; it isn't turned the same way', as if this model series had a special fixed direction corresponding to the cylinder revolving in the direct sense. As for Bar, he will not go beyond the final term when we start from an intermediate term (otherwise he gets on very well), for the reason that the model line 'can't help me any more, now it's another way': it is sufficient to say, though negatively, that it constitutes a rigid and self contained whole. If we consider the series EFDCBA as 'in order' and 'regular', in opposition to EFABCD which is 'not regular', we understand by that, like Pie, that this dual movement in opposite directions starting from the intermediate term (E) reproduces the order of the revolving cylinder itself. Deni, finally, is completely precise: the series CDEFBA is more correct than CEDFAB 'because up to here (F) it is like the model und then it starts again with (BA)', while the order DEFABC 'is wrong: ... on the cylinder it's not the same thing'. Even more, for inverse order, he executes a circular gesture designed to imitate the rotation of the cylinder and which unites CBA to DEF as if these two fragments of the series, which start off from C in opposite directions from each other reproduced one complete rotation! In a word, since the elements constituting the beginning of the model series will have to form the end of the new series, the subject brings them into harmony by reversing their respective directions of travel, thinking thus to imitate the actual rotation of the cylinder: the 'rigidity' of the intuitive series (model series) thus prevents them, when starting from an intermediate element, from using 'operations' on the rotation as such, and they then replace it by a reversal of the order of the terms preceding this starting point. Three quotations of Rog, Cha, and Ma, picked out at the end of the list (prior to Deni) together express the whole matter quite clearly.

Altogether, the various reactions of stage II (sub-stages IIa and IIb) and this is the essential characteristic of the rigid or intuitive series as opposed to the mobile or operational series of stage III, all add up to a confusion or want of differentiation between the objective order of the elements turning on the cylinder and the subjective order of the perceptions and actions occurring in the construction of the model series. So long as the actual activity inherent in this construction (or simply in the series constructed earlier) agrees with the external order of events, the child builds up the correct series: this is why every series starting with A is properly constructed, and correctly extended in the form A . . . FA . . . FA. But as soon as one starts from an intermediate term X, either the child does not even manage to foresee the series X . . . F (sub-stage IIa) or else he succeeds in doing so but cannot continue beyond F (sub-stage IIb): in the first case IIa, either he preserves the direction but fails over proximity, or else he proceeds using pairs of elements which are neighbours but reverses the order, and in the second case (IIb), either he pursues the latter method, or else he systematically reverses the elements preceding X. In all these cases we can therefore say that the characteristic series of this stage are rigid, because intuitive, and intuitive because (both when correct and when faulty) they depend upon actual previous activity rather than on abstract relationships established by virtue of true operations.

4. The third stage and conclusions

The reactions of stage III (7 to 8 years on average) finally free themselves from the foregoing errors by attaining operational mobility. Here is an example:

REN (8; 0) constructs A . . . FA . . . F: is that difficult? *Oh no.* And if we begin at (C)? *(CDEFABCDEF).* And with (E)? *EDC . . . You are sure? It depends which way you turn it. Like the last time. Oh, then its (EFABCDEF).* How can you tell? *I look at this* (model series) *but now I can do it even without looking.*

And if I turn it this way (inverse direction) what comes after (F)? *FEDCBA.* And with (B)? *(BAFEDC).* And with (D)? *(DCBAFE).*

We can see that the different questions no longer present any problems, inverse order even being spontaneously foreseen by the subject ('It depends which way you turn it') and the series starting with intermediate terms no longer evokes accidental inversions.

In conclusion, let us first note that the stages established correspond to a chronological progression. Out of seventy-three subjects interviewed, stage I gave an average of 4; 9 (4; 3 for Ia and 5; 2 for Ib) and stage II 6; 5 (6; 0 for IIa and 6; 9 for IIb).

But let us, above all, point out how much these stages agree, despite appearances, with those we obtained in the course of Chapter One with the study of the construction of linear order. On the course of stage I direct linear order gives rise to a correct forecast, but inverse linear order as well as direct and inverse cyclic order are forecast incorrectly. Now it is clear that direct linear order requires only a simple perceptual intuition while its inversion, and equally direct cyclic order, imply an additional difficulty, which is notably similar in both cases: that of imagining the order obtained when making a half-turn, or when describing a circle, and thus returning to the starting point. It is noteworthy moreover, to observe in both cases that the relationship 'between' is absent during the first stage and precisely because of these difficulties, whether of inversion (linear order) or of periodicity (cyclic order). In the course of stage II inverse linear order is acquired, but the child still does not understand (or not immediately) the reversals of order due to the half-rotations or rotations either of the apparatus or the observer (from his personal point of view). Now, so far as cyclic order is concerned, we observe in the course of stage II successes and failures exactly equivalent in their degree of difficulty of intuition: direct cyclic order is acquired, which therefore corresponds to inverse linear order, but only if one starts concerned, we observe in the course of stage I successes the same for inverse cyclic order, which corresponds perfectly to the obstacles respecting partial or full rotation of linear apparatus. On the other hand, in both cases (Chapter One and Two) there persist certain difficulties in the course of the second stage, relative to the relationship 'between' (which in cyclic order appear in form of problems of proximity). Articulated, but rigid, intuition therefore is very characteristic of stage II in both areas. Finally in stage III all questions are solved in both cases.

Such a parallelism is of the greatest interest in studying the problem of the relationship between intuition and operation: from simple or perceptual intuition to articulated intuition on to rigid representational anticipations and from there to operations. There is therefore the same continuity in the construction of both types of order. There must be added, alike for both of these, that the difficulties relative to inverse order start off by being greater than those relative to direct order, while this time lag progressively diminishes as one moves away from the earlier intuitive levels and approaches that of operations, i.e. precisely towards articulated intuition becoming reversible.

PART 2

Change of Location

Having studied relations of order in terms of operations of 'location' we can now undertake the analysis of movement itself as a 'change of location'. We shall see in fact how far the idea of the path traversed, which adult intuition would be inclined to consider as basic, is actually a derivation compared with intuitions of order (primacy of the point of arrival of movements in contrast to the interval included between the points of departure and arrival) and how its ultimate operational constitution is itself subordinate to that of operations of location. The first chapter of this second part is designed to show this connexion and Chapters Four and Five study changes of location as such.

Let us recall here what we said earlier in the Foreword of this work: that is how greatly the primacy of the point of arrival of movements, as opposed to the actual path traversed, is tied up with the finalism which impels the child to consider each change of location as directed towards some goal, i.e. precisely towards its given finishing point. That is why the hierarchy of values, which determines the successive concentrations of the perceptual and image-using intuition of movement remains constantly as follows: first, consideration of the point of arrival, next, of the point of departure, and only lastly of the interval between these two, i.e. of the path traversed. Moreover, if the matter is already clear-cut as far as change of location itself is concerned, it will be even more so in comparison of speeds.

On primary intuitions these comparisons are based exclusively on the actions of preceding and overtaking while starting points, distances travelled and times taken are ignored.

CHAPTER THREE

The Path Traversed

By what characteristics will a subject at the level of pre-operational intuitions evaluate a movement? Will it be, from the outset, by the path traversed, as with operations allowing a co-ordination of distances with the sequence of changes of location? Or will the idea of the path traversed begin by being undifferentiated from the order of succession itself, and tied up more with starting points and, above all, points of arrival rather than with distances as such?

To answer these questions, we ask the children to compare two paths taken, one in a straight line, the other an indirect line, but such that the points of arrival and departure of the moving objects can always be visually correlated according to the relationships 'above' or 'below'.

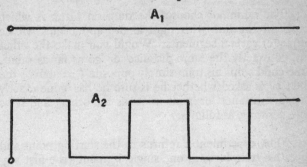

In fact we stretch out two pieces of string on each of two planks of wood, horizontally. One is straight. On the first plank A, the second piece of string describes a kind of

Greek frieze, all the segments being equal and at right angles to each other.

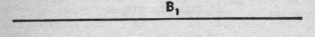

B_1

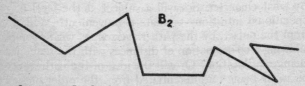

B_2

On the second plank B, the second piece of string is stretched out in irregular zigzags with variable angles and unequal segments. A moving bead on each string on both planks represents a tramcar. The child also has some cardboard measuring strips: for plank A, one single measure the length of the identical sections of the figure, and for plank B, five measures corresponding to the five different lengths of segments.

Q 1. The examiner chooses the tram on plank A which travels on the line with right angles and begins with a journey of several segments: 'Would you make the other tram go exactly the same distance' or 'go as far as mine'. If the child stops his tram simply opposite (= above) the other, he is asked whether he is sure he has 'gone exactly the same distance' or 'gone as far as the other', and if he is, we continue as follows:

Q 1a. The experimenter returns to the starting point and moves his tram forward one single segment (the first segment is perpendicular to the child's straight piece of string) and thus it is left opposite the starting point of the child's tram. When we invite him to do an equal distance on his straight length of string, either he refuses to make any change because his tram is still opposite the examiner's or else he discovers that 'going the same distance' does not necessarily signify arriving at the same level.

Q 1b. When the child has stopped his tram opposite the experimenter's after a number of segments, we may also suggest covering the distance back to the depot: then we move the tram along our right-angled line segment by segment, each time asking the subject to travel an equal distance. The child thus notices that he reaches the depot before the other tram and we ask him why.

Then we ask question one again for the outward direction.

Q 2. After a change of location several segments long in the outward direction on plank A we ask the child if he is quite sure that the pieces are equal: 'Could you get any help from this bit of cardboard (measuring one segment in length)?' If the subject hesitates the cardboard is moved closer to one of the segments, but without placing it over it.

Q 3. If the child understands the measuring of the distances on plank A we go over Q 1 and 2 on plank B, but offering all five cardboard strips at the same time. In the case of the most advanced subjects we suggest measuring B with a single one chosen from the five strips.

Out of forty-nine children interviewed between 4 and 9 years of age (mostly 5 to 8 years) we were able to pick out three chief stages, corresponding to those in Chapters One and Two. During stage I, the length of the paths traversed is evaluated in terms of the intuitive order of the points of arrival. In the course of sub-stage Ia this is so in spite of any suggestions to the contrary; in the course of sub-stage Ib the questions relating to the first segment (1a) and to the return journey(1b) change the child's attitude to the first segments, but he returns to his first conception over a longer distance. In the course of stage II the child separates the length of the paths travelled from the intuitive order of the points of arrival, but fails to find a measure and is content with intuitive approximations. During sub-stage IIa, he begins as in stage I then adapts, little by little; during sub-stage IIb he evaluates the path from the outset according to its length, but fails with the measure. in the course of stage II, finally, the measure is discovered.

In what follows, we shall not stress the measure as such, this is a problem we shall take up in later studies of the child's conception of space and geometry, but we shall bring the analysis to bear only on the question of the relationship between the order of the points of arrival and the length of the paths traversed. Nevertheless from this point of view itself, it was apposite to examine, in passing, the reactions to the measure, which in this particular case go towards showing whether this length is conceived intuitively or operationally.

1. *The first stage: Length of the paths traversed evaluated in terms of the intuitive order of the points of arrival*

We recall that during stage I the notion of order remains entirely intuitive: if direct linear order is preserved, it is not yet capable of inversion; on the other hand cyclic order is in no wise understood and with inverse linear order, equally with direct cyclic order, we may observe the existence of systematic difficulties respecting the idea of interval or relationship 'between'. It is very interesting that it is precisely this intuitive linear order on which the child in stage I relies for the evaluation of the length of the paths traversed. This relationship has nothing intrinsically absurd in it, since it amounts to determining the distance as an interval between two fixed points; but, precisely because of the fact that only direct linear order gives rise to a correct intuition, this method (estimating the length of the journeys according to the order of the arrival points only) leads to accurate results in so far as the moving objects follow the same lines in the same direction and start from the same spot. In contrast, when the two lines traversed are different, as in the present experiment where one is straight and the other indirect, the incomplete nature of the initial intuition of order, and in particular the lack of understanding of the relationships of interval (or relationship 'between') leads to the surprising result that two paths are considered equal when their points of arrival coincide (or when one of them is 'opposite' the other) independently of the distances formed by the respective linear intervals.

Here are some examples of these early responses.

LIL ($5; 5$). The examiner travels the first five segments of A_2: the child places his cube exactly opposite this: Is that the same distance? Yes. Quite sure? Yes. Let's go back to the depot and see if it's the same thing (going back segment by segment: Q 1b). (Lil sets his cube opposite the other each time, without moving it when the segment of A_2 covered is perpendicular to his line A_1). Now I'm going only up to there (two segments). You do the same distance. There! (opposite). And now (one segment). I can't go forward. Why? Your train is there (points underneath the starting point of his own). But you have to make the trip (Lil moves forward 2 millimetres). Is that the same now? Yes. And now (four segments) (Lil follows those segments which are parallel to his own, without attending to those segments of A_2 which are perpendicular to A_1, and arrives exactly opposite). Let's start again (two segments). (Same again).

JOC ($5; 5$). Same reactions at first. The train is moved one segment, the first on A_2: Joc starts off by moving his 2-3 millimetres. Is that the same distance? (Does not know what to say). Let's carry on (second segment). There! (opposite). You think you've done the same distance? Yes. And could this cardboard strip help you to measure (bringing it nearer to the first segment)? (shakes his head) Let's go back to the station travelling the same distance (bringing the train back one segment on A_2, Joc does the same on A_1). But you're already at the station. I'm not. Have we gone the same distance on the way back? . . . (at a loss) Then let's change trains (experimenter does a trip on A_1 and child takes up position directly underneath on A_2). Do you think you have gone exactly the same distance as mine? Yes.

CHA (5; 6). Same responses, but justifies this each time saying: *It's the same distance, because this one here is here*, i.e. above) *and that one there is there* (right underneath).

MIC (5; 8) Begins as the foregoing and does not move his train when the first segment only of A_2 is traversed. With two segments of A_2 he limits his move to one segment of A_1 placing it directly above the other. Are you sure you have gone as far as mine away from the depot? *Yes.* Point with your finger to your route and mine (he follows them with his finger). Is it the same distance with your finger? *No.* Which is longer? *The blue train's* (A_2). Why? *Because of the squares* (right angles). Then I'll carry on (third segment), i.e. perpendicular (to A_1). *I'm going to stay where I am.* But with your finger which of the two routes is further from the depot? *That one* (A_2) correct. Then go back to the depot and go the same distance as mine—but as far as mine has gone! (He starts again from the beginning and once more places it directly above).

With plank B: exactly the same thing.

FRE (5; 9). Same responses: Do you think that you could measure with this strip of cardboard whether you have gone the same distance? *Yes.* He then places the cardboard on top of the two beads at the same time to show that the points of arrival coincide and does not concern himself with the intervening distances from the starting point.

It is clear that none of these children imagines that four or five segments of the indirect line with right angles, A_2 , are equal in length to one segment of the straight line A_1 , which has the same starting and finishing points: perception alone is enough to register that the straight line is shorter. And amongst the subjects, Mic proves to himself, by passing his finger along each of the lengths of string, that A_2 is longer 'because of the squares', i.e. the right angles. If the child declares that the paths are equal in both cases it is because he thinks of the actual movements or changes of location, and not of the distances covered; or more precisely, he does not make distinction between distances and movements. Principally, he conceives of the movement or 'change of location' as being, in the strict and limited sense, a 'dis-placement' or 'change of position', while the 'positions' themselves are located by the intuitive order of the positions of starting and mainly of finishing. Two movements are thus held to be the same length when they arrive at the same finishing point. If this is the principle, then detours made enroute matter little. 'It's the same distance' says Cha, 'because this one here is here and that one there is there' (one above the other).

But one difficulty persists: what if the child had not understood what we required of him? It could in fact be that his reactions proceed from a sheer verbal difficulty or as the mathematicians would say purely a question of definition. The equality of the two routes is defined by us as an equality of the actual distances travelled, but this could be conventionally defined as a coincidence of finishing points: the child faced with the question, 'Have they gone the same distance?' could simply understand 'have they travelled without overtaking one another' and everything would be explained by that.

Two reasons, however, each sufficient in itself, oppose this interpretation. The first is that we shall find the same response in many other fields, and most particularly in that of speed; primary intuition of speed is, as we shall see, that of overtaking, i.e. of a change of order, and it is by means of this criterion alone that in stage I the child estimates differences in speeds without concerning himself with the distances covered in a given time. If then it is a question of a general mechanism, one could not attribute the foregoing reactions to a verbal misunderstanding. In the second place, the subjects at sub-stage Ib, who begin like the foregoing, manage to correct this initial reaction during short journeys but later fall back into their mistake with longer journeys. The analysis of their reactions thus allows us on the other hand to verify the meaning of those in sub-stage Ia. Here are some examples:

RAY (5; 6). The experimenter chooses the straight line A_1 and moves his train the equivalent of two segments. Ray then moves his five segments on A_2 which has the effect of putting it directly underneath the first: Is that the same distance? Yes. Let's go back to the station and change trains. Look, I'll go up to here (one segment of A_2). And I move to here. (Ray moves correctly along A_1 about one segment). Is that the same? Yes. Why? . . . Right. Let's go on then (five segments on A_2). There! (He places it opposite). Is that the same thing? Yes. Sure? Yes. Can you measure with the cardboard strip? (He places it across the two beads like Fre).

REN (6; 7). We move forward the equivalent of three segments on A_1. Ren moves his train six segments on A_2 so as to be opposite: Is that the same distance? Yes. Quite sure? Yes. Why? (he traces with his finger). It's longer down below (A_2). Then go back to the station and do the same length as mine. (He starts again and arrives at the same point). But you just told me that the blue one (A_2) has travelled further? Yes, but you have to straighten out blue's route (=the piece of string A_2 so as to compare it with A_1). Could you find out with this strip of cardboard (=measuring one segment)? (he tries to measure, but inaccurately leaving the strip obliquely without following each of the segments at right angles). It won't work, because there are these little squares (the angles). It would have to be straight. (Attempt to show him, but he does not understand). Let's change trains. (We cover the first segment on A_2, perpendicular to A_1). (He stays put at starting point of A_1 . . .) It's the same. But I moved and you didn't! (He moves forward a little, about one segment's length) Is that exactly the same? (He measures one segment and corrects it). Yes. Now I'm moving here (nine segments). (He tries to measure). There, there, and there (arrives directly above).

Plank B. Experimenter travels three unequal segments of B_2 and Ren places his directly above. Is that exactly the same distance? Yes. Why? Because they're opposite. Is it the same length? No. (he moves forward a little). Is that right now, or not? No, it's more correct when it's right opposite (he puts it back above the other). You could measure it. (He puts the cardboard over both beads like Fre and Ray).

By their difference from subjects in sub-stage Ia, these children through their very hesitations leave no more doubt as to the significance of the early response we are discussing here. Everything happens as if the conceptions of the path travelled on the one hand and of change of location evaluated by its arrival point on the other (displacement or change of location), were at first undifferentiated (sub-stage Ia) and as if they were only beginning to be differentiated at the level we are examining now. Ren, e.g. explicitly says that the route on the indirect line 'is longer' but he proves unable to compare it with the route on the straight line if the former is not itself made into a straight line. 'It would have to be straight'. And then when he cannot find any criterion for estimating the distances, other than the order of arrival, he returns to this early system justifying it explicitly: 'It is more correct when it's right opposite'. Ray on the contrary returns to it as it were automatically, after succeeding briefly in separating the distance in the case of a single segment: as soon as this is increased again he falls back on the criterion of the point of arrival. But why does Ren, who is further ahead in this attempt at separation, not manage to measure the series of segments? We saw that he knows perfectly well how to measure a single one, but as soon as it is a question of several at a time, and placed in different directions, he remains unable to add up these segments, as if measuring the path traversed should be carried out only towards the point of arrival. It is clear then that the obstacle once more arises from the conception of order: the early intuition of order, which is that of direct linear order, is in reality that of straight-line sequences, and as soon as it is a question of indirect lines and especially of the Greek frieze form of A_2, this order then presents for the subjects at stage I the same difficulties as cyclic order, and the relationships of interval (or 'between') are no longer mastered. Thence the evaluation of the path traversed by the arrival point alone, and thence, even in the case of subjects who like Ren begin to separate distance from order, the difficulty of comparing by measuring the straight line A_1 and the indirect line A_2.

2. The second stage: Separation of path traversed from order of finishing points, but failure in measuring

In the course of sub-stage IIa, subjects begin as in Ib, but instead of returning, when distances are increased, to evaluation according to arrival point, they continue to separate distance from order. Here are some examples starting with an intermediate case between Ib and IIa.

PAN (4; 8) superior: We move the bead five segments on A_2. Pan places his block above: *What does it mean, going the same distance: to travel the same length or to arrive at the same spot? To travel at the same speed.* And do these two travel at the same speed? *No, the red one (A_1) goes quicker.* Why? *The blue one went round about and the red one went straight ahead.* Then make the red one be as tired as the blue one. (He moves red forward on straight line A_1). Could you get any help measuring with that? *No.* Starting again (two segments). (He places his block above the other). Is it as tired as mine? *Yes* (four segments). (He moves forward several segments, but without being able to measure one-to-one).

Plank B: We move three unequal segments on B_1 and Pan places his block directly above, then corrects himself right away, pushing it further on and measuring very approximately with his finger.

ER (5; 7). Five segments on A_2: he places his head opposite. Do you think that's the same distance? *Yes, because the two trains are like that* (one above the other). What does it mean: going the same distance? *Arriving at the same spot.* How long did (A_2) the blue one take? *Two or three minutes.* And the red one (A_1)? *The same.* And now? (first segment)? *I have to leave it* (does not move his train). But mine did move? *Oh, yes!* (He moves it forward). (Five segments). *It wasn't right before* (he moves it a long way). Could you measure with that? (He tries) *No.* Plank B: moves it forward from the first.

AND (5; 8). Six segments: he puts his train directly above, then forwards, back, forward, etc. without deciding between the two systems: Could you find out using this (cardboard) *No, I want to go round it* (he traces path with his finger on

A_2). And now (five segments)? (Places opposite). *No, that's
not right* (hesitates as before). (One segment, perpendicular).
There! (goes forward at once). (six segments). *There!* (forward several lengths).

Plank B: goes forward from the first gauging distances by
eye, after laying measure on first segment.

JAN (6; 2). Experimenter moves forward three units on A_1
(straight line): Jan sets his train opposite, underneath, which
represents seven segments. With one segment on the straight
line he does the same (=three segments on A_2): *Is that the
same? Yes* (he traces with a finger) *No, it's longer. Well
let's go back to the station and start again* (one segment).
There, that's the same, that's one (correct, the first segment
of A_2, perpendicular to A_1). *And that* (five segments) (At
first he moves underneath, then counts) *No, that would be
ten* (moves back).

Plank B: at the outset he moves ahead on A_1. Tries to
measure but very inaccurately, without placing the units together one by one, and hindered because he always points the
strip of cardboard in relation to the point of arrival.

UL (7; 7). Exeprimenter travels two units on A_1. U1 moves
directly beneath (five segments of A_2): *Are you sure it's the
same distance? Yes. No* (he goes back and starts again). *There*
(correct). *I'm moving here* (five segments). *There!* (seven
units) *How can you tell? Because I look at the sizes* (checks
with fingers). *And could you use that* (strip)? *No. You see*
(putting it on two segments)? *No.*

Plank B: he moves on B_2 farther than B_1, at the outset,
then measures the route on B_1 using two strips placed next
to one another and carries these over to B_2, angling them a
little but not taking every contour into account.

We see that at the beginning of the interview these
subjects make the same distinction between the equality of
the paths travelled and that of the arrival points as in
stage Ib. Er is quite explicit about this (going the same
distance is 'arriving at the same spot') and Pan gives us
the key to this response: making two equal journeys is
'going at the same speed', i.e. precisely, according to the
intuition of young children, arriving at the same spot (see

Chapter Seven). But later, observation of the detours (in the case of Pan) and above all the experience of the path travelled on the first segment of A_2, perpendicular to A_1, shows the child that the order of the arrival points does not correspond to the length of the paths traversed: in particular if we divide the whole route into successive lengths, there is no longer any correspondence between the two kinds of values. The child then seeks to evaluate the lengths themselves, and does so either by eye or by measuring with his fingers. In fact it is by first tracing the paths travelled with a finger that he best sees their disparity, as if he had to relive the movement in order to understand the difference between the paths. 'I want to go round it' says And, e.g. But as the journey is still experienced as an expression of a unique and total movement, it may not be broke up into stationary lengths, hence the refusal to use the cardboard strip. Added to this is the fact that, attracted always by the preferred direction determined by the point of arrival, the child using the cardboard tends to point it in relation to this spot (cf. Jan and Ul at the end of the interviews) whence the impossibility of splitting up the route. However Jan was close to measuring when he counted the segments.

The subjects at sub-stage IIb immediately make the distinction between lengths of journeys made and the order of the arrival points, but they scarcely respond any better to measuring.

Luc (5; 10). Three units on A_1: Luc puts his train at the top of the first segment of A_2: Is that the same length? No (he moves on to the third segment). There: that's three squares. Could you use this strip (placed on the line)? No.

Plank B: Two segments: Luc measures with his fingers and stops a little ahead. Because you came from here and mine from here (he checks by making the trip again with his fingers).

Dor (6; 0). Two segments of A_2: correct; and one, the same (immediately). Six segments: at first places it further on. Why? Because there are these little squares there. But why just there? *There are six of them* (counts by eye but refuses the measuring strip). Continuation: same reaction.

Plank B: moves forward immediately, takes strips 1, 2, and 3 for these segments of B_2, then places 1, 4, and 2 on the straight line B_1 and says *That makes three there and three here*, as if it were a case of equal units. Which is longer? *This one here* (B_1 where the longest strip, i.e. 4, is placed). Put these strips (1, 4, and 2) back down here (on B_2). (He only moves 4 and 2). Following this he refuses to use a single cardboard unit. *You can't do it like that.*

EL (6; 4) gauges three segments on A_1 by eye, following up three on A_2: Is that right? *Yes . . . no, not quite three times* (he moves it on a little). Could you measure with that? (putting strip against one segment) *No.* We start again: he calculates by eye, without keeping units equal.

Plank B: he places his train, and covers the two pathways with measuring strips, not concerned with their disparity: *This comes to three, and here it's five.* But he does not alter the location of his bead. He fails in the use of a single measuring strip.

CHRI (7; 1) always moves the train on A_1 ahead of the other, but refuses to measure, saying *You can see what it is.*

GIL (7; 2) reacts in the same way at first, tries with the cardboard strip then discards it, preferring to measure with his fingers. But he finally picks it up again and is successful in measuring, thus moving on to stage III.

We can see that from the outset, these subjects all distinguish between equality of lengths traversed and coincidence of point of arrival, but the problem is to know whether this dissociation is complete, or whether within the conception of the path traversed by the child at this level, there remain certain intuitive attachments derived from the idea of the order of arrival (and if it may not be precisely these attachments which hinder measuring as yet). Indeed, there could not be complete differentiation between the two kinds of concept under consideration except by means of a dual operational system: points of arrival, here, arise from an arrangement of elements coming in succession (A before B, B before C etc.) while lengths or distances imply the dovetailing of the gaps inherent between these successive points. Now we have been able to note, in the course of Chapters One and Two that the subjects belonging to this second stage are still far from mastering the use of operations of order, since they still work from 'rigid' intuitions (for sub-stage IIb, see Chapter One, §2, and in particular Chapter Two, §3), although these are articulated: forecasting of sequences is only possible starting from the commencement of a series and not from an intermediate term, etc.

If this is the case, one may go on to wonder whether this linking up of the intervals, or the operational conception of distances travelled, is already achieved. It is here that the examination of the responses relating to measuring is very instructive, even without emphasizing the mechanism of the latter.

Why in fact does none of these children manage to measure the distances by means of the cardboard strips available? All measuring implies at least three conditions: (1) a division cutting off from the main body one part selected as the unit; (2) a change of location allowing the unit part to be transferred to the remaining parts of that same whole, or to those of a separate whole; (3) a transitional relationship permitting the conclusion that if A=B and B=C, then A=C. Now the behaviour of the subjects quoted (except Gil at the end) quite sufficiently reveals that these conditions are not met and this for a reason never expressed but which runs through every interview: the fact is that the movement is an indivisible whole, and the path traversed is directly formed out of the series of positions successively occupied in the course of this movement, thus division into homogeneous units is impossible.

What in actual fact do our subjects do when we coax them to measure? Either they trace the path with a finger as in sub-stage IIa or else they completely cover the tracks with disparate measuring strips (Dor and El) as if the spectacle of these last would allow of a clearer estimate than the sight of the lines themselves! Hence it is obvious that we cannot as yet speak of division resulting in the parcelling of the whole into homogeneous parts or units. So it is that Dor, after putting cards 1, 2 and 3 over the indirect line B_2, and cards 1, 4 and 2 upon the straight line B_1 says 'That makes three and three', as if it were a question of equal units, and El on the other hand, having covered both lines with unequal strips says 'That makes three there and five here' without shifting his train any the more for that, as if the distances being equal or not, were unrelated to this measuring business. None of these subjects on the other hand can use one single strip selected as a unit. When they finally count the segments, like Luc and Dor (at the beginning), it is the stages of the movement itself that they are enumerating and not units of length (although A_2 is formed of ready-made units) since they do not concern themselves with making up equal units on the straight line A_1. As for the change of location of the measuring strip it is not grasped any better than the subdivision aspect: when the child measures with his fingers, the point is that he is trying to imitate the intrinsic motion of the moving object, and when he is given one single measuring card, he cannot transfer it through the sequence of new positions. And why is that? The fact is that he does not even understand the transitional relationship in itself ($A=B$, $B=C$, therefore $A=C$) or at least he does not have the idea of applying it to the comparison of the two lines. E.g. Dor having put cards 1, 2, 3, on B_2, and cards 1, 4, 2 on B_1, in no way attempts to transfer either of these two groups to the other line, and when 1, 2, 3 are removed from B_2 and he is asked to transfer cards 1, 4 and 2 over to B_2 he is satisfied with moving 4 and 2. In a word, there is neither the formation of one unit by means of subdivision, nor is there any transfer of the measuring unit, nor even any measuring unit in common.

Now the significance of these responses is undoubtedly that distance for these subjects is not yet entirely differentiated from the actual movement, although identity of length is beginning to be separate from identity of arrival points. The distance or length of a path travelled always constitutes a spatio-temporal intuition in its entirety of the journey to be made in order to reach the goal. That is why at this level there is not yet sufficient operational inter-locking of the gaps to permit the formation of a measuring system.

3. The third stage: Operational Comparison of paths traversed and conclusion of measurement

Before examining clear cases of this final stage, here are some intermediate cases between stages IIb and III which show the progressive discovery of measurement.

Mon (7; 2). Six segments on A_2: he moves his train a great way ahead of the other: Can you use this card to help? Don't know. We'll begin again (three segments). There! (he measures the three segments correctly and transfers this to A_1).

Plank B (three segments): he takes cards 3, 4, and 5 then lays them aside, and finds No. 1, applies it to the first segment of B_2 and transfers this to B_1. He then does likewise with cards 2 and 3. And if you only took this one (card 1)? (He again measures the first segment but does not know how to go on).

Eli (7; 11). Five segments (equal) on A_2: counts and trans-fers these approximately. He is given the card: he transfers it five times.

Plank B: at first as with Mon, then when the experimenter takes train B_1 (the straight line), Eli measures six equal units on B_1 and tries to transfer these to the indirect line B_2, but seeing that the unit does not correspond as before to the other segments he confines himself to counting them without allowing for their disparity.

Jo; (8; 0) at first refuses to measure then takes the card, tries out and transfers five segments. How did you do it? I counted five spaces.

Plank B: proceeds in the same way as the foregoing sub-jects, moving his block forward as he transfers each card in turn Nos. 1, 2, 3 . . . And using just one card? (He tries with No. 5, then takes No. 2, then No. 1, which he transfers as on plank A). Once, twice, etc.

PIE (8; 6). Plank B: That won't work, because the cards aren't all the same (puts down 1, then 4 and 2, and tries with No. 1 by itself, which he uses correctly as the unit).

And here are some clear cases:

GEO (7; 8) meausres the distances on plank A right from the start. With B, he first applies one or two strips, which he tranfers, then he takes No. 1 and applies it successively, transferring it the same number of times.

He is shown the two planks at the same time and asked to find on the zigzag line B_2 a distance travelled on the right-angled line A_2, and vice versa: he manages quite correctly using card 1.

MAR (7; 11) meausres from the very start by counting the segments on A_2 and transferring the unit strip an equal number of times. With B he transfers the various cards: And with just one card?—(he takes no. 5 and puts his finger on the spot where each of the segments in turn ends on this longest strip, then uses card 1, which he transfers correctly).

We can see that at the culmination of this evolution, paths traversed are not only differentiated from the position of points of arrival, but are also conceived as distances independently of movement as a change of location or dis-placement: by virtue of being the intervals contained between the points of departure and arrival, they are therefore considered as being lengths whose potential sections may correspond, from one line to the other. This 'qualitative' divisibility and transferability comes a little before the discovery of the idea of the unit (Mon and Eli) but it is quickly followed by the formation of the latter, through the combination of repeated 'dis-placement' (successive transfers of a single measuring strip) with subdivision. Whence comes the understanding of measurement. One may therefore say that at the level of concrete operations (7 to 8 years) the idea of the path traversed is operationally acquired under its dual qualitative and metrical aspect ('jointing' of distances comprehended as intervals between points of departure and arrival; and measurement through transposition of the unit section).

In conclusion, so long as the idea of order remains intuitive (stages I and II) the path traversed remains undifferentiated from this order and from movement conceived as travelling directed towards a given goal, whereas once order is operationally constructed (the operations of 'placing' of stage III) the path traversed is distinguished from the interval between the extreme points of the change of location, and the order of successive positions no longer interferes with the addition of intervals or distances.

CHAPTER FOUR

The Composition of Displacements

So far we have been able to observe that even if direct linear (normally rectilinear) order is given intuitively, the various relations of order (inverse linear order and cyclic order in both directions) are completely formed only when 'grouped' into an operational system which might be called a grouping of 'placements'. Turning now to movement or 'displacement', which viewed qualitatively is only a change of place or order, we have already been able to establish that the path traversed, or the interval between starting and finishing points, remains undifferentiated from the order itself, so long as this last remains intuitive: on the one hand, the distances covered are at first gauged solely by the finishing points, and on the other hand the integral and indivisible nature of movement as a change of position directed towards a goal or end-object prevents their measurement. It is only when order reaches the level of concrete operations (7 to 8 years) that paths traversed are conceived as intervals or distances capable of subdivision, and open to operational qualitative or metrical evaluation. Thus it is now apposite to study the actual operation of change of position, which, if the foregoing analyses are accurate, may be conceived either in terms of operations of order, as a change of position or dis-placement, or else in terms of the intervals contained between the sequence of positions, as a summation of distances.

In order to do this, we shall simply ask the child if, on a straight line, the distance covered on the outward journey from O to X is equal to the distance travelled on the way back from X to O, and if a series of part distances covered between O and X is equal to the same series travelled in the opposite direction. We shall in some cases analyse the problem on an inclined plane, i.e. asking for a comparison of ascents and descents (Section I) and sometimes on a horizontal plane (Section II). These very simple questions are enough as we shall see, for the study of the responses of each stage from 4 to 11 years. In the course of the next chapter, we shall complete this investigation by turning to the problem of relative movements.

SECTION I Ascents and descents

The apparatus used consists of a cardboard mountain with a doubled string stretched down one of its slopes, and fixed by a nail at the top. A bead travels along this string and represents a funicular railway or 'teleferoc' (all our subjects know the one at Salève). Between the base O and the summit D of the mountain, trees and houses are placed giving points of reference, A, B, and C. Let a be the trajectory OA; a^1 the path AB; $b^1 = BC$; and $c^1 = CD$; also let b = the path OB $(b = a + a^1)$; c = the path OC $(c = b + b^1)$; and d = the whole path OD $(d = c + c^1)$; finally let the same letters preceded by the minus sign stand for the return journey (descents). Strips of cardboard corresponding to these different lengths a, a^1, b^1, c^1, b, c, and d are also used; one set is red and the other blue, so that the child may distinguish between those used to measure the journeys in the direction OD (red) and those in the direction DO (blue). Three kinds of questions are asked.

Q. 1. We begin by making the bead climb up from O to D and down from D to O, asking the child if the funicular 'went farther going up or coming down.' The red and blue cardboard strips are given to the child from the beginning for measuring the journeys, or are placed upon the paths if he does not measure of his own accord, so that the meaning of both question and reply may be more distinct.

Q 2. The string extends up to C, comes back down to B and then travels back to D, finally returning in one journey from D to O. The partial trajectories are thus: $a + a^1 + b^1 - b^1 + b^1 + c^1 - d$. Therefore the question is to find out whether the ascents were equivalent to the descents, i.e. if $(a + a^1 + b^1 + b^1 + c^1)$ or $(c + b^1 + c^1)$ is equal to $(-b^1 - d)$. If there is some ambiguity we point out the two ascents $(a + a^1 + b^1)$, i.e. OC, and $(b^1 + c^1)$, i.e. BD, and then the two descents (b^1), i.e. CB, and (d), i.e. DO. The cardboard measuring strips are once again at the child's disposal, and if he cannot manage to use them correctly on his own, we measure along with him. But the following three reactions have to be noted: the child's response before he himself measures then this measurement together with the answer which follows, and the response after the adult's measurement.

Q 3. A further section is added when we take the following route $(a + a^1 - a^1 + a^1 + b^1 - b^1 + b^1 + c^1 - d)$, i.e. OB, BA, AC, CB, BD, and DO. The problem is to find out whether the sum of the ascents is equal to the sum of the descents $(-a^1 - b^1 - d)$ which is obvious if one reasons deductively (formally) but gives rise to difficulties if one tries to recall all the sections intuitively. But on the one hand, the zigzag route of the string round about the seven nails fixed at O, B, A, C, B, D, and O is enough to recall the paths travelled and on the other hand, above all, the red and blue card strips are always at the child's disposal, so that the question is reduced to establishing that the sum of the red lengths (placed end to end) is equal to the sum of the blue lengths.

The reactions observed are at the same time very simple and very instructive. In the course of stage I, the child is unsuccessful in the very first question, i.e. he thinks that the bead travels farther when climbing than descending. He does not attempt to measure the paths, and if we place upon these the card strips $+d$ and $-d$ to show him that they are equal, he is by no means convinced. Q 2 and 3 are therefore insoluble. In the course of stage II the subject continues to think that ascents are greater than descents, but measuring with the cards leads him to recognize that the two movements are equal. On the other hand the subject cannot manage to measure the paths in Q_2 in his own; but after measurement he again recognizes their equality $(b+b^1+b^1+c^1=-d-b^1)$ which he originally denied. Finally Q_3 is either insoluble, or is also solved by means of measurement and with the help of the experimenter. In the course of the stage III (7 to 8 years) Q_1 is solved: the child knows from the very start and before any measurement, that the displacements are equal whether travelling up or down. Q_2 and 3 on the contrary give rise to different reactions at the beginning and the end of the stage. During sub-stage IIIa Q_2 cannot be solved a priori by a formal method of deduction, but the subject manages to measure the zigzag route unaided and so establishes by his own measurements that ascents and descents are equal. Q_3 does not produce an a priori solution either, for lack of formal generalization, but it too is solved by another set of measurements. In stage IIIb this progress is maintained with the addition that Q_3 is successfully solved by direct generalization once the solution of Q_2 is obtained (by measurement). Finally, in stage IV (10 to 11 years) the child manages to solve all three questions formally, by a a priori deduction without any need for concrete measurements and foreseeing the results of these.

1. The first two stages: Inequality of ascending and descending movements

For most young subjects, the funicular goes farther on the way up than on the way down. Subjects in stage I even maintain this after having observed the identical cards used for measuring, whilst subjects in stage II change their minds on observing measurement.

Here are some examples of stage I.

Luc (4; 0) agrees that the train went *straight up* and *straight down*. Then *did it go farther going up or coming down? Going up. Why? Going up, to get right up to chalet* (=D).

(The red and blue cards are placed on the two tracks.) Look at these two bits of cardboard. Yes. Are they the same length? Yes. Then did it go farther on the way up or down? *On the way up.*

Q2: The train went farther going down than going up because the descent is made in a straight line. Luc remains unable to dissociate the partial ascents and descents of the outward route, and a *fortiori* to measure them.

FANC (4; 9). Farther going up or down? Going up. Why? (Points to the track with an all-embracing gesture). Could you show me with these cards? (Fanc herself places the red on the ascent and the blue on the descent). Put them on the table. Are they the same length? Yes. Then did the train go farther upwards or downwards? *Upwards.*

Q2: same response.

CHRI (4; 9) (her twin): same reactions.

BIA (5; 0). *Farther going up. Why? Because it's right at the top there.* Do you think we could see with these pieces of card if it went farther upwards or down? (We place blue on the descent and he puts red on the ascent). Now what about these strips? *They're both the same length.* Well, then, if the train climbed up along this red strip and down along this blue one, and the two cards are the same length, did it go farther upwards or down? *Upwards.*

Q2: *Farther downwards.* Show me how it goes up and where it comes down. (He points correctly to ascent and descent). Then was it farther going up or down? *Up.* Why? Could we measure with these cards? He cannot do so. We then place the red ones on the two upward journeys $(+b)$ and $(+b^1+c^1)$ and the blue ones on the two descents $(-b^1$ and $-d)$ and draw attention to the equal lengths of each set. Well, then? *It went up farther.*

CAT (6 years). *Farther up. Why? Because the wire is longer.* Could you show me with these cards? (Does not move. We put red on ascent and blue on descent). *It's the same thing.* Is one longer than the other. No. Then farther up or farther down? *Farther up.*

Q2: *Farther down. Why? Because this one is longest (d).* And with the cards? (He cannot do it but we help and point out their equality). So then? *Farther down.*

And here are some examples of the reactions of stage II, which begin as before but give way to correction after measurement. The first two cases quoted are intermediate between stages I and II, because the understanding resulting from measurement only appears in Q 1 and not in Q 2.

JAC (6; 4). *Farther on the way up.* Why? Can you show me with these cards? (He puts them on the lengths of string and compares them of his own accord). *No, they're the same length.*

Q2: *It's farther going down.* Why? *Over there* (b) *is shorter than this* (d). Show me where it goes up and where it comes down. (He does this correctly and we measure with him). Well then? *It's not so far going up as coming down.*

ROB (6; 6). *It's farther going up.* Can you show me with your finger? (He goes over the ascent and the descent). So? *Farther on the way up.* A little or a lot? *A lot more.* Try it with these cards. (He puts them in place). Look again (he follows with his finger). Well then? *Oh, no, it's no farther on the way up, so it's the same thing.*

Q2: *It's further going down.* Can you show me with the cards (he becomes completely confused through not aligning them end to end. We do this with him and he notes their equality). So? *It's farther going up.*

GIS (7; 4) hesitates, then: *Farther going up.* Can you point to where it climbed up? (He places the red card on the ascent). And where it came down? (He puts the blue card on the descent after following it with his finger). So then? *Farther on the way up.* Put the cards on the table. *They're the same.* What are? *The red and the blue.* Then did it go farther going up or coming down? *The same going up and coming down.*

Q2: *It's farther going up.* (He places the cards with our help, then he is asked to put them on the table and he himself puts them end to end). *They're the same thing, because one is just as big as the other.*

Q 3: Same responses, no anticipation.

NEL (7; 6). *It's farther going up.* Why? *Because the way up comes to a little bit longer.* Can you show me how much with these cards? (He places red and blue). *It's the same thing.* Why? *Because the cards are the same length.*

Q 2: *Farther going up.* Show me. (He places the cards with our help). So now? Put them on the table. (He himself puts them end to end). *It's the same thing.*

Q 3: Same reactions (no generalization).

Sim (8; 0). Same reaction to Q 1. Q 2: *Farther going down.* Why? *It's longer.* Try to measure. (He places the cards but forgets one section, then finishes with our help). So? *Farther going up.* Put them on the table. *Oh, they're both the same.*

These are the first two types of reaction observed. According to children seen in Geneva, in a variety of schools (public and private) only two-sevenths of subjects between 4 to 5 years understand from the very beginning that the journeys are equal ascending and descending; among normal subjects, a half at 6 years, three-quarters at 7 to 8 years, and all at 9 years recognize this equality in Q 1. Out of the estimates of inequality, only two doubtful cases reckoned the descent as greater than the ascent, one being a far from normal subject and the other bringing in the speed. Thus it would seem permissible to assume that children begin by considering an upward movement as greater than the corresponding downward movement.

Now this initial intuition is of some interest as indicating the lack of at least two forms of differentiation: no distinction being made between the path traversed and the placing of the finishing points (as in the last chapter, but the order being here defined by the relationship of 'high' and 'low'); nor between the dynamic or physical elements of the movement and simple spatial change of location, so that vertical and horizontal are idiosyncratic and not isotropic, as compared to any other direction.

It is true that the possibility of a child's misunderstanding the question could be raised: the adult could be thinking of the path traversed as a distance, while the child could be answering in terms of energy, duration or order. To clarify this confusion it is by no means enough to multiply the questions and vary their form: all the terms are ambiguous and the idea of a longer journey can always be taken in a temporal as well as a spatial sense. On the other hand, if there is no differentiation between the path traversed and the order involved nor between the spatial and dynamic factors of the movement, it goes without saying that this general want of definition involves verbal misunderstandings, these being not causes then, but effects of the former. Now the reaction of the subjects to measuring are enough to show that this second answer is the right one. Amongst the youngest children (stage I) who do not understand measuring, seeing that the cards placed on the table are equal has no effect on their belief that ascent and descent are unequal. But subjects in stage II, who without perfectly executing the measurements understand their meaning, do expect this inequality to figure in the actual measuring. Seeing that this is not the case, they then modify their supposition and recognize this equality: proving that their first response was not simply verbal.

What then constitutes the idea that from O to D the train climbs farther than on its return from D down to O. There is (to the extent that the results of Chapter Three are general, this follows as a matter of course) first of all a lack of dissociation between the distance travelled and the order of the points of arrival. If the length of a path travelled really does begin by being evaluated according to its arrival point, then even on a horizontal plane young children will experience some difficulty in understanding that the path OD= the path DO since it requires permutation of departure and arrival points: we shall in fact see in §5 that in the course of stage I a resistance does persist against admitting this basic equality, i.e. against abstracting from asymmetrical journeys O→ D and O← D the symmetrical distance O↔D. Now in the case of an ascending path there is the addition of an intuitively still greater asymmetry yet: D is 'above' O, or 'at the top', and O is 'below' D, or at the bottom. The vertical order which thus appears, therefore invests D, the point of arrival in the ascending direction O↑D, with a positive bias in relation to the point of arrival O, in the case of the descent D↓O. This is what Bia explicitly states: 'it went farther on the way up . . . because up there it's right at the top'. And Luc 'It went farther so as to go right up to the chalet'. More over, whilst the equality of the symmetrical distances between O and D, and D and O, is universally recognized from stage II on, upon the horizontal plane (see §4) at first this is not the case on the vertical plane amongst the subjects of this same stage and only by measurement are they convinced of their mistake.

But why does order judged by 'at the top' and 'at the bottom' create a stronger and more lasting asymmetry then horizontal order? It is because the ideas of vertical and horizontal are of a physical,[1] not a geometrical[2] nature: now, initially space shows no basic distinction between these two, and is therefore not isotropic.[3] Indeed apart from the subjects whose response is explained by bringing in the order of 'up above' and 'down below', there are some (and each type of motivation implies the other from the very start) who explicitly declare that the path of ascent is 'longer' than that of the descent, or who expect this implicitly. E.g. for Cat (stage I) the ascent is greater than the descent 'because the cable is longer'. Now, it is an interesting fact that the equality of the cardboard strips used to measure the two lengths does not enlighten him, not only in the absence of transitivity, but doubtless also because once these cards are placed horizontally on the table they no longer express the inequality of the paths which are on a slope.

As for subjects in stage II, they so confidently expect inequality in the upward and downward paths that they try to check by measuring (and when it is a case of the paths in Q 1 in a continuous block they already know how to measure them with single strips unlike the measuring of the segments arising in Q 2 and 3): they are thus quite taken aback to find the lengths equal, and unlike Cat they conclude from this the equality of the paths, E.g. Nel: 'It's the same, because the cards are the same length',

---

[1] Pertaining to the world of matter and energy.
[2] Treating of spatial magnitudes using simple figures.
[3] Having the same properties irrespective of direction.

and above all Rob: 'The way up isn't any longer (comparing the red card with the blue one) so it's the same thing. Gis is even clearer: looking at the cards placed on the sloping paths, he continues to think the ascent is longer than the descent, but seeing the cards on the table end to end, he changes his mind and ends up: 'The way up was the same as the way down.' It is thus quite clear that the first statement made by these subjects introduces an inequality of distance or length according to which the train climbs farther from O to D than it returns from D down to O. Now this inequality which is included in stage one in evaluations based only on the finishing point, thus persists in the course of stage II and disappears only when the results of measuring are observed. On the contrary, when the paths are horizontal (see §4) it disappears at the end of stage I: therefore vertical and horizontal directions are not isotropic before stage III.

The reason for this is clear: in the earliest intuition of movement, and consequently if our hypotheses are correct in the initial intuitions of order itself, there occur factors which exceed the purely spatial and which are connected with time, speed and effort expended. That the child thinks when he declares that the object travels further on the way up than on the way down, or that the stopping point 'at the top' takes precedence over the stopping point 'at the foot,' is thus simply that there is more to the action of ascending than descending: there is an effort, a muscular activity, which may equally well be represented by a greater distance covered or a longer time taken. 'It's a longer journey', as it might be expressed in common speech. It is this egocentric element which invests the order 'at the top' and 'at the foot' with its special character, which therefore prevents the distance OD from being symmetrical, i.e. equal to the distance DO and which, in a word, blocks the reversibility of 'displacement' or movement: a distance uphill is not equivalent to the same distance downhill, because the act of descending is not yet directly the inverse of the act of ascending, but constitutes an action intuitively different.

It is this fundamental irreversibility which we find in

the responses to Q 2 in these stages, but with this further complication that the distances this time are composite and no longer in a continuous block, the distances $+b^1$ and $-b^1$ being respectively added to the paths OD $(=+d)$ and DO $(=-d)$. There often arises in this respect a verbal difficulty devoid of interest, when the child thinks we are calling the whole of the outward journey the ascent including $(-b^1+b^1)$ and of course he then judges the ascent to be longer than the descent. But to remove this ambiguity it is usually sufficient to go into greater detail, tracing with one finger, or putting the measuring cards in place, to show that we are comparing $(+d+b^1)$ with $(-d-b^1)$. What happens then?

The youngest cases (Luc, Fanc and Chri: 4 years) cannot understand that $(-b^1)$ on the outward journey is downhill, and is to be joined to $(-d)$ on the return journey. Therefore they do not manage to understand the actual question, because of inability to dissociate into 'composable' parts what seems to them an indivisible movement. But Bia, Cat etc. (i.e. the great majority of cases between 5 and 6 years in stage I) do manage (some right away and some with our help in removing misunderstanding) to understand which are ascents and which descents. And yet they still unanimously think (with in addition the cases of Jac and Rob intermediate between stages I and II) that the sum of the ascents does not equal the sum of the descents. But there is no longer a general primacy of the ascents here: in half the cases (and this remains true in stages II and III) it is the ascents which are favoured and in the other half, the descents. In other words, the child is impressed by the fact that the upward journey is made in two almost equal parts $(a+a^1+b^1)$ and (b^1+c^1) and the downward journey in one large and one small part $(-d$ and $-b^1)$ and sometimes he thinks the first two are bigger than the second two and sometimes thinks the opposite.

But why does he not succeed in 'composing' them accurately? The fact is that there occurs a phenomenon analogous to but not identical with that of the replies to Q

1. Since in the case of initial intuition the order of the finishing points and the movements themselves are not dissociated from the driving force which is at the same time objective (speed etc.) and subjective (feeling of effort etc.) then on long journey and two partial journeys cannot form the same displacement: the impetus is broken, speed different etc. That is why sometimes the subjects quoted think that the downhill trip is greater because implying a single long trajectory (− d) and sometimes that the uphill journey is greater because it rests on a series of separate journeys. And in both cases simply measuring the lengths (as opposed to the movement) does not convince the child. In the course of stage II on the contrary (the clear-cut cases of Gis, Nel and Sim) the child begins to dissociate movement from motor intuitions, and without as yet expecting any equality, he does, nonetheless, allow himself to be convinced by measurement. If on the other hand he is unable to measure the sectional journeys unaided (as opposed to the paths in Q 1 where measuring involves only the placing of a single card), it is precisely because dissociation remains incomplete: to the extent that movement is still coloured with dynamism, the child does not understand why he must measure the distance as such, but once measurement is achieved with the experimenters' help, their equality is recognized.

Reactions to Q 3 are the same at the corresponding levels.

2. The third stage: Groupment of changes of position by means of concrete operations, but without formal generalization

The essential characteristic of stage III is the understanding acquired by the child of the equality of ascents and descents. In other words, if we accept the interpretations given so far, the dissociation of the actual change of position from the dynamics of movement. It is interesting to note how far this acquisition converges with the reactions of this same third stage described in the course of

Chapters One and Two. Operational inversion of linear order replaces intuitive inversion when children approach the age of eight years. Consequently, position and change of position begin to constitute one and the same grouping. It is at the same level that cyclic order is acquired, and above all that the distance covered is dissociated from the order, and takes the form of the symmetrical distance or interval between the starting and finishing points. It is at this same third stage that temporal order becomes differentiated from spatial order[1] as dynamic factors become dissociated from changes of position and that as we shall see (Chapters Six and Seven) operational realtionships of speed are constituted in place of the generalization of 'overtaking'. It is thus easy to see why Q 1 is solved in stage III, through dissociation of the change of position as such. An important consequence follows with Q 2: the child becomes able to measure the partial journeys uphill and downhill unaided and so to conclude their equality by means of concrete operations. But, unlike Q 1, where he anticipates the results of the measurements, since it concerns two complete journeys requiring no mental combination, he cannot do so in Q 2, where he would have to reconstruct mentally the details of the paths to and fro: so he imagines that the ascents exceed the descents or vice versa, and only discovers their equality by measuring. As for Q 3 subjects solve this empirically like Q 2 in the course of sub-stage IIIa while at stage IIIb they foresee the result by generalization from the result of Q 2.

Here are some examples of reactions belonging to sub-stage IIIa, beginning with an intermediate case between stages II and IIIa, solving Q 1 right away but still not achieving entirely spontaneous measurement in Q2:

JUL (6 years) Q 1: Is it farther on the way up or on the way down? *It's the same.* Why? (He puts the cards in place). *They're the same length.*
    Q 2: *It's farther going up.* Why? . . . Show me with these

[1] (See: 'Origins of the Child's Conception of Time').

cards. (He measures OD and DO). *It's the same thing.* And that? (CB and BC) (he measures). *It went the same distance up and down.*

Q 3: *It's farther uphill.* Check it? (He measures correctly). *It's the same.*

BRAN (6; 11) Q 1: *It's the same. Why? You can see it is.* Look at it with these (cards). (He measures). *Yes.*

Q 2: *It's farther going up. Why? It twists more on the way up.* Measure it. (He measures it all correctly after hesitating over — b^1, puts them down end to end, and concludes): *They're the same.*

Q 3: *It's farther going up. Why? Because there are all these* (ascents) *to do.* Check it. (He measures all the upward journeys and sets them down end to end, then hesitates, considers, and does the same with all the downhill journeys. Then, without placing the series of red cards next to the blue ones, he concludes): *It's the same. Why? Because they're the same length.*

PIE (6; 11) Q 1: *Same thing. Why? Because it's the same distance.*

Q 2: *The way up is longer, no, the way down is longer. No, it's the same thing. No, it came down farther because of that one* (−b^1). Are you sure? *Yes.* Check it with the cards. (He puts d in place then $a^1 + b^1$, then chooses a as the unit and transfers it to each uphill section). *That makes five times.* (He measures the downhill sections in the same way). *That makes five too. They're the same.*

Q 3: *Wait, I'm going to see* (he measures in units again). *It's the same thing.*

MARC (7; 7) Q 1: *Same thing. Why? Because the strings are the same length.*

Q 2: *It's farther going up. Why? Because of these* (the zigzags). Trace with your finger where it goes up and where it comes down. (He does this correctly). So then? *It goes farther on the way up.* And with this? (He puts the cards in position, lays them down on the table, places them side by side, and finally says). *It's the same.*

Q 3: *The way up is farther* giving the same reasons, then same methods leading to correct result.

ELI (8; 10). Same replies. With Q 3 repeats exactly the same steps as in answering Q 2, slightly faster.

SOL (9; 2) Q 1 correct. Q 2: *The way down is faster* because the two ascents $(a+a^1+b^1)$ and (b^1+c^1) together seem to him shorter than the descending sections $(-d-b^1)$. Q 3: *The way down is farther* as before. He starts to put the cards in place then says: *I think they're nearly the same*, but unlike answers in sub-stage IIIB he has to finish measuring to be quite sure.

The vital achievement affirmed by these replies is thus complete reversibility of the operation of displacement: the descent from D to O is now nothing but the ascent from O to D only in reverse: $-d=-(+d)$, so that the interval separating O from D becomes the same in both directions and forms the 'distance', now differentiated from the psychophysical dynamism of movement and constructed in a rigorously symmetrical relation (=the relation O↔D as distance from O→D and D←O). Q 1 is thus solved directly before any measurement simply by stating the operational properties of a change of position conceived as a reversible operation.

In the second place, this reversibility of the basic operation of displacement allows the subject to solve Q 2 and 3 by totalling the ascending vectors and the descending vectors respectively in order to verify their equality. So long as change of position remained irreversible there was, in fact, no point in measuring, since the length of the cards could neither express the actual dynamism of the movement nor its individual character. On the contrary, with the reversibility of changes of position, the problem becomes simply a question of distance or the path travelled and measuring therefore becomes possible as we have already observed amongst the subjects of stage III described in the previous chapter (Chapter Three, §3). With this measurement (which in the case of Pie is metric as he makes use of a unit, but remains 'intensive' in the case of those who simply place the cards side by side) operational composition of changes of position independently of any directional bias becomes a possibility.

But why does this incipient grouping remain limited to the concrete level, i.e. why does the solution of Q 2 and 3 necessitate the child's measuring the trajectories instead of deducing a priori that $+b^1-b^1=0$, and that $(a+a^1+b^1 +c^1) =(d)$? In the case of the problem studied in Chapter Three measurement is clearly necessary to transfer the segments of the zigzagging lines on to a straight line, whereas here reasoning should be enough to show that corresponding to each upward segment there is an equivalent downward segment. Now, not only do the subjects have to measure to solve Q 2, but even after solving this, they use the same method for Q 3 instead of deducing at once that an extra zigzag will not alter the equality of ascents and descents. Subsequent reactions may help us to understand these difficulties.

In the course of sub-stage IIIb in fact, i.e. from 9 to 10 years on average, the child still reasons as before in Q 2, but once he has measured and found the solution, he manages to forecast by direct generalization, that the result of problem 3 is again equality. Here are some examples of this level IIIb.

CLAN (8; 1) Q 1: *It's the same thing.*

Q 2: *It's farther going up because there are lots of zigzags.* Show me where it goes up and where it comes down. (Correct). So then? *It's farther coming down, no, it's farther going up, no, it's the same thing . . . But I still think that it went farther on the way up because of the bends . . . No.* (He measures). *Yes, it's the same.*

Q 3: *It's the same as before.* Why? *Because I know it's the same amount. We've only to put on these cards.*

THES (9; 2) Q 1: *The same thing.* Why? *They're equal.*

Q 2: *It goes farther up.* How much farther? *That much* ($+b^1$). Prove it. (He places the cards). *Oh, no, it's the same thing: there's one going up and one coming down!*

Q 3: *It's the same thing.* Why? *There* ($+a^1$ and $-a^1$) *there's one uphill and one downhill and here as well* (second bend: $+b^1$ and $-b^1$). *Yes, they're still equal.*

JAC (9; 5) Q 1: *Equal.* Q 2: *Further uphill.* Much farther? *No, that much* ($+b^1$). Could you prove that? (He puts the cards in place and says) *Uphill is longer.* Why? (Looks again without taking them off the slope and says) *No, equal.* Can you show me? (He puts the cards on the table and places them side by side). *Yes it's right.*

Q 3: *They're equal.* Why? *Because it goes up here* $(+b^1)$ *and it goes down here* $(-b^1)$ *and the same here* $(+a^1-a^1)$. *If you add together the distances uphill, and the distances downhill, it will come to the same amount.*

Ros (9; 7). Same reactions, but taking the opposite point of view (downhill is farther in Q 2 because of $-b^1$. Q 3: (Long reflection). *It's the same.* Why? (Measures each vector separately and its inverse). *There!*

An (10; 10) Q 1: *Equal.* Q 2: *It's longer uphill.* How much? $(+b^1)$. Can you prove that? (He places the cards on the paths). *It's the same: they're the same lengths.* (Q 3) *The same.* Why? *It's the same amount.*

The interest of these replies is evident compared with those of sub-stage IIIa. The difficulties of Q 2 are still much the same: because the child does not analyse where the journeys begin, he either feels the ascents exceed the descents, pointing out the segment $(+b^1)$ or the reverse, pointing out $-b^1$. And then, often as soon as measurement begins, he observes the factor of compensation. When we go on after this to Q 3 on the other hand there is immediate generalization, and measurement is unnecessary.

Let us note first that there is true generalization and not simply 'transfer'. In the course of sub-stage IIIa the child applies the method which was successful in Q 2 just as it is to Q 3: to the extent that applying the same procedures makes them easier to use and reduces the time required to reach the answer, there might be said to be transfer. On the contrary, in the case of the subjects just quoted it is the actual solution, discovered in Q 2 which is adjusted to Q 3 by an act of direct understanding and therefore there can be said to be generalization. Now, what does this comprehension consist of? Clearly the subject no longer has to analyse the partial ascents and descents in detail: by some kind of formal mechanism, he grasps from the out-

set that each partial ascent is compensated by a partial
descent, and vice versa. Therefore he succeeds in mastering the system in its entirety as it were because he does
not analyse each element. Whereas with Q 2 his attempts
at analysis confuse him and he is lost. But this early
formal thinking, which bypasses actual reconstruction by a
deduction depending directly on the generalized factor of
compensation, can only be achieved so far at this level
IIIb if the way has been paved in Q 2 by the actual
experience of measuring the paths. During stages IIIa and
IIIb the subjects lack the ability to adopt, right from Q 2,
an abstract and formal method which would save them
analysis section by section. In the absence of this method
of reasoning they engage in the reconstruction of each
separate element and are confused by perceptual difficulties.

3. The fourth stage: Correct solution of all three questions by the method of formal deduction

The advance which characterizes this final stage is the
release of this formal method whose origins we have just
described and which in stage IV appears right from Q 2,
i.e. without further need to prepare the way by a series of
actual measurements. The average age for the commencement of this stage IV is 10 to 11 years, with some exceptional cases beginning at 9 years and even 8; 10, intermediate between stages IIIb and IV.

Here are three examples, beginning with one of the
transitional cases.

RAY (8; 10) Q 1: *Same thing. Why? Because you could say
that each journey is a half.*

Q 2: *Uphill is farther, no it's the same thing. Why? Because it's obvious.* Show me. (He places the cards on the sections and lays them in a heap on the table). *It's the same
thing.* Are you sure? *You can see it* (only then does he place
them side by side).

Q 3: *It's the same thing as before.*

MAR (11; 2) Q 3 (before the others): *I think it's the same thing. Why? Because it goes up here.* (He points out the three segments) *and goes down there* (likewise). *It's the same. And if I say that the way up is longer, could you show me? Yes* (he measures without difficulty). *It's correct.* Q2 likewise.

LAUR (11; 4) Q 2: *Perhaps its' farther going down. Oh, no: They're equal, it comes to the same thing because it goes up there* ($+b^1$) *and it comes down there* ($-b^1$) *and here* (the second b^1) *it goes back up the same distance that it came down then it goes on climbing up* ($+c^1$) *and comes all the way down* ($-d$).
Q 3: *They're still equal because if it always goes back up the same distance that it came down, it comes to the same amount.*

The great difference between these subjects and the earlier ones is evident: instead of losing their way in a preliminary analysis of the paths they start from the beginning with a formal kind of anticipatory scheme formed of the hypothesis that the various ascents are compensated by the descents, and only then do they examine the elements to verify if their hypothesis is correct. The formal method is therefore hypothetico-deductive, i.e. it proceeds by the co-ordination of hypotheses, before proceeding to check by experiment. This is what one clearly sees in the cases of Mar and Laur. On the contrary Ray who is just beginning this type of reasoning is still partly at the stage of direct inspection of details, and is in advance of the subjects in stage IIIb only through his ability to analyse. Certainly the children in stage III (concrete operations) already know something of deductive reasoning, since the measurement of the paths implies a deduction: this is obvious when comparing the subjects of stage III with those of stage II, who cannot manage without help to measure the routes in Q 2 and 3, and it was particularly evident in the course of Chapter Three. But this deduction is made from actual experiment, since the use of the cards as intermediaries is indispensable to its conclusion. Subjects in stage IV on the other hand are convinced of equality simply by the logical calculation of direct and inverse operations, without further need for measurement: the grouping of changes of position is therefore reconstructed on the formal level after the mastery of concrete operations and earlier sensori-motor compositions. It remains to be seen, however, why the solution of Q 2 and 3 requires formal anticipation instead of being solved by concrete deduction: this will be shown by what follows.

SECTION II *Horizontal movements*

The question might be raised as to how reactions to the same questions would develop when ascents and descents were not involved. Thinking that the problems set would then be too simple, we used two techniques, one corresponding to the previous one and the other involving several moving objects changing position at the same time. We felt the latter would be much more difficult, but it is interesting to note that they proved of nearly equal difficulty and we shall write about both sets of results at the same time.

Technique 1 consists simply of presenting on a straight line OD certain points of reference at equal or unequal distances, and strips of red cards for the outward journey and blue for the return: we then move a single (chess) piece, e.g. from O to D ($=+d$), then from D to B ($=-c^1$ $-b^1$) then from B to C ($=+b^1$) and finally C to O ($= -b^1-a^1-a$). For the sake of variety we did not have fixed strings but as we went along we merely recorded the paths travelled on a separate piece of paper using our two colours. The journeys on the other hand are made directly on the coloured cardboard strips, which we set aside after each part journey, in two heaps (red and blue): the question is then simply to find out whether the sum of the red cards or tracks would be equivalent to that of the blue ones (return journeys). In Technique 2 we begin by placing five chess pieces O, A, B, C, and D on these five positions. Then we place, e.g. O upon C, C and B upon B and O: then with or without drawings, according to the case, the red cards OC ($=+c$) and blue ones CB ($=-b^1$) and BO ($=-b$) are set aside and the question is to see whether ($+c=-b^1-b$). After the reply measurements are made and then the questions are varied on the same model but complicated or simplified according to the child's reactions.

Now, two interesting results were obtainable in this way. One of course was that the reactions to both techniques corresponded chronologically. The other is that these two kinds of reactions are themselves in agreement with those we have just studied on the inclined plane. The only difference to be pointed out is that Q 1 (is the distance OD equal to the distance DO?) is naturally easier on the horizontal plane since the dynamic factors (effort, speed and time) are the same in both directions, unlike the contrast of ascents and descents. Nonetheless, it is not usually solved in the course of stage I. It is solved right away in stage II unlike reactions relating to the inclined plane.

The stages observed are therefore as follows. There is no operational composition in the course of stages I and II, i.e. neither anticipation nor induction after alignment of the paths travelled, and this verification does not help with later forecasts. Stage III gives rise to concrete compositions in the form of a progressive induction by virtue of observations made and stage IV shows formal deduction anticipating each result.

4. The first and second stages: No operational composition

Subjects in the first stage not only do not foresee the result of the itineraries, but even after observing the equalities or disparities (according to whether one returns to the starting point or not), they cannot find the rule for the following questions:

Rot (5 years). Technique 1. Itinerary $+d$ and $-d$ ($=Q\ 1$). Is it the same? *No, it's longer towards your end.* And now? (same thing). (He measures). *Yes, it's equal.* And this time ($+d-c^1-b^1+b^1-b$)? *I want to think about it.* Which way did it go? (He points it out correctly). What are you going to do? Look at these. (He aligns the cards). *It's the same thing: it did this and this* (pointing out the details of the journeys). And now ($+d-c^1-b^1-a^1+a^1-a^1-a$)? *Don't know* (aligns the cards). *Oh, yes, it's the same.* And now (same combination)? *Don't know* (aligning). *Same thing again.* And this way (another combination)? *It's complicated. You'd have to count.*

Cri (5 years). Same beginning: And this way ($+d-c^1-b^1+b^1-b$)? *Red will be longest.* Why? *It went farther that time.* Look (we put them in line and he understands). And this ($+d-b^1-a^1+a^1-b$)? *Don't know* (he aligns them). *Oh, the same thing.* And now ($+c+c^1-d$)? *More blue ones, because it went farther on the way back,* etc.

Jac (5 years) ($+d-c^1+c^1-d$): *Don't know. In any case one is longer than the other. I think blue.* Look. (He aligns them). *Oh, its' equal.* Could you tell what it was beforehand? *No,* etc.

Wil (6 years) ($+d-d$) ($Q\ 1$): Same length? *No.* Why? (he compares the cards). *Yes.* And now (Technique 2): ($+b-a^1+a^1+b^1+c^1-d$). Are they the same? (He aligns the cards). *Yes.* And this way? ($+c-b^1-a^1-a$, putting the cards aside). *No, red is longer.* And this way (Technique 1) ($+d-c^1+c^1-d$)? *No.* Why? *Red is longer again.*

Clearly no composition is possible: estimates are either random or based upon the longest section perceived.

In the course of stage II all the subjects solve Q 1. ($+d-d$). Moreover they often manage to guess the result, but without being able to justify it. To find out whether real composition exists it is enough to introduce an unequal return trip without returning to the starting point: if the child is satisfied merely to guess then he believes they are equal. Here are two examples:

SER (6; 6) recognizes that the outward journey $+d$ and the return $-d$ are both the same. And this way? (another itinerary). Still the same. And now? (Another combination but without coming back to the start: stopping at B). Same thing. Look carefully. Yes, it's still equal. He is therefore not making a calculation.

PIE (7; 10) agrees that outward and return journeys are equal in the case of $+d$ and $-d$. Technique 2: $(+d-c^1-b^1-c)$? Red is longer (he aligns them). No, equal. And this way (another combination)? Same. And now (another combination)? Just about the same. Why just about? A little more towards me. Look carefully. It's confusing. You'd have to count how many journeys it does. Now look (Technique 1: $+d-c^1-b^1+b^1-c)$? Red is longer. Now you are going to do it yourself (we get him to walk along a line in the room). You start from here (O), you go up to the window (D). You come back here (B) you go back there (C) and you're back at the start (O). Did you go farther in one direction than in the other? I went farther towards the window than towards the door. Which way did you go towards the window? (Points to $OD=d$ and $BC=+b^1$). And towards the door? (Points to $DB=-c^1-b^1$ and $CO=-b^1-b$) Now then? Went farther towards the window. And if I told you it was the same thing? No.

One can see that even while replying correctly to Q 1 on the equality of the single journeys in one direction and the other, and even while occasionally guessing the correct results the children are not in fact 'composing' the segments of the itineraries any more than in the course of the first stage.

5. The third stage: Understanding through concrete operations without formal deduction

The subjects of stage III (7 to 8 years up to 10 to 11 years) do not solve the problem beforehand either. This anticipated solution would in fact imply formal deduction, as seen in Section I, and the moment has come to try to explain why this is the case. But when, after one or two

wrong forecasts, these children observe the result of aligning the segments, they correctly forecast the subsequent
ones and understand the rule by reconstructing the operations involved. The question is thus to grasp why they do
not manage to deduce beforehand what they understand
in retrospect. Here are some examples:

PAR (7 years). Technique 2: $(+d-c^1-b^1+b^1-c)$. *No.
There's more red. Look,* (he aligns the cards). *Yes. And this
way* (another combination). *That must be equal in both directions. Why?* (He reconstructs). *Yes. And now?* (new
test). *Same thing. And this way?* (New combination but two
pieces rest on one line)? *No. Why? That's missing* (right).
Technique 1: same thing.

AND (8 years). Technique 1. Outward and return journeys:
Same thing. And this way? $(+d-c^1-b^1+b^1-b^1)$? *Red is
longer, because it hasn't come back to the start* (right). *And
now* $(+d-c^1-b^1+b^1-c)$? *Red is shorter. Try to see if that's
right.* (he himself measures the journeys by means of a sheet
of paper without aligning the cards). *No, they're both the
same. And now?* $(+c-b^1-a^1+a^1+b^1-b^1)$? *Blue is shorter
because it doesn't come right back to the start* (correct). *And
now* $(+d-c^1-b^1-a^1+a^1+b^1-c)$? *Same thing because it
went this way and that* (points out the route taken to and
fro). *And this* (new combination)? *Same thing. And this
counter test: unequal. No. And this? Same thing because it
made one whole journey and several partial ones in each direction* (correct).
  Technique 2: same responses.

LUC (8 years). Technique 2: $(+d)-(c^1-b^1)-b)$? *Same
thing. Why? Because the two blue paths* (c^1+b^1) *and* (b)
are half the red one (d: correct). *Now look* $(+d-c^1-b^1-
-a^1-a)$? *No red is longer. Try it.* (He aligns the cards).
Yes. (another combination). *Yes, because the men cover the
same journeys.* (Another test). *Still the same journey* (correct).

JEA (9; 3). Technique 1: $(+d-c^1-b^1+b^1-c)$? *Blue is
longer, because the road is farther towards me.* (He aligns
them). *Oh, no, the same journey.* (Another try). *Same journeys, because the man came back to the starting point.*

(Another trial but stopping at A on the return journey). *Not
the same. Why? Because of the journeys out and back that he
made: he didn't come back here* (O). (Another test). *Not
equal, no: equal because its' the same journey, in both directions.*

Technique 2: $(+d-b^1-c^1+b-b^1-c^1-b)$? *It's the same.*
(cross check: two men on the same line). *Same thing. No,
more blue, because they are not all in place.*

DRE (9; 6). Technique 1: $(+d-c^1-b^1-a^1-a)$? *Same
length because the man came back to his starting point. And
this way* $(+d-c^1-b^1+b^1-c)$? *A longer distance in this
direction* (red). Try to draw it. (He does so). *Oh, yes.*
(Another try). *Same amount because it went forward three
times and came back three times.* (Another trial, but stopping
at A on the return journey). *More red than blue. And now*
(another try)? *More red than blue. And now* (another try)?
*Same thing, because there are several zigzags in either direc-
tion.*

Technique 2: *Same thing because the men are in the same
place as before.* (Another try). *Still the same.* (New trial
with two men at the same spot)? *Longer in your direction
than in mine* (correct) *because the men have all come back.*

We can see the interest of these facts and their parallelism with those of the corresponding stage studied in Section I. None of these subjects in fact solves the question of
the partial zigzags right away. In contrast, when there is a
single journey outwards $(+d)$ and return journey in two
parts $(-c^1-b^1)$ and $(-b)$ the problem presents no difficulties (see Luc). The subject Dre even solves the question of a return journey in four stages but with all the
segments facing the same direction. It is therefore partial
journeys out and back which still hold the child back. But
as soon as he has observed the result once or twice (by
aligning the cards, or by measuring of his own accord or
even simply drawings involving analysis of the tracks) he
then reconstructs the operations quite easily (see And,
Luc, Jean and Dre at the end of the interviews) and even
manages to forecast correctly the result of the subsequent
combinations, with or without their being equal.

Furthermore it can be seen that Technique 2 which

involves permutations between five objects is scarcely
more difficult than Technique 1, i.e. the partial outward
and return journeys of a single piece. Now it would seem
that having to combine the changes in position of five
moving objects which replace each other at the points O,
A, B, C and D, the child ought to become a good deal
more confused than in displacing a single moving object
between the same points, even with variable journeys out
and back. The fact that this is not so is highly instructive
and allows us finally to solve the question, left unresolved
till now, of the difference between concrete and formal
operations.

The question may indeed arise as to why subjects, who
like the foregoing are able to reconstruct fully the operations carried out, cannot manage to deduce them beforehand? We saw in the conclusion of Section I, it is true,
that the anticipatory schema grouping all the changes of
position arising in these questions (Technique 1) is necessarily hypothetico-deductive and consequently formal,
since it implies beforehand the hypothesis of general compensation and only comes to verify it in retrospect. But
why does this anticipatory schema not appear from the
age of 7 to 8 years, i.e. as soon as the reversibility of
dis-placement is achieved and allows measurement and
concrete grouping of the segments of the path travelled.
We have already observed, in Chapters One and Two how
far the child in stage III had mastered the question of
multiple inversions in linear and cyclic order and what
subtle compositions he was capable of in this respect (two
inversions=direct order, etc.). Why is he blocked here
simply by the interplay of partial journeys to and fro?

In actual fact, if (as everything has led us to believe so
far) a dis-placement really is in essence a change of order
or placing then the complex track of an object traversing
paths such as OD, DB, BC, and CO is comparable to a
system of permutations. If M is the moving object, these
tracks are in fact equivalent to the succession of positions
MABCD, OABCM, OAMCD, OABMD, and MABCD,
as if M in turn replaced O, D, B, C and O. It follows that
it changes its number in the series 4+1 times in one

direction and $2+3$ times in the other, whence the equation $5 = 5$. In the case of Technique 2, if we put O on D, D upon B, B at C, and C on O, we obtain the series CADBO which likewise involves five changes of position in each direction (four for O replacing D plus one for B replacing C in one direction, and two for D replacing C plus three for C replacing O in the other direction). The two operations are thus in fact equivalent, but in both cases they involve a system of permutations: permutations between M and the fixed points not occupied by it, in Technique 1, and permutations between 'men' corresponding to these points in Technique 2.

Now a study which we have undertaken on the development of the operations of permutations and combinations shows precisely that the discovery of a complete system only takes place towards 11 to 12 years, contrary to operations of simple seriation or ordination which are acquired at about 7 years of age. The reason for this is clear: a system of permutations or combinations implies that the mind accomplishes several seriations simultaneously rather than in succession, i.e. given a set of facts in one field of thought, seriation would simply spread them out in either direction. But operations of permutation must arrange them in series according to any possible order. In other words, the operations of permutation are formal and not simply concrete.

Generally speaking, in fact, formal operations are to be conceived as operations effected upon other operations, hence as operations of the second degree. The operations of permutation, e.g. consist of arranging seriations into series. The operations of the first degree, upon which the secondary ones bear, are themselves concrete operations. Whence the analogy of content between formal operations and concrete operations. As for the operations bearing upon the primary operations, they are either fresh concrete operations (but of the second degree) as in permutations, etc. or else simply systems of implications and incompatibilities established between the propositions which represent the initial concrete operations: this is the case with all formal operations expressing in colloquial or mathematical language those operations which might be performed concretely and which formal thinking merely constructs symbolically. This explains why formal operations, being operations, of the second degree or operations bearing upon other operations, are at the same time akin to concrete operations and nevertheless much harder to use.

It is undoubtedly for similar reasons that the construction of the anticipatory schema indispensable to the solving of Q 2 and 3 is more difficult than concrete operations. The subjects in stage II manage to solve the problems of equality when the return journey is made in several stages, though always in the same general direction, because in that case they only have to add concretely, while they fail when the various directions are mixed up and so call for reconstructions and analogous to those which occur in operations of pure permutations.

6. The fourth stage: Immediate solution by formal deduction. Conclusion: The grouping of changes of position

Unlike the subjects of the previous stage, those whom we shall quote here have no longer any need actually to align the partial journeys in order to understand the solution, but construct the equalities or disparities deductively from the very start. Here are three examples:

GER (9; 10). Technique 1: *Same length. Why? Because there are the same journeys coming towards me as towards you.* (Another combination). *Same thing. Why? Because the journeys are long or short but it's always the same going towards you or towards me.* (Numerous trips to and fro but stopping on the way back at A). *Red is farther. Why? Because the man didn't come back to the starting point.* Are you sure or are you guessing? *Sure.*

Technique 2: *Blue is longer because they've gone more often towards you than towards me . . . Oh, no.* (Other permutations). *The same because they all travelled in both directions.* (Another combination with two men on a single line). *Not the same because that one hasn't come back here.*

NERA (10; 3). Technique 1: *Same thing because it did the same journeys in both directions.* (Another combination stopping at A). *Same thing because it does six trips each way. Oh, no, five here.* (Very rapid changes so that he should not be able to count). *The same thing because to come back to the start again he has to cover the same routes.* (Cross check, also very rapid). *Not the same because it didn't come back to the starting point.*

Technique 2: *There are too many men to count but still it's the same thing in both directions.*

LAUR (11; 4). Technique 2: $(+d-c^1-b^1+b^1-b^1-b)$? *They're equal because they always go back to where they were: they only replace each other.* (Other combinations). *Equal.* (Still more, but two men on A). *No, these are not equal, because there's this bit here* (OA) *short.* (Same thing). *They're not equal either because there are more return journeys than outward ones if it started off from there* (correct).

Technique 1: *They're equal. It only made some zigzags but each time it came back the same amount that it went forward.*

Thus we can once again see the synchronism of the levels of reactions to Technique 1 and 2. Bearing these results in mind we can now reconsider the nature of movement and the operations of dis-placement, and likewise of the groupments of groups which permit their construction.

Comparing these results (parallel to those of Chapter Three) with those of Chapters One and Two, it is impossible not to observe the close connection between operations of order or placing and between operations of change of position. The former in fact imply the latter, at least from the spatio-temporal or infra-logical point of view.[1] From the point of view of pure logic, order is given independently of its construction and then the relations

[1] For the distinction between logical and infra-logical operations, see *Le Developpement de la notion de temps chez l'enfant*, Conclusions (at the end of Sect. II) and *Le Developpement des quantities chez l'enfant*, Conclusions.

characteristic of it may be 'composed' in the direct or inverse form, without any movement being involved. But if we shift the analysis on to the infra-logical area of the operations constituting space, time, movement and speed, then every ordered series involves movement and there are two reasons for this. Firstly, in order to construct the series under consideration its elements had to be placed or followed up in a particular order and this order or 'placing' is therefore the result of a displacement; secondly, in order to pass from direct order to inverse order, i.e. from A→B to B→A, one must either 'dis-place' the elements or else 'dis-place' the subject who is observing, i.e. in abstract terms to change the 'direction of travel'. This is what we saw in Chapter One: the passage from direct order to inverse order involves partial rotation either of the apparatus or of the observer. In their turn operations of displacement imply placing as we learned from Chapter Three (evaluation of paths travelled judged by the order of the finishing points and then purely by the intervals between the starting and stopping points) and the present chapter (parallelism between understanding of changes of position and of permutations). And this is likewise the case for two reasons: firstly, objects changing positions relative to one another involve a change of order or placing; secondly, the dis-placement of a single moving object is also a change of order, but relative to its co-ordinates, i.e. to ordered points of reference.

If then, by taking up an exclusively genetic standpoint, and not being influenced by any other preoccupation, we attempt to characterize the qualitative operations at the root of order and movement, we can see that these two conceptions proceed from one and the same reversible operation, of which the direct form is 'placement' and so the inverse form is 'dis-placement'. Let A→B be a placement, the inverse placement B→A constitutes a displacement, and the inverse displacement (which is therefore the reverse operation of the inverse) returns to the placement A→B. Consequently from this point of view there will be complete correlation between the two kinds of operation and each movement may equally well be considered as a displacement or a re-placement.

Only difference, but it too is altogether relative, may legitimately be maintained between operations of order and of movement, and this suffices to dissociate them in practice: it is either the subject who arranges the objects, whether by his actions, or by following them with his eye, or by the internalized movements of his thought and who changes his place to obtain inverse order, and then one would speak of 'placement' in both directions of travel; or else it is the elements which change places with each other, and then one would speak of 'dis-placement', direct and inverse. But the fact remains in both cases that all placement is relative to a dis-placement and vice versa.

The qualitative operations of order (placement) and of displacement are thus in themselves equivalent on the infra-logical level to what on the logical level would be seriation of mobile, asymmetrical relationships. And then, just as a system of symmetrical relations defined by the intervals contained between the terms of the series may be drawn from any seriation, there may also be found in every system of placements and displacements a corresponding system of intervals contained between the sequence of positions, and so these intervals form the distances or paths travelled. In fact we were equally able in Chapter Three, by measuring the paths traversed, and in Chapter Four, by comparing the total journeys in terms of the successive partial journeys, to observe that the idea of distance covered is only understood in the third stage, once the operations of displacement have become reversible.

In a word, qualitatively, it is the changes of order which constitute displacement as such, and the intervals between the series of points which form the distances or paths traversed. These two kinds of qualitative operations are thus distinct, though inseparable, and relations of order or displacement are added non-commutatively because they are asymmetrical while distances or intervals are added commutatively because of their symmetry.

As for the passage from these qualitative groupings of a

purely logical nature (or to be precise infra-logical)
towards the mathematical group of dis-placements, it is
sufficient for the understanding of this, to introduce measurement into the two factors of placement and displacement involved in any movement. From the point of
view of 'placement', i.e. of the system of ordered points of
reference to which every movement is relative, it is enough
to construct 'co-ordinates', i.e. precisely, a sum of ordered
points whose intervals constitute measurable distances.
From the point of view of change of position, it is then
sufficient to measure the path traversed in unit distances
relative to the system of reference defined so far. This is
why in mathematical construction 'displacement' arises
from metrical geometry while order itself starts with topology because one is disregarding the actions of the subject
in the inversion of 'directions of travel' and likewise in the
act of arranging in order, itself. But this dissociation,
however legitimate, should not obscure the operational
nature common to both placement and dis-placement
when the latter is viewed qualitatively, and independently
of any measurement.

In the case of the child, the passage from qualitative
groupings of placements and dis-placements to the metrical group of dis-placements is on the other hand complicated by the fact that the ideas of straight lines, parallels,
and angles are 'given' intuitively long before they are
operationally constructed. It follows that there exist intuitions of lengths and distances almost as early as the initial
intuitions of order and partly independent of them—
which does not mean that one type is more correct than
the other.[1] On the contrary, being based on perception
they inherit all its illusions as well as its character of
immediacy. It is only when the qualitative operations of
placement and dis-placement are organized in into coherent reversible systems that distances are constituted as
systems of intervals, and not before; because two qualita-

---

[1] On the contrary, an initial non-conservation of distances and
lengths was observed during the research into the spontaneous
geometry of the child.

tive grouping form one metrical group, first on the level of concrete operations (7 to 8 years) then on the hypothetico-deductive or formal level (10 to 11 years).

CHAPTER FIVE

Relative Movements

The results to which the foregoing chapter has just led us—the initial difficulty in 'composing' displacements then a successful conclusion in the form of a grouping of formal operations—lead naturally on, by way of a counter check, to the study of relative movements. The movements used in Chapter Four are movements in series and the composition of these simply consists of adding them together as if two changes of location made up only one single one (this is moreover, the essential characteristic of 'groups': the two operations combine into but one). On the contrary, relative movements are simultaneous, e.g. the movement of a passenger on a boat in motion. Their composition then consists of considering them as if they were in succession and adding them up in the same way as the previous ones, e.g. the boat, has moved ahead the distance X and the traveller (on the boat) the distance Y hence the total journey (in relation to the shore) in (X plus Y) if they are going in the same direction or (X minus Y) if their directions are opposite. But it may be seen at once that intuitively this relativity of movement appears to be more difficult to grasp than the composition of movement in succession, since attention must be brought to bear on the two movements simultaneously. Operationally, on the contrary, the composition of the movements is the same whether they are in succession or simultaneous. It is therefore of interest for us to compare a problem of relative movements with the earlier problems in such a way as to make clearer the respective rôles of intuition and operations.

Finally, it should be noted that questions of speed will

not arise at all in this chapter: we shall meet them again in
the relative movements analysed in Chapter Eight.

1. Technique and general results

The presentation of the test is as simple as possible: a
small snail shell is placed on a board or a piece of cardboard between 10 and 15 cms. long and between 3 and 5
cms. wide. The subject is told that the snail is going to
take a walk on the plank and that because of its slowness
we can watch its movement very closely. Only, while he is
moving along we shall play tricks on him. We are going to
move the card quite slowly too, without his noticing it:
sometimes in the same direction as him and other times in
the other direction. The snail is then put down on one end
of the cardboard, a clearly visible line of reference being
marked on the table at the same time, and the snail and
the card are moved along simultaneously (or one at a
time, at first, if the child does not understand at the
outset) according to the various possible combinations.
The child has at his disposal some strips of paper for
measuring the path of the board starting from the line of
reference and likewise the path of the snail on the plank.
The problem is to locate again the point the snail had
reached, after the materials have been removed, or else
where he will arrive, given certain conditions which are
stated verbally.

As a general rule we asked the following four questions.

Q 1. The snail and the card are proceeding at the same
time in the same direction (with the path of the card either
longer or shorter than that of the snail). Q 2. Same
reconstruction with aid of the paper strips, but the paths
are in opposite directions. Q 3. We tell the child, but this
time without actions, simply by a verbal statement or by
sketching the movements in gestures but without the subject being able to observe the result), that the snail and the
card are going in opposite directions from one another,

but both travelling the same distance at the same time: the child should therefore foresee that the snail will stay in the same spot. Q 4. The snail is placed at one end of the card (on the guide line): to forecast whether he will arrive on the right or the left of this line according to whether the path he covers is longer or shorter than the card, while this is moving in the opposite direction.

From the responses of sixty-seven children, between 5 and 14 years of age when interviewed, we were able to distinguish the following stages, in correlation with those which have been described in the preceding chapters. In the course of the first stage the subjects do not manage to pay attention to more than one of the two movements: usually that of the snail. But as they do not succeed in measuring even one single track taken as a whole, their reactions will not detain us long. On the contrary, we find some intermediate subjects between stages 1 and 2 who manage to use the paper strips to measure the paths and who continue nevertheless, to consider only one of these. In the course of the second stage the child measures the two paths but in order to reconstruct the path travelled by the snail, he confines himself to putting them down side by side, both starting from the guide line, being unable to understand that they are added to or substracted from one another: the subject therefore does not even manage to resolve Q 1 for want of placing the two tracks end to end. From stage III on, (concrete operations beginning about 8 years or so) Q 1 (paths in the same direction) is solved by addition of the paths and Q 3 (equal paths in opposite directions) by subtraction. In the course of sub-stage IIIa solutions are found to these problems only, whilst during sub-stage IIIb (9 to 10 years) the other questions (unequal paths in opposite directions) gradually produce empirical solutions. Finally in stage IV (10 to 11 years) all four questions are solved from the very start.

We can therefore see, by comparing this development with that of the solutions analysed in Chapter Four, that if the composition of relative movements is more difficult intuitively than that of movements in succession, this delay is only noticeable during the early stages. As we

reach stage IV on the contrary there is synchronization
between the operations and on the hypothetico-deductive
or formal level, the two developments join up.

2. The first and second stages: No composition
of movements

Here first of all are some examples of the first stage (no
measurement) and some intermediate cases between stages
I and II (beginning of measurement of paths) amongst
which only one of the two movements is considered when
reconstructing the point of arrival of the snail.

TON (6; 7) does not know what to do with the strips of
paper for measuring. To find out where the snail got to Ton
confines himself to reproducing approximately the movement
of the card, but without paying attention to the guide line
nor to the change of location made by the snail on the card
independently. Same reaction for the movements in contrary
directions. For the reversed movements of equal length, on
the contrary, he does not concern himself with the displacement of the card, but only with that of the snail. Placing the
end of the card on the guide line, he says of the snail: *He
started off from here,* (guide) *and he arrived there* (other
end of the card). And what did the card do? . . .

NIS (7; 6) measures the path of the card and that of the
snail; What does this paper stand for? *The measurement of
the snail, the measurement when he moved forward.* Show
me where it got to. *Up to there* (takes the strip back to the
guide line). And what did the card do? *It moved forward too.*
By how much? (He points to the measure of the path of the
card). Well then? . . . Did it make any difference that the
card moved forward while the snail was moving? *No.* Where
did the snail get to? *There* (as before). An explanation is
given and the two paths are put in a line.

Q 2: Nis transfers the measurement of the snail back. And
the card? *You moved it backwards.* Then where did the snail
arrive? *There* (points to the same point as before).

NAL (7; 8). *There* (snail alone). But the card moved too?
Where did it get to? (Points to it approximately). Did it

make no difference for the snail that the card moved at the same time? *No*.

Q 2: Same reaction.

And now here are some examples of stage II, in the course of which the children transfer the second movement, as well as the first, but without adding them together, and confining themselves to placing the two measuring-strips together and both starting from the guide line.

IAC (7; 7). Now the snail is getting off. He has finished his trip. Where did he get to? *Here* (points approx.) Don't you need to measure? (He measures and transfers it to the guide line) And the board? *Yes, it moved forward*. (He measures and places the measuring strip at the side of that of the snail). But look: when the board moved forward from there the snail travelled on top of it (we slide the paper which measures the path of the snail upon the paper showing that of the board, until the former extends end to end from the other). Now let's start again (new attempt). Where did it get to? *Here* (he again puts both papers side by side starting from the guide line). Look (we put the two papers end to end). Now where did he get off? (Seems to understand).

Q 2 (opposite directions): He thinks he is making a long trip but you see I am pulling the board like that. Where will he arrive? (Iac measures the two movements, then places the strip of the snail's journey on the left of the point of departure and the paper for the board on the right). *Here*. Why? *The snail goes on this side and the board on that*. But look carefully (starting again). Where does it finish? *Here* (once more sets the two paper strips in reverse direction from the line of reference and points to the end of the snail's strip without bothering about that of the plank).

COL. (8; 1) measures from the very start (Q 1) the two paths and places the two paper strips parallel, each starting from the guide line. *The snail gets to there* (end of its strip, without thinking of that of the board). And the board? *There*. But the snail was on the board when it was moving? *Yes, but he started out from there* (absolute point of departure). But the board moved forward even further? *Yes*. Then, where did the snail get to? *Here* (end of its strip starting from the reference line, and still without concerning himself with the path of the plank).

Q 2: Col like Iac places the paper strips on either side of

the starting point: *The snail arrived here* (on the left at the end of its paper strip). *But the board went which way? The other way.* Was the snail carried along too? *Yes.* Then where did it arrive? *Here* (as before). Why? *Because he went this way and that's the distance he travelled.*

We can see the interest of these last reactions. The fact that the subjects of stage I do not manage to pay attention to both movements at the same time, and forget one when they are reproducing the other, is in no way decisive, for this could only be a difficulty of attention or of focusing intuition. But the fact that the subjects of stage II measure the path of the snail on the board, then of the board on the table, and carefully transfer these two movements to start from the starting line without managing to combine them by simple addition or subtraction, is truly the index of a systematic difficulty in the composition of displacements. Now this difficulty is exactly analogous to those which we have analysed in Chapters Three and Four, on the level of this same stage II: inability to measure journeys when they are not integral but composed of segments which must be co-ordinated amongst themselves, non-reversibility of the directions of travel and, above all, no differentiation between lengths and their order in succession. In the present case two points are specially to be noted. When the snail and the board move in the same direction the child sees quite clearly, at the same time as he notes what is given, that the board carries the snail along, but at the time when he is reconstructing the path of the latter by transferring the measured length, the subject does not understand that the starting point of this journey was itself carried along by the board nor that the problem is to know just how far it was carried along: the fact that this starting point coincided, at the commencement of the movement of the board, with the guide line from which the board and the snail started, simultaneously, makes the child persist in calculating the path of the snail from this line as if the starting point of the snail were absolute, and not relative to the actual board. In other words it is the absolute character attributed to the starting

point of the comparative movement which prevents its
composition with the absolute movement: it is therefore
once more a question of order which faults the composition of the lengths in the case of Q 1. As for Q 2, when
the snail travels in one direction and the board in the
other, the movement of the snail is conceived as taking
place entirely in the first direction: if it started from the
left of the guide line, the child will place the paper strip
used as a measure altogether on the left without counting
the fact that the board carried the movement to the right.
On the other hand he will put the strip measuring this
second movement altogether on the right of the starting
line as if it were a question of two movements, quite
absolute, starting in opposite directions from the same
point. Here too the relationships of order determining the
directions of travel are weightier than the consideration of
the lengths covered, whence the impossibility of composing the latter. In both cases (Q 1 and 2) everything,
therefore, carries on as if the movement of the snail
stayed independent and could be transferred singly. The
only progress shown by stage II compared with stage I is
that the movement of the board is likewise measured and
transferred, but it is separate and unco-ordinated with the
first.

3. *Composition (by concrete operations) of movements in
the same direction, and also of movements in reverse of
equal length, but failure in composition of unequal movements in opposite directions*

We recall the characteristics of stage III described in
Chapter Three and in the two sections of Chapter Four:
now capable of concrete operations, the subject manages
to measure the segments of paths through the 'composition' of the partial journeys. As for the reverse directions,
he conceives the journey on the way back as necessarily
equal to that of the outward journey (including the case of
ascents and descents), even when the return journey is
completed in several stages, provided that they are all

facing in the same direction (inverse). On the contrary in the case of several partial outward and return journeys he only arrives at a gradual empirical solution. Now, the situation is very similar when it comes to comparative movement. The subjects in stage III, in fact, are successful in composing the two movements when they are in the same direction. Moreover they succeed in solving in advance i.e. without experimental observation, the question of equal movements in contrary directions: quite definitely, composition of movements in the same direction has become operational, since from the operation A+X the subject infers the operations A−A=O, i.e. the inverse and the identity. But when the inverse movements are unequal i.e. A−X (where X is greater or less than A) either he fails in any composition (sub-stage IIIa) or else he only arrives at the solution empirically and by gradual 'groping' forwards (sub-stage IIIb).

Here are some examples of sub-stage IIIa starting with an intermediate case between II and IIIa (who do not manage Q 3 right away).

ROL (7; 10) Q 1: Places the papers representing the paths of the snail and of the board end to end but without taking the starting line into account. Do you remember where the plank was? *There* (he adjusts it). Where did the snail stop? *Here* (the end of the plank's path). *No, there!* (he adds on the path of the snail again). Why there? *Because the starting point is there and then the board moved forward; then, because the snail was on top, it's there* (correct). And now (Q 2): opposite directions with unequal journeys). *The snail moved back* (he says this upon perceiving the movements, then he measures the paths of the snail and the board and puts the paper corresponding to the former on the left of the line of reference and the latter paper on the right). The snail did which journey? *On this side here.* But since the board moved back did it do a longer or a shorter journey than the other? *Longer* (the movements are repeated). *Oh, shorter!* So then? (He puts the two papers end to end, but both on the side of the snail!). Did it do all this journey? *Yes.*

Q 3 (equal movements in opposite directions): at first he points to the left, then to the right and finally discovers that the snail does not change its position.

FRAN (8; 1) Q 1: (He places the measures end to end right away). That was the journey of the card, and then the snail was on top. (Q 2: contrary motion). Where did it arrive? *Here* (he places the track of the snail on the left of the line and that of the board on the right and points to the end of the former). You think that he went such a long way? *Oh, no, you pushed the card back to there.* And where was the snail? *On the card.* Then does that make a difference? *The card got pulled back and he went off this way.* And all this time was the snail going forwards or back on the card? *Forwards* (the movements are reproduced). *Oh, because when the snail went off* (=began to move), *the card moved back, and then the snail was not going along with it* (=in the same direction). Would the snail have arrived in the same place if I had not moved the card? *The same thing.* Where did it arrive? *There* (still the same spot). Another test: he places the two papers this time side by side on the same side of the starting line and points out the end of the snails' track as if that of the plank played no part in it.

Q 3 (equal journeys in opposite directions): He stays there (correct right away).

VIL (9; 0) Q 1: points it out approximately, then places the two paths end to end pointing out the end of the second.

Q 2: puts one track on each side of the starting line, like Rol and Fran. What did the card do? *Went backwards.* Then did the snail do a longer or a shorter road? *Longer.* Longer than if he had gone by himself? *No, shorter* (he puts them back as before). But where did the snail stop? *There* (end of its own strip, on the left) *and then the card went back there* (towards the right).

Q 3: brief hesitation then: *He does not move.*

We can see the progress of these reactions in relation to those of stage II: the subject understands from the very start that if the snail is carried along by the board, the starting point of its own path is to be placed at the end of the latter and not on the absolute starting line, which marks the beginning of the path of the board. This is what Rol says very clearly: that is the starting point there (=the line of reference) and then the plank moved forwards: then, because the snail was on top (=on the board) that's where it is (=he places the path of the snail in continuation of that of the board). In a word, the starting point of the snail ceases to be absolute and is conceived as being carried along, whence the composition by addition of the paths travelled. It follows that when the movements are in opposite directions, the child also understands that they cancel each other out when the lengths are equal (Q 3).

But why do they not manage, in that case, to 'compose' the paths going in opposite directions by simple subtraction when they are unequal? Now, the solutions given to this Q 2 simply carry on those of the preceeding stage. Rol however says right away 'the snail went backwards' but unable to subtract one journey from the other, he places the first on the left and the second on the right of the starting line, as in stage II. We ask him, as with the later subjects who arrive at this same impasse, if the snail's path is actually longer or shorter than if the board had not been moved back: to which Rol and Vil at first reply 'longer' because there are thus two movements instead of only one, then 'smaller' only because in fact it is backwards. So we can understand why they hesitate to subtract journeys which seem to them basically to be added together: whence the final solution of Rol, who places them in a line. As for Vil and Fran their conclusion is made explicit by the latter: 'the card went back and then the snail was not going along the same way', thus the movements are independent.

In a word, the concrete operations which appear with stage III do not at first permit anything but the solution of compositions all in the same direction or else in opposite directions when the paths are equal, because then there is complete compensation and the composition of the direct journey $+A$ with the inverse one $-A$ produces the identity $A - A = O$. But when the inverse journeys are unequal, concrete operations are no longer enough and a formal mechanism is necessary. Why? That is what the examination if the following reactions will allow us to analyse. In fact in the course of sub stage IIIb Q 2 is solved little by little through empirical trial and error.

Ed (8; 10) Q 1: correct right away. Q 2: He will go backwards (Ed places the papers end to end as for Q 1 on the left of the starting line, then he moves the one which represents the path of the board backwards without knowing what to do with that of the snail). Will the snail travel farther than before? *No, he will travel a shorter way.* What was the snail doing when I was pulling the board? *He was going forwards, but not far* (he pulls the track of the board on to the right of the guide line and places that of the snail astride of this line to mark this move backwards, but without being able to co-ordinate it with the paper belonging to the board.) (Further attempt). *He came beyond the line* (right, but without accurate co-ordination).

Q 3 (equal journeys in opposite directions): *He stays put.*
Q 4: foresees correctly whether on the left or the right.

Aud (9; 5) Q 1: correct right away. Q 2: *He will go a shorter way* (he lines them up as before, on the left, then draws the path of the board back, on to the right of the line of reference, and lays upon the latter line the paper belonging to the snail. After which he moves the last paper back, arriving more or less at the right spot, but without co-ordinating it with the paper representing the path of the board).

Q 3 and 4: correct.

Lil (10; 0): with Q 2 begins by putting the snail's track to the right of the starting line and the track of the board on the left, then reverses these positions and places the snail's track astride the line. Finally, he puts both papers on the right of the line, as in stage II but in the right hand direction, to mark the general move backwards.

Q 3: *He moved back: he is still on the line.*
Q 4: *The plank does this and the snail does that: on the right.* The same for the contrary relationships (correct).

Hub (10; 7) Q 2: *That's the path of the board* (puts it right away on the right of the line: correct). *The snail did that* (puts him on the left of the line, as in stage II, then moves back). *In any case, you don't need that* ('path' of the board). *He comes beyond the line* (moving that of the snail back farther) *no, not so far.*

We can see that these subjects are starting coordinating, or at least are trying to co-ordinate movements

in contrary directions even when they are unequal (Q 2).
But they are not successful with precise subtraction. They
correctly place the paper upon the right of the line of
reference representing the track of the board, which therefore measures the movement backwards. As for the snail's
track, they fail to find its relative starting point, i.e. to put
it at the end of the other paper. They well know nevertheless that this starting point is carried by the movement of
the board; above all they know, contrary to the subjects of
sub-stage IIIa, that the total journey of the snail is shorter
than if it had moved by itself: 'he will not go so far' (Ed)
and a 'shorter journey' (Aud). They therefore find that
one must subtract or diminish something, but do not know
how to do it, nor how much to subtract.

What does this curious situation depend on? Why does
the child not understand that it would be enough to make
the starting point of the snail's track coincide with the end
of the board's path going backwards, when he grasps
perfectly well that the total is made less? It all takes place
as if the subject did not conceive of this diminution as a
subtraction properly so called, and this for want of clearly
imagining the movements in question either as simultaneous or as in succession. In order to understand the relationships of these two movements, it is necessary in fact
that one's thinking should be able, at will, to call up each
separately in succession, then to harmonize each with the
other in a simultaneous whole. Now, if the subjects quoted
have attained the level of concrete operations, one must
allow that these are not enough to ensure this passing from
the simultaneous to the successive and vice versa, and that
only a deductive mechanism working on hypotheses as
such, hence a formal mechanism, permits of a solution to
the problem. Let us examine from this aspect the intermediate subjects between this sub-stage IIIb and stage IV
and let us look for the way in which they discover the
correct solution.

GAB (9; 8) Q 2: he begins by placing the measuring strips
on both sides of the starting line, then draws back the paper
for the board gradually from left to right (correct direction)

whilst he places the paper for the snail astride the line of reference. He then moves it slowly back, until reaching the right hand end of the first paper, and then cries *That's it. He starts off from here.* Finally he points out the spot where the snail stopped.

Q 3: Equal paths in opposite direction: *He stops at the same spot where he started.*

REN (10; 5) Q 1: at once says *You have to add the two together.* (Q 2: opposite directions). *You have to add them together as well* (places one strip to the left and the other onto the right of the line). *No, you have to take that away* (the measuring strip for the plank) *from this* (snail's strip). *There will only be this left* (he points out the difference after putting the paper on that of the snail). Good. So where did it stop? (He places the measure for the plank on the right of the line, and that of the snail beside it, making the ends coincide). *That's where he stops* (correct).

GER (10; 6) Q 1: *There's the path the card made: the snail did the same journey on the card. So you add the papers end to end.* That's right. And this way? (Q 2). *The snail was in front and the card behind.* (He lays the snail's strip on the left of the line, and that of card on the right, then reverses them, then lays the paper for the snail astride the line, and the one for the card on the right, and finally adjusts the ends together).

Q 4: *Here* (correct) *because you drew the card back farther than the snail went forward: he ended behind the guide line.*

We can see how the child arrives at the correct answer: by making *simultaneous* again the movements under consideration after having measured them as if they were in succession. In the case of Gab the thing happens without verbalization, but with Ren and Ger the mechanism is clear: sometimes it is the awareness of the subtraction to be carried out which leads them to reconstruct the two movements in opposite directions as if simultaneous, and sometimes their simultaneous nature which leads to the subtraction. Ren begins by stating explicitly that you must 'add' the movements in the same direction, and after wanting to do the same with those in contrary directions he recognizes that you have to 'take away' one length from the other: that is when, in order to carry out the operation, he places the measuring strip for the board upon that of the snail, which sufficiently expresses their simultaneous nature and allows him, at length to make the ends coincide correctly. As for Ger, who also starts with the explicit addition of the movements in the same direction, he, from the outset, plans the subtraction of the movements in contrary directions, conceived as simultaneous, then feels his way towards the actualization of this operation.

In a word, in order to arrive at the subtraction of movements in opposite directions you must first allow for their simultaneousness, without which their arrival in succession, or rather their measurement in succession, gives the impression of an addition or of a 'longer' journey, as we have seen in sub-substage IIIa, but in order to visualize them as simultaneous after having measured them one after the other, you must have the intention of 'composing' them by one single operation of subtraction. Now, it is precisely the potentiality of formal thinking to manage to fulfil these two conditions at the same time, 'by passing' what is actually there through a hypothetico-deductive reconstruction which allows one to think of the simultaneous as if in succession, and vice-versa at will. But, an interesting thing, in the case of the present test, as in that of the journeys in succession studied in Chapter Four, it is only when partial movements occur in contrary directions that this reconstruction of a hypothetico-deductive nature is necessary. When, on the contrary, the simultaneous movements are in the same direction (or when it is a question of movements in succession in opposite directions but with a single reverse movement, or else in several steps but always in the same direction) concrete operations are enough because they already manage to bypass reality by anticipating the inverse motion of the changes of location observed.

The subjects who we have just examined are therefore on the boundary of formal thinking, which they arrive at (or rather replace in part) by a series of gradual tentative procedures. Those whom we are going to analyse now, on the contrary, solve from the very start, and with one single thought process, this double problem of simultaneous representation and of operational co-ordination.

4. The fourth stage: Immediate solution of the question by formal operations

The average age at which children enter this last stage is about 11 years but naturally we find exceptional cases from 9½ years on, and particularly from 10 years:

GUI (9; 6) Q 1: *You have to add them up.* (Q 2). *The board travels like this, and the snail like that* (from the very beginning he places the measure of the snail's journey opposite the end of the strip for the board's movement). (Further attempt with snail's journey shorter than that of the board). (Same). (Q 3). *He will stay in the same place.* (Q 4: correct).

DO (9; 11) Q 1: *The snail moved forwards too, at the same time as the board* (he adds the journeys). (Q 2). *The card went back and the snail forward. Since the snail did this distance and the plank that, the snail did this journey on top of the plank* (he puts one measuring strip on top of the other). *This piece* (the difference) *is the distance the snail did farther than the plank.* (With the proportions reversed). *The snail did this much less because the board went farther back* (points it out exactly).

GIL (10; 3). Same responses. Gives as reason for subtraction (correct positions): *The card made the snail do a shorter journey.*

IAC (11; 4) Q 1: *This is what the board did, and that is what the snail did, over the board: you have to put one following the other. Q. 2. The snail did this journey and at the same time as he goes forward, the board moves back this much* (he subtracts).

AND (12; 3) Q 2: *This* (strip) *is how far the snail went forward, and that is how far you took this back: I'm finding out what the difference is.*

DOL (12; 8). *It's as if the roadway were moving backwards while he is going forward* (from the outset he tries to find the difference).

As always, at the end of a complex evolution, we are struck by the simplicity of the final reaction. Reading these few words, it seems that the subject does no more than translate what he has just perceived into words and measurements; the snail is going forward and at the same time the board is moving backward, thus the total journey consists of the difference between the two. In actual fact, as we have seen from stage I to stage III, in spite of seeing the two movements simultaneously the subjects at the earlier levels do not manage to think of them as simultaneous, since to do so is quite different, being at first a question of measuring them in succession and then of reconstructing their synchronization operationally. In the course of stage I, only one of the movements is considered while the other is as if pushed aside by the attention which is centred on the first. In stage II this situation seems to be past since the two movements are measured, and the two measurements of the journeys are placed on the table, but they are only laid side by side and not added together, with the result that only one of the two is actually considered. In stage IIIa the two movements are added together when they are in the same direction, but when they are in opposite directions co-ordination is attempted without being arrived at, since one of the measuring strips is set down on the left of the guide line and the other on the right: the child thus loses any idea of simultaneous co-ordination as soon as the movement of the board carries with it the starting point of the snail's journey in the opposite direction.

Being forced to think of these movements successively in order to be able to measure them, the subject can no longer reconstruct them as simultaneous for want of knowing where to place the starting point of the latter, since the plank has moved away from the fixed line of reference. In the course of sub-stage IIIb, the child seeks to make the co-ordination accurate, but does not manage precise subtraction for lack of the reconstruction, as yet, of their complete simultaneousness. Finally, the formal thinking of the subject in stage IV just quoted puts this situation right, by virtue of a hypothetical-deductive mechanism which allows one to translate at will the simultaneous into the successive and then the successive into the simultaneous. It is thanks to this ease of reconstruction, a mobility which is itself due to the habitual manipulation of hypotheses or assumptions, that the subject finally manages to submit the relative movements which he perceives to the ordinary operation of subtraction in so far as these are the reverse of addition (on the logico-arithmetical or spatio-temporal level).

As a general rule, formal operations are distinguished from concrete operations in that the former constitute operations of the second degree carried out upon the latter. Concrete operations, in fact, bear upon reality itself, perceived or conceived, whilst formal operations proceed simply upon verbal supposition, or on hypothesis based on symbols (as in mathematics) which represent the former. Concrete operations are consequently enough for the solution of the 'composition' of movements in the same direction (Q 1) or of contrary movements of equal length (Q 3). This last question is solved even from stage III on the verbal level, (of course, because an operation is verbal it does not necessarily become formal); the subject in stage IIIa has already understood that contrary movements of equal length will compensate each other exactly. The fact is, therefore, that it is possible to construct a single reversible system by concrete operations, whether it is a question of movement in the same direction or a contrary movement whose compensatory nature is understood to be due to a simple outward and return journey. In the case of movements of unequal length in opposite directions, on the contrary, it is in vain that the child perceives the simultaneousness of the movement and that he is able to manipulate his measuring strip in any direction, the operation must be formal because it is a question of thinking of two concrete systems at one time, arrived at by measurement in succession, and to be co-ordinated in a single simultaneous whole. It is the same with the operations in the last chapter, when they bring in partial outward and return journeys (as opposed to complete journeys, even when they are made in several attempts, provided that the partial vectors have the same direction): although in succession these partial outward and return journeys must be co-ordinated amongst themselves as if they were simultaneous, and it is this reunion in a single whole of several successive systems in different directions, each of which taken separately is understood concretely as a reversible movement, which gives to complex questions of change of location the character of formal operations. (See Chapter Four end of § 5).

But formal operations add nothing to concrete operations as regards the nature of the actions involved, (apart from their hypothetico-deductive nature and the consequent logic of propositions by means of which they perfect the logic of classes, relationships and numbers, as well as infra-logical or spatio-temporal relations), they simply translate them on to a different level, which is that of suppositions or hypotheses, The subtraction of the journeys, in Q 2, by the fact that it is formal, does not differ from a concrete subtraction such as that which arises in Q 3 and both of them obey the same operational laws.

On the whole the operations proper to movement only (independent of speed) are as follows:

1. The qualitative grouping of displacement, conceived as changes of position or of order (asymmetrical) . . . (grouping identical to that of position—'placing'—from which it differs only by reference to movements on the part of the subject or of the objects themselves).

2. The qualitative grouping of paths travelled or "(symmetrical) intervals included between the points in order, of departure and arrival.

3. The metrical group of displacements implying measurement of the distances travelled along with those defining the axes of the co-ordinates acting as their system of reference (this dual measurement both synthesizing and quantifying the relationships of place, of displacement and of intervals).

4. Finally, the reconstruction on a formal level of the

foregoing three systems: while groupings 1 and 2 and group 3 are completed by 7 to 8 years, this formal reconstruction becomes effective only at the age of 10 to 11 years, under its dual aspect of co-ordination of movement in succession in opposite directions and of relative movements of unequal length in opposite directions.

PART 3

Qualitative Speed

There appears to be nothing simpler than a change of position: setting aside its speed, it seems obvious that movement should be immediately understood intuitively as a path travelled. Now we have just seen that displacement consisted essentially of a change of position or placing, movements being evaluated at rest by the order of succession of their stopping points alone, and we saw that the idea of the distance travelled finally took shape as the interval between the starting and stopping points only after the formation of the operations of placement or order.

Speed, on the other hand, may appear more complex: in so far as it is a relationship between space and time its formation would seem to have to wait until the operations relating to the construction of the ideas of the 'path travelled' and of duration had been completely formed. But if this is indeed the case with the 'metrical' conception of speed, would there not exist a basic intuition of 'rapidity' and perhaps even a system of qualitative operations basing speed on order just like movement itself? And if the speed of a single moving object remains unanalysable from this point of view, because it is an absolute, might not the comparison of two speeds follow on from this other idea of order, namely change of position?

CHAPTER SIX

The Intuition of Speed

The first problem which we have to solve when beginning to study the conception of speed is, of course, to determine what initial intuition or intuitions this concept proceeds from. Of course, every movement experienced is at first attached to an impression of speed, and as we have seen, it is a long time before the idea of a pure 'displacement' is constructed, i.e. a movement viewed independently of its speed simply as a path travelled in a particular direction. Thus one possibility of analysing the intuition of speed at its source might be to start with kinaesthetic sensations and with dynamic impressions or regulations of effort (or acceleration) and of fatigue (or deceleration). However, in the child's case these subjective impressions do not give rise to conceptualized intuitions, except when attached to external movements or to movements of his own body but perceived from the outside. Therefore, we shall only arrive at the effect of the internal factors in speed indirectly and in view of other basic given factors. We shall, therefore, confine ourselves at first to tracing the early intuitions of speed in the data relating to movements perceived from the outside, and since on our scale there are no absolute speeds either in the perceptual field or in the sphere of intelligence, we shall start our analysis with the comparison of two movements.

The facts indicate that the simplest intuition of speed, as well as of movement, is based on an intuition of order: at any age a moving object is held to be faster than another when it overtakes it on a path parallel to its own, i.e. when it has originally been behind the other one according to the direction of travel, or side by side with it, and afterwards is ahead of it. In order to analyse the problem more thoroughly our subjects undertook the following three types of test, corresponding to the three sections of this chapter: (I) judging the respective speeds of two moving objects when the starting and the stopping points alone are visible: the paths are unequal in length though parallel and running in the same direction but remaining out of sight (e.g. two tunnels of unequal lengths); (II) determining the respective speeds of the two moving objects travelling along paths which are altogether open to view and unequal in length though the starting and the stopping points are the same (or with stopping points side by side); (III) judging the speed of two moving objects travelling 'neck and neck' along two concentric tracks of widely differing sizes, and visible throughout.

SECTION I. The speed of two movements where only the starting and stopping points are visible

The children are shown two straight tunnels, of unequal length (55 and 40 cms.) and two dolls with rigid wire rods attached to their backs. The two dolls are placed at the entrances of the two tunnels (and these entrances are themselves placed side by side along the same starting line) and they set off at the same moment and stop together at the other end. Then we simply ask whether one went faster than the other.

It is important before asking questions about speed, to point out clearly the disparity in length of the two tunnels, requesting the child simply to point out the longer of the two. Moreover the child should be seated in such a way that he can keep a watch on the two exits as well as the two entrances of the tunnels, and he himself gives the starting signal. If he clearly fails to solve the questions on speed, the two movements are repeated with the tunnels removed: when the child has seen which of the two dolls was travelling faster and has explained why, the tunnel apparatus is replaced and the original questions are again put as before.

Three stages of response were observed. In the course of the first the child fails to solve the problem of the tunnels, even after seeing the dolls travel the same paths in full view on the table. During the second stage, the child at first fails in the question of the tunnels, but later gradually reaches the correct solution, in particular when he has seen the dolls run on the table. In the third stage a correct answer is given immediately.

1. *The first stage: Failure in comparison of speeds*

Here are some examples of the initial reactions:

BERN (5; 2) recognizes that one of the tunnels is longer than the other and that the dolls started and stopped simultaneously: Then did one of them go quicker than the other? No. We then remove the tunnels and reproduce the same movements: was one of the dolls faster than the other? Yes, *this one* (correct). Did they set off at the same time? Yes. And stop at the same time? Yes. Did they travel for the same length of time? No. *This one longer* (=farther). And like that? ('A' starts first and 'B' catches it up. Both stopped at the same time). This one caught the other one up. Did one of them go faster? No. (We replace the tunnels. Starting and stopping simultaneously). And now, did one of them go quicker? No. Thus the greatest speed is attached to visible overtaking. With the same simultaneous stopping points their speeds are judged equal even if one moving object set off after the other from the same starting point.

IOS (5; 6). Did they set off at the same time? Yes. And stopped at the same time? Yes. Did one of the dolls go faster than the other? No. Are the tunnels the same length? No, *this one is smaller and this one bigger*. Then was one of the dolls faster? No. Watch again (repeat experiment). Yes, *the same speed*. In the smaller tunnel is the road shorter? Yes. And they arrive at the same time? Yes. Then does one go quicker than the other? No. Does it make no difference if one of the tunnels is bigger than the other? *Of course not!* Which is the longer road? *This one*. Then does one of them go faster than the other if they arrive at the same time? No.

The two paths travelled under the tunnels are marked with chalk and the tunnels removed: If they start at the same time and stop at the same time, does one go quicker than the other? *Yes—the first one goes quicker because the path is longer.* (We rub out the chalk and replace the tunnels). Do they start and finish together? *Yes.* Does one go faster than the other? *No.* Why? *They stop at the same time.*

MAR (5; 11). Do they set off at the same time? *Yes.* And do they stop at the same time? *Yes.* Does one of them go faster than the other? *No.* Did they go at the same speed? *Yes.* Why? *Because they were both going faster.* Faster than what? *. . .* Was one of them faster than the other? *No.* Did both of them take the same time? *No, not the same. One took longer.* Which one? *The one in the big tunnel.* Then one went faster than the other? *No.*

We get the child to run across the room from A to B whilst the experimenter walks from A to B (starting and finishing simultaneously on an audible signal): Did we start at the same time? *Yes.* And stopped at the same time? *No.* Did one of us go faster? *I did because I ran harder.* Did we travel the same length of time? *No.* Why? *I went farther than you.* And did we stop at the same time? *No.* (This time the experimenter and the child run towards each other, the former on the path AB and the child on the path DB— which is longer than AB). Did we start together? *Yes.* And stopped at the same time? *Yes.* Did one of us go faster than the other? *No.* Did one of us run a longer distance? *Yes, I did.* Then did one of us go quicker? *Oh, yes, I did.* We return to the tunnels again: same reactions as before.

LAV (6; 0). Is one of these tunnels bigger than the other one? *Yes, this one.* Look at these dolls. They set off together and they stopped together. Did one of them go faster than the other? *No.* Why? *They were travelling for the same length of time.* Did they travel the same distance? *No, this one is longer.* They started at the same time? *Yes.* And stopped at the same time? *Yes.* Did one go quicker than the other? *No.* Both the same speed? *Yes.*

The two dolls with the tunnels removed: Did they set off at the same time? *Yes.* Did they stop at the same time? *No, that one there is longer: they did not stop at the same time.* You must tap on the table counting: 1, 2, 3. On 3 the dolls will stop. (We start again, stopping on 3). Did they stop at

THE INTUITION OF SPEED

the same time? Yes. Did they go at the same speed? *No, it was more there* (right). Then we'll take the tunnels again (experiment). Did they set off together? Yes. Did they stop at the same time? Yes. Did they go as fast as each other or not? Yes. Did one go a longer distance than the other? *Yes, that one there* (right). Was it going faster, harder than the other, or the same? *They were both going just as hard.* They were travelling for the same time? *Yes, both the same.* Did they travel the same distance? *No, that one went farther because it is a bigger tunnel.* And the other? *Less, because it is shorter.* Then did one of the two go faster than the other? No. But this one (big tunnel) went farther than the other? *Yes, it went the length of its tunnel.* Then didn't one of them have to go faster than the other? *No, they both went the same.*

As we can see, these initial facts show from the very start the contrast between the ease of intuitive solution when the moving objects are visible throughout their journeys and the difficulties of the operations which become necessary when these given factors are no longer perceptible.

When the two journeys are completely visible, the subject has no difficulty in recognizing that one of the moving objects is moving faster than the other, provided that they set off simultaneously from the same point and travel in the same direction. But is it then a question of an intuitive understanding of speed as a relationship between a duration and a path travelled? One might sometimes think so, e.g. when Ios says: 'the first one goes faster because the road is longer'. However, even in the case of visible paths, two good reasons prevent us from accepting this interpretation. The first is that the length of the path travelled is only brought in if there is some overtaking. Mar e.g. is already lost when the two movements to be compared are directed towards one another and we shall see in Section II of this chapter and in Chapter Seven how little notice the child takes of distances to be covered when no overtaking takes place. On the other hand, if it were the relationship between time and space which gave rise to the intuition of speed, it would at least be necessary for equal-

ity of synchronous times to be recognized. Bern attributes
a longer time to the longer of the visible paths even while
he recognizes the simultaneousness of departure and of
arrival (after which he judges the speeds of two movements travelling equal paths in unequal times as equal,
which shows how little he is concerned about time). Mar
also supposes 'a longer distance= a longer time', and Lav
even denies that they stop simultaneously. We have in any
case discussed elsewhere[1] this question of the time common to two movements of different speeds sufficiently to
know that at this level the equality of synchronous durations still has no meaning for the child.

The intuitions of speed could not therefore consist of a
relationship between distance covered and time, for want
of general interest in the former and of understanding of
the latter: it can therefore only be the perception or the
visualization of a practical rather than an intellectual relationship, that of 'overtaking'. This relationship may be
perceived or felt directly in terms of one's own bodily
activity when one voluntary movement is more effective
than another, in particular where effort is involved, i.e. (as
Baldwin and Janet have clearly shown) a feeling of acceleration, or conversely of deceleration. But overtaking can
also be perceived when two given moving objects are
following two parallel paths in the same direction, and it is
in just this particular situation that the intuition of external speeds begins.

Now, if this is the case, we can understand at once why
the child is unsuccessful when the movements to be compared in speed are not visible, and only the simultaneous
starting and stopping points are perceptible: in fact no
overtaking is then open to observation. But, in the absence
of perceptual observation, could the subject not imagine
this overtaking going on under the tunnels, as he eventually visualizes it (cf. Mar when we pursue the point) when
he has seen two runners going towards each other? But, in
this latter case, the child does not imagine the potential

[1] *Origins of the Child's Conception of Time*, Chapters Three to
Seven.

overtaking, by relating the time and the distance travelled: he estimates directly through his eye movements as he watches the two movements, where the runners would be if they were going side by side. On the contrary, in order to imagine the overtaking inside the tunnels, it is actually necessary to begin with the idea of the lengths in order to relate them to the equal durations. Now, as the child at this level does not even manage this correlation within the restricted field of perception, of course he is even less capable of this in the case of hidden movements.

But why then does he come to consider the two speeds as equal instead of answering at random? The fact is that estimates of simultaneousness cause no difficulty in this case whereas they do when the paths are visible: the starting points are compared directly with one another and the child then switches his attention to the exits of the tunnels, in order to verify the simultaneousness of the stopping points regardless of the speeds and the actual movements, as the latter are out of sight. Since the two movements thus have simultaneous starting and stopping points, the subject infers that the speeds are equal. When asked, he infers that the durations are also equal, but the basis for this is the speeds (it is in fact only in the case of dissimilar speeds that the child denies the equality of synchronous durations).

2. The second stage: Intermediate responses

The subjects of stage II begin as the previous ones by affirming that the speeds of the movements in the tunnels are equal. But then, whether on reflection the lengths appear to them to contradict this equality, or whether a comparison made when observing the speeds without the tunnels leads them to this reflection, they modify their original opinion. Here are some examples:

FRAN (6; 0). Look at these tunnels. Are they the same size? *No, this one is better.* Right, off we go. Did they start at the same time? *Yes.* And did they arrive at the same time?

Yes. Did one go quicker than the other? No. Is one of the tunnels bigger than the other? Yes, this one. Now watch again (experiment repeated): *Did one of the two go quicker, harder than the other? No.*

Now look: I am taking away the tunnels. How do they travel, one faster than the other? *No, Yes. Which one? That one* (short journey) *because the path is shorter* ('fast' is thus taken in the sense of 'arriving first at equal speeds'). (Races with the child in the room). *Which one went quickest? I did, because I ran harder* (right). *And which of the two little men* (on the table)? *That one went quicker because he raced along on his own* (=harder). And this way (B starts after A and catches him up). *(B) is quicker, because he caught the other one up.* And this way (A on a straight line and B on an oblique line but with a longer trajectory; starting and stopping simultaneously). *That's the one that went quicker (B). How do you know? Because it was ahead* (=longer journey translated into terms of overtaking.)

I'm putting them back in the tunnels (exp.). *Did one of the two go quicker than the other? Yes, that one* (the one in the bigger tunnel). *Why? Because it's first* (=space translated into overtaking). *But did they stop together? Yes.*

GIL (6; 0) recognizes the unequal lengths of the tunnels and the simultaneousness of starting and stopping. Nevertheless he believes the speeds are equal. The movements are then repeated without the tunnels. *Does one go quicker than the other? Yes, that one* (correct) *because it runs harder.* And this way (inverse ratios). *That one* (right). And now (same paths but not starting simultaneously). *That one was faster because it caught the other one up.*

We replace the two tunnels: *Are these the same size? No, this one is bigger. Did they set off together? Yes. Did they stop together? Yes. Did one of the two go faster than the other one? No, but that one* (big tunnel) *was ahead, because the tunnel is longer.* Then did one of the two go faster than the other? *No.* But is one of them more out of breath than the other? *Oh, yes, one went a bit farther, this one.* And one went harder, faster than the other? *Yes, that one went quicker. Why? To reach the other end of the tunnel* (at the same time).

Iac (6; o). Is one of the two tunnels bigger than the other?
Yes, that one. Did they stop at the same time? *Yes.* Did one
of them go quicker than the other? *They were both the same.*
Is one of the tunnels longer? *Yes.* (Experiment repeated).
They both went at the same speed. Does it make no difference if one of the tunnels is longer than the other? *One of
the dolls goes farther.* And in the same time? *Yes.* Then does
it go quicker? *They both go at the same speed but one goes
farther than the other.* How's that? *It has to go right to the
end.* Did they travel for the same time or not? *One took a
little longer than the other.* And did one go harder? *No, both
the same.*

Without tunnels: Does one go faster? *That one goes faster.*
Why? *Because the path is longer.* And did they travel for the
same time? *No, that one* (the same one) *took longer.* Faster
or not so fast? *It went faster.*

(The tunnels are replaced). A little faster or the same?
That one (big tunnel) *was faster, because it has a longer
way to go.* Did they start at the same time? *Yes.* And did
they stop at the same time? *Yes.* And did they travel for the
same time? *No, that one* (the same one) *travelled longer
than the other one.* And just as hard? *That one* (still the
same one) *went harder than the other one.*

These three examples of intermediate reactions allows
us to watch the gradual passage from the early intuitions
of speed, attached to visible overtaking, towards a correlation leading to the unification of time and distance
travelled.

Fran e.g. reacts at first as those in the first stage: but
when paths are visible, he shows a step forwards, extending the concept of overtaking, by a kind of articulated
intuition or imaginative reconstruction to trajectories
which are not actually parallel. 'That one there is faster
because it is ahead', he says for example, which undoubtedly signifies that if the paths were parallel, overtaking
would take place. When we eventually return to the experiment with the tunnels, he answers correctly this time that
the doll going through the big tunnel is going faster than
the other, and again expresses this in terms of overtaking:
'because it is first'. What the child evidently needs then in
order to discover the right answer at once is a certain

articulation or regulation of representational intuition permitting him to convert differences in length into relationships of overtaking, and once this generalization is achieved in connection with visible paths of different lengths, he also applies it to hidden paths.

Gil begins in the same way, but when we return to the tunnels his response is curious. He recognizes that overtaking must take place, applying what he had just observed with the tunnels removed, and so infers that the moving object in the big tunnel is 'farther ahead because the tunnel is longer'. But since this overtaking is not visible, he hesitates at first to interpret it straight away as a difference in speed and he has first to recognize that the doll must be more out of breath before finally consenting to state that 'he went faster to reach the very end of the tunnel'. Similarly, Iac begins by saying in the experiment with the tunnels, 'they both travel for the same time, but one goes farther than the other': it is only after seeing the dolls without the tunnels that he translates this 'farther' into overtaking involving not only the stopping points but the actual movements and their speeds ('that one was faster because it had a longer distance to go'). But on the other hand, he also concludes from this disparity of lengths that it travelled 'longer' which is enough to show that he stays within the intuitive sphere and does not achieve an operational relationship between the distance travelled and the time taken.

The conditions necessary for the passage from initial intuition to operations are thus revealed, since the earliest intuition of speed is that of overtaking, and this is not visible in the case of the tunnels, it is necessary to transpose lengths and times into visualized overtaking. The subjects of the first stage remain incapable of this translation, whilst those of the present stage when they see the movements repeated without the tunnels understand that the greater space traversed by one of the moving objects implies the fact that it overtakes the other. When they subsequently return to the experiment of the tunnels, some like (Fran and Iac) immediately transpose what they have just seen and so have no difficulty in implying from the length of the bigger tunnel a hidden overtaking, hence a greater speed; others on the contrary like Gil, interpret in two steps: the length of the large tunnel entails that this moving object gets 'farther ahead' than the other, and this order of succession of the stopping points then brings about the idea of overtaking and greater speed.

But the conclusion from this rather more mobile articulation of intuition should not be that these subjects are liberated from intuitive methods and have arrived at operations. They still in fact think in terms of real overtaking and cannot yet manage to generalize so far as to correlate time and space traversed. Concerning space it cannot be said that relationships of order (overtaking) are already co-ordinated in every case with relationships of distance (length of the path travelled) since overtaking has to be visible briefly for the disparity in length of the tunnels to be interpreted in terms of speed. Concerning time, it is evident that Iac still attributes a greater duration to the longer journey in spite of the recognized simultaneousness of the starting and stopping points respectively. Moreover, Fran wavers between two contradictory meanings of the word 'fast': the temporal sense (to stop quicker=before another one moving at equal speed) and the meaning actually relating to speed. In short these reactions do not go beyond the level of intuition, but due to a greater mobility in imaginative anticipations and reconstructions the child succeeds in visualizing to some extent what is going on under the tunnels. These forms of imagination or mental experiment undoubtedly constitute regulations of the initial intuition, exclusively perceptual, decentring it in the direction of reconstruction and anticipation, hence towards operational reversibility. But this reversibility is only completely achieved with the grouping of all the relationships involved—distance, duration, and order.

3. Third stage: Operational solution of the problem

In contrast with the foregoing subjects, those of this third level manage to establish the difference of the speeds simply by correlating the given factors of time and space traversed.

AND (6; 6). Did they start at the same time? Yes. And stopped at the same time? Yes. Are the tunnels the same length? No, that one is bigger. Did they travel for the same time? Yes. And at the same speed? That was one quicker, because it is longer: it's farther so it went quicker. This one went more slowly because it stopped farther back: it was a little behind that one. Why? Because it was closer there (closer to the other one at the starting point: he points to the starting line) and you pushed it.

LAM (7; 4). Did they stop at the same time? Yes. Did one go harder than the other? No, the same, because they got there at the same time. Are the tunnels the same length? Oh, no! Did one of the dolls go faster than the other? Yes, the one that goes through the bigger tunnel. Why did it go quicker? Because it is longer.

PAR (6; 11). That one went faster. Why? Because the tunnel is bigger. Did they take the same time or not? No . . . Yes. Why? They set off together and they stopped together.

CLAN (7; 2). They didn't travel at the same speed, because one of the tunnels is bigger: so one went faster. Did they take the same time? Yes.

GO (7; 6). Did one go faster than the other? Yes, the one which went the longer distance. Recognizes equality of durations.

The progress made is evident in comparison with the second stage. The youngest of these subjects, And, directly translates the disparity in length of the tunnels in terms of order of succession, hence as overtaking: since one of the tunnels is 'bigger' than the other, then the moving object which travels through it has gone 'farther': it is longer so it was 'faster', whereas the moving object which goes through the little tunnel went 'slower because it stopped farther back: it was a little behind that one'. So once again it is overtaking which is the criterion of speed, but an invisible and operational overtaking since the orders of succession 'ahead' and 'behind' or 'after' are translatable in terms of intervals or lengths and are themselves the result of a translation originating in lengths perceived (the lengths of the tunnels). On the other hand, in the case of And there is equality of synchronous durations: overtaking has therefore actually become a relationship between space traversed and time taken. In the case of the other subjects it is no longer even necessary to imagine any overtaking inside the tunnels or to reason from this actual overtaking: the distance travelled (lengths or intervals in space between the starting and stopping points) and the time taken (duration or interval in time between the simultaneous moments of departure and the simultaneous moments of arrival) are directly correlated in the form of speed. And since the lengths are unequal and the durations are held to be equal, the speeds are recognized to be dissimilar.

Such a co-ordination of the relationships involved thus implies understanding of the equality of synchronous durations and this is why the operational conception of speed, unlike the intuitive conception, implies a spatio-temporal construction of the whole. Indeed, if this present development is correlated with the evolution of the conceptions of time and movement (see Chapters Three to Five) it is clear that the operational relationships of speed is formed in necessary correlation with the relationships of duration and the distance covered itself, since duration appears as a result of co-ordination of speeds, the idea of the distance travelled implies grouping of relations of order, and speed involves co-ordination of duration and distance. The intuition of overtaking becomes truly rational when the order of the starting and stopping points of the movements being compared is conceived as simultaneously determining spatial intervals and temporal intervals. The spatial intervals (displacements) constitute the distances travelled (lengths). The temporal intervals (co-displacements) constitute the durations. Together these form the speeds themselves.

SECTION II. *Wholly visible movements with starting and stopping points coinciding or in alignment but unequal in length*

The results obtained so far seem simple; the earliest intuition of speed is overtaking conceived simply as an inversion of order. But gradually as the intuition of overtaking becomes articulated due to its generalization and regulation by means of imaginative reconstructions and anticipations, starting and stopping points are considered to the same extent as points of overtaking or actual inversion of the order of succession: a system of intervals is then formed between the starting and stopping points, and these intervals determine on the one hand the paths travelled (lengths or distances), and on the other hand the durations (intervals of the order common to both movements or system of co-displacements) from which eventually proceeds a restructuring of the idea of speed, conceived from then on as the relation between these two kinds of intervals.

For verification of this hypothesis, or at least the first part of it, a very simple method emerges, suggested by the parallelism thus implied between the construction of the concepts of speed and of movement itself: this is to apply to speed the schema of the tests in Chapter Three, i.e. to question the child on certain fully visible movements of different speeds where overtaking is absent. Let us for example have two moving objects start simultaneously from the point A which are to arrive simultaneously at B, but one of which will travel in a straight line, while the second will make various detours: will the child understand that the latter was moving at a greater speed? Or else let us have two moving objects start off from A, but while one moves in a straight (horizontal) line as far as B, the other at the same time is travelling along a line AC, where C is directly above B, and AC forms the hypotenuse of the right-angled triangle ABC: will the child then see that the speeds are not equal? Finally, a special case of particular interest is that of two circular movements on two concentric tracks. This case of speed in cyclic order is postponed until Section III, while this second section is confined to the speeds of movements in linear order.

This is the technique adopted. Q 1: two rectilinear paths AB and AC, forming an angle. We ask first if one of the paths is longer than the other, then we state that the two cars are going to travel along them at the same speed: will one finish before the other? Finally we do the experiment and ask why the object travelling along the oblique line (AC) arrived at C after the other had reached B.

Q 2: same questions with one straight line and one wavy line between A and B (starting and finishing simultaneously in both cases).

Q 3: we state that the two cars are now going to travel along two lines AB and AC, (forming an angle)—setting off together from A and finishing at the same time, one at B and the other at C: does one of them have to go faster than the other? The experiment is done, and we ask if the speeds were equal.

Q 4: same, with one straight line, and one wavy line AB.

Now, the stages observed were found to be the same before.

4. The first stage: No understanding of differences in speed

Here are some examples of early reactions showing inability to structure either speed, or durations, and frequently not even the path to be travelled, before the movements are perceived:

Jac (4; 9) Q 1: Is one of these paths longer than the other? No. If these two cars start at the same time and go at the same speed, will one of them finish first or both at the same

time? *They will both finish at the same time.* (Experiment).
This one finished first (AB). Why? *It went faster.* Watch
(experiment repeated) . . . Q 2: same reactions. Q 3: if these
two cars start together from here (A) and stop together there
(B and C) will they have travelled at the same speed? *Yes.*
Watch (experiment). Did they both go at the same speed?
Yes, the same speed. Q 4: same.

HEL (4; 8) Q 1: Are these two routes the same length? *No,
this one* (oblique AC) *is longer.* If these two cars start at the
same time and go at the same speed, will they arrive at the
same time at the other end (pointing to B and C)? *Yes, at
the same time.* Watch (experiment). Which one was first?
That one (AB). Why? *It went faster—No, it was the same
speed.* Did you tell me that this path is longer (AC)? *Yes.*
Which one got there first? *That one* (AB). Why is that? *It
went quicker because it reached the very end.*

Q 2: Which is the longer of the two routes? *That one*
(detour). Why? *Because it makes detours.* If these two cars
start off together and go at the same speed, which will finish
first? *They will get there at the same time.* Watch (experiment). *That one finished first.* Why? *Because the road is
shorter.* Then which one goes faster if they finish together
(Q 4)? *The same speed.* Watch (experiment) *That one
(straight road) was faster.*

DOL (4; 11) Q 2: states that one of the lines is longer because *it makes detours* but thinks that at equal speeds the
two cars will arrive at the same time at the other end. After
the experiment, says *No, that one arrived first, because the
road is quite straight.* Q 3: If they start at the same time and
finish at the same time, do they move at the same speed?
Yes. (Experiment). *That one went faster* (oblique). Why?
Because you pushed it so it would be first. Q 4: *They won't
go at the same speed.* Why? *It has to go faster on this road*
(the straight one). But if they both finish at the same time?
They must both be moving slowly.

MOO (5; 6) Q 1: Are these two roads the same length? *Yes.*
Look carefully. *No, that one* (oblique) *is longer.* Will both
cars reach the end of their road at the same time if they go
at the same speed? *Yes.* (Experiment). *No, because this road
is longer: that's why the other one finishes first.* (Q 2). *This
road* (with detours) *is longer.* And if these cars go at the

same speed when will they reach the end, at the same time, or one after the other? *At the same time.* (Experiment). *No, because this road is longer.* Q 3: If both cars reach the end at the same time will they have gone at the same speed? *Yes.* (Experiment). *Yes, it's the same speed.* Look again carefully (suggestion). *That one's faster* (direct perception). Why? ... Q 4: same.

Ros (5; 8) Q 1: If they go at the same speed ... etc.? *They will finish at the same time.* (Experiment). *That's because you didn't go fast enough. No, the two cars went at the same speed. It's because the road is longer.* (Q 2). Is one of these roads longer? *That one because there are detours.* If the cars go at the same speed will they take the same time to reach the end or not? *The same time.* (Experiment). *That one got there sooner.* Why? ... Q 3: *The same speed.* Q 4: *The same speed as well.* (Experiment). *Both cars go at the same speed.* Do they? *That one is faster* (straight line).

Hen (5; 11) Q 2: *Both roads are the same length* (measures with a bit of string). *No, that one is longer.* If they start together at the same speed, will they reach the other end together. *Yes.* (Experiment). *No, because of the detours.* Q 3 and 4: same speeds, and after the experiments, similarly.

Ton (6; 2) Q 1 and 2: same lengths and simultaneous arrivals forecast. Q 3 and 4: same speeds.

Let us begin by stating that these subjects are by no means unanimous in recognizing the inequality of the lines they see: Hen e.g. at nearly 6 years old, and Ton at 6, still consider a wavy line equal to a straight line and they have to use pieces of string to discover the difference in lengths. Moo at first considers the straight oblique line (hypotenuse AC of the right-angled triangle ABC) as equal to the horizontal AB etc. As for those who see the disparity from the very start, it is a matter for conjecture whether this is because the movement has not yet taken place, for (as we saw in Chapter Three) at this stage changes of location are still evaluated in terms of the order of succession of the stopping points. In the second place, even the subjects who agree at once at the inequality of the lengths to be

travelled forecast that at equal speeds, in spite of the
different distances, the two moving objects which set off
simultaneously will reach the end at the same time: the fact
is that once again, but this time in the case of durations,
they are judging in terms of the stopping points and not of
the actual distances. This tendency is so strong, in the case
of the youngest subjects of this first stage, that even after
the experiment, i.e. after they have seen the moving object
following the longer road stop after the other one, they
continue to think, that at the same speeds they should
arrive together, and that if one of the two does not 'reach
the other end' as Hen says, the fact is that it did not go
fast enough. Some other subjects, on the contrary, enlightened by the experiment, recognize that the moving
object which had the longer of the two roads to travel
finished after the other 'because of the detours' etc. But
let us note that this judgment is still not concerned with
the actual speed: it is confined to the observation in retrospect that at equal speeds the longer of the tracks take the
longer time. Since the speeds were stated to be equal from
the start, there is no longer any problem on that score,
the child's reply simply amounts to saying that the duration of the journey is proportional to the distance
travelled. Now, this intuition of duration based on the
space traversed is only true at equal speeds and we have
seen elsewhere (Origins of the Conception of Time, Chapter Five) how deceptive this is when the speeds are dissimilar, i.e. precisely where the question of speed begins
to arise.

This is what is revealed by the responses to Q 3 and 4:
given that two paths are recognized to be unequal, do
respectively simultaneous departures and arrivals correspond to equal or to unequal speeds? Now, in this instance
the subjects of this level are unanimous in expecting that
the speeds should be equal and the reason is immediately
obvious, according to the results of Section II which are
confirmed in this way: the fact is that, in spite of the
inequality of the paths traversed, there is no overtaking
since the two moving objects reach the same point or
points on the same finishing line. Moreover, when he sees

the two movements effected afterwards in front of him, the child may continue to say that the cars were going at the same speed, in the absence of overtaking (Jac, Moo, Ros, Hen etc.) or he states that the one which travelled along the shorter road went quicker because it is a shorter distance to travel, or finally he recognizes that the speed of the other was greater, but without being able to say why, i.e. confining himself to perceiving this greater speed and not relating it to the longer distance travelled.

The first of these reactions confirms the rôle of overtaking, which is not invalidated by the latter. As for the second, we shall find it again and again in Section III. Let us confine ourselves for the moment to noting that it rests on an ambiguity common to the child's logic and also to speech itself. The intuition of speed, which is that of overtaking, amounts to supposing that the moving object which is fastest is the one which arrives first at the finishing point. Now, this can have two meanings: overtaking due to greater speed, or finishing first because the road is shorter. In the second case both the child and everyday speech use 'finished quicker' but that may mean 'earlier' where the speed is the same or lower.

5. The second stage: Intermediate reactions: solutions of Q. 1 and 2 but failure with Q. 3 and 4 (sub-stage IIa) and success after the experiment (sub-stage IIb)

Here now are some examples of children who manage without difficulty to solve Q 1 and 2, i.e. judging that the time is proportional to the distance travelled regardless of the order of the stopping points (cf. Chapter Three, stage II) but who fail in problems of speed properly so called (Q3 and 4), even after the experiment (sub-stage IIa).

CLAN (5; 6) Q 1: *The oblique route is 'longer'. If these two cars start at the same time, and at the same speed, will they finish at the same time? No, one will go quicker* (pointing to the straight road). *But they travel at the same speed. Then this road is longer, and it will arrive later.* (Q 2): *No. When the car on this road* (the straight one) *is at the end, the car*

on the other road (the winding one) will be here (middle).
(Experiment). *Yes, it is longer.*

Q 3: They set off at the same time and finish at the same
time. Will the speed be the same? *Yes.* (Experiment). *Was
it the same speed? No, the car on this road* (the straight
horizontal one) *went quicker: it is shorter.* Q 4: the same.

MIR (5; 9) Q 1: Will they finish at the same time? *Yes.*
(Experiment). *No, because this road is longer.* (Q 2): *No,
that one will finish after the other one because this road
makes detours.* (Q 3): Same speed? *No, this car* (winding
road) *goes slower.* But if they finish at the same time? *Then
it is the same speed.* (Experiment). *Yes.*

LUC (6; 3) Q 1 and 2: *No, because this road is longer.* Q 3:
That one (the straight horizontal one) *goes quicker.* (Ex-
eriment). *Both of them go quicker* (equality). But watch.
*Both of them arrived at the same time, because you made
them go at the same speed.*

TEA (6; 5) Q 1: *No, because this road is longer.* Q 2: *No,
because that road zigzags, that takes longer, and this car here
only has to go straight ahead* (Q 3): *Both the same.* (Experiment: it is Tea himself who travels along the hypotenuse:
he 'brakes' so as not to go faster than the experimenter, and
thus does not go so far). Did we finish together? *No.* What
is to be done? *Go faster.* (New experiment: finish stimutan-
eously at the end of each line). Well? *That was the same
speed.* Q 4: same.

BAR (7; 5) Q 1: *This car finishes first, because the road is
shorter.* (Q 2): (Same thing). (Q 3 and 4): *They will both
go at the same speed.* (Experiment). *Yes, it was the same
speed.* Why? *Because they arrived at the same time.*

These reactions carrying on from those of stage I are
the more interesting because the child, in replying correctly to Q 1 and 2, seems to master the problem of the
relationship between time and space covered. In point of
fact this understanding is limited to seeing that at equal
speeds the times are proportional to the spaces. But as we

saw in connection with *The Origins of the Conception of Time*, there is not even any true understanding of duration because the latter is only dissociated from space or movement where there are differences in speed: in the absence of this condition, time simply remains undissociated from space, and when different distances are travelled at different speeds, the child at this level can no longer distinguish succession in time from succession in space, or durations from movements or distances themselves. Now this is precisely what one observes in connection with Q 3 and 4. If duration were dissociated from space, speed would be conceived as the relationship between space and time, since duration itself would be the relationship between the space traversed and the speed. Now, in the case of these last two questions, the children of this second stage react like those in stage I: they think the speeds are equal where different distances are traversed in the same time, and this is simply because there is no overtaking. The experiment does not enlighten them and if they do conclude by recognizing a difference in the speeds, it is only to attribute the greater speed to the car which travels along the shorter road.

In sub-stage IIb, on the contrary, gradual discovery of the correct solution is observed but only after experiment.

MGR (6; 4) Q 1 and 2: correct. Q 3: Shall I be moving at the same speed as you if I get over there (extremity of the oblique line) at the same time as you? *Yes.* (We walk at the same speed, without reaching the end of the line). You see, I did not get to the end. *You must go faster.* (Experiment). And now, were our speeds the same? *You went a bit faster.* Why? *Because the line is longer.* Q 4: same beginning, then after experiment: *One is faster than the other, because the road is longer.*

NIN (6; 5) Q 1 and 2: *This car does not go so far because the road is shorter.* (Q 3): *They both go at the same speeds.* (Experiment). *That one is faster.* Why? *Because the road is longer.* (Q 4): *That one must go faster.* Why? *Because it zigzags.*

Obviously the answers to Q 3 and 4, although correct, are not yet operational since they are only reached after some tentative activity and by progressive organization of the experiment. They normally appear gradually from age 6 to 7.

6. The third stage: Operational solution of the problem.

This third stage is characterized by immediate solution of all four questions, by means of groupments of 'concrete operations':

BER (6; 8) Q 1 and 2: *They won't arrive at the same time because one of the distances is longer. Q 3 and 4: They will not go at the same speed because one of the roads is longer. Which one will go faster? The one which does the longer distance.*

WEI (7: 0) Q 1: *This road is longer. The other car will get there first, unless this one goes faster.* (Q 2): *This road is longer: the car will not reach the other end.* (Q 3): *This car will have to go faster. Why? Because it has a longer road to go. Q 4: the same thing.*
BUS (7; 3) Q 1 and 2: *This car will still be moving when that one is already there* (correct). *Q 3 and 4: That one will go faster because the road is longer.*

In conclusion it is evident that the results of this test entirely confirm those in Section I; the development of the responses is the same in both cases, and the corresponding stages appear at the same ages. The differences in speed are not forecast at first and they are not even observed in the experiment, in the absence of overtaking, whereas in stage III these differences are understood and even deduced beforehand on the basis of the relationship between the space traversed and the time taken. The fact that the starting and stopping points of the two movements each coincide or are simply in line with one another no longer dominates the child's thinking. The reactions in § I showed that the earliest intuition of speed was restricted to observation of visible overtaking, hence to a perceptible inversion of the order of the moving objects, whereas later the starting and stopping points are both considered, and the intervals of space and time between them permit the conception of speed as a ratio of lengths and times. The present reactions have completed the picture by revealing that in the beginning the order of the stopping points alone determine the speed even when the paths are entirely visible, while later the relationship of the spaces traversed and the durations is formed in spite of the absence of overtaking.

SECTION III. *The speed of circular movements with concentric paths*

In order to complete the foregoing analysis there remains the problem of examining the question of circular movements effected on concentric tracks. A particularly interesting difficulty is raised in fact by cyclic order, which in this case replaces the linear order considered so far. It is possible for two moving objects travelling along two concentric circumferences to start off from two points side by side and to return to these same points having travelled continuously neck and neck; will the child attribute different speeds to them although there is no overtaking and no dissimilarity in their paths?

Two large concentric circumferences are drawn, with radii in the ratio of approximately 2 to 1, representing race tracks or roads. A straight line starting from their common centre intersects the two circumferences horizontally towards the left. Two cars, or better still, two dogs, set off at the same time from this guide line and return to it together, one having travelled along the 'big circle' and the other the little one. This simultaneousness of starting and stopping is stressed, and the movements are repeated twice or thrice quite quickly with repetition of the given factors. Then we simply ask which of the dogs (or cars) went faster, 'the one on the big circle or the one on the little circle'. In order to translate the problem in terms of inner experience, we also ask which one had to 'hurry' more and especially 'which one is more out of breath'.

In addition, thanks to Mr. Andre Rey, an apparatus was devised consisting of a bar fixed at one end to a pivot around which it describes a horizontal movement. Two dolls are fixed upon the bar, one near the centre of rotation and the other farther away from it; these are moved through 45°, and we ask whether one of them moved faster than the other.

The test results with the two concentric tracks are altogether comparable qualitatively with those discussed so far: during the first stage the child either thinks that the speeds of the two moving objects are the same, or else that the one on the little track goes faster than the other; intermediate reactions characterize the second stage, and the correct answer comes in the third. But, from the point of view of average ages, whereas subjects of 7 years who belong to the third stage, may be found quite easily, nevertheless there is normally some delay with the tests of Section II because of the much greater intuitive difficulties of the relationships. As for the question of the dolls fixed on the same rotating bar, it is only solved towards 11 years, in a fourth stage, for it implies formal or hypothetico-deductive operations to dissociate factors which are in actual practice not separable.

7. The first stage: Speeds judged equal, or inverse ratio of speed and distance

The spontaneous reaction of younger children is to consider the speeds equal, in the absence of overtaking. But if their attention is drawn, particularly through the suggestions of the experimenter, to the unequal lengths of the two tracks, they then state that the speed is greater on the smaller track. Here are some examples:

MAT (6; o). Does one of them go faster than the other? *They go at the same speed.* Why? *Because they finish at the same time.* But are the tracks the same length? *No.* Well then? *That one* (small circle) *goes faster, because it has a shorter road to go.* Mat is shown the straight roads which are very dissimilar, one of the movements being considerably faster than the other, and he answers correctly. *That one goes faster, because it has a long way to go,* but when we return to the circular tracks, he states *the one on the little circle goes faster because it has the shorter journey.* Are you sure? *No, they go at the same speed.*

Ros (6; 4). *They both go at the same speed.* Why? *Because they finished at the same time.* But which one has the longer road to go? *The one on the little circle.* Then which one goes quicker? *They're the same.* Why? *Because they started off at the same time.* But did they both hurry the same or was one hurrying more? *Both the same.*

Mey (6; 6). *They travel at the same speed.* Why? *They go very fast.* But are the tracks the same length? *No, that one is longer.* Then does one go faster than the other? *No, because they have to get there together.* But is one more out of breath than the other? *No, the same.* Why? *They both go very fast.*

Col (6; 5). *The one on the inside goes faster than the other one.* Why? *Because it's got more speed.* How's that? *Because if there is a little circle, that's quicker because there is less to be done.*

Fau (6; 6) likewise thinks that the car in the little circle goes faster because the circle is smaller. Why is that then? *Because it has less turns to do.*

Nan (7; 10). Did one of these dogs hurry more than the other one? *No, both the same.* Why? *Because the tracks are the same length.* Would you like us to measure them? *No, that one is smaller* (little circle). Then did the two dogs run at the same speed? *Yes.* How's that? *They were both going at the same time.* But how did they manage to finish at the same time then? *Because the one on the outside went slower to be at the same time as the one on the inside.* Then do they go at the same speed? *Yes.* One of them isn't hurrying faster than the other? *No, they're both hurrying the same, because the one on the outside goes slowly, because he wants to keep going at the same time as the one on the inside.*

TER (7; 11). *Does one go faster?* No, they went at the same speed, because they finished at the same time. *Are the tracks the same length?* No. *Well then?* The one on the inside goes faster than the other one because it has a shorter road. *But does it finish first?* No, at the same time, but it goes quicker because it has a shorter road.

ROU (8; 5). *They go at the same speed. One of them isn't going faster?* No, they both hurry the same. *Are the tracks the same length?* No, the one on the outside is longer. *Then is there one who will get more out of breath than the other?* No, they are both out of breath the same. *Why?* They always go at the same time (points out their positions always neck and neck). *Now you must make them go round once* (he does so, but the dog in the little circle sometimes overtakes the other, since he gives them both the same speed). *Same speed?* No, the little one a bit quicker, because it sometimes went ahead of the other one. *But did it finish at the same time?* Yes, so they went at the same speed.

DES (8; 7). *They go at the same speed because they start and finish at the same time. But will one be more out of breath than the other?* Of course not, since they are doing the same thing. *But doesn't one of them make a big circle and the other a little one?* Yes. *Well then?* But they start at the same time and they finish at the same time.

WIL (8; 8). *The same speed. Has one of them a longer way to go?* That one (large circle). *Then which one goes faster?* The little one because it has a shorter road to go. *But which one is more out of breath?* The little one (doll in the little circle). It goes faster.

CHAL (8; 10). *They both hurried the same. But at the same speed?* Yes. *Are the tracks the same length?* No, the one on the outside is longer. *Then was one more out of breath than the other?* No, they both hurried the same. *Have you got a friend who lives farther away from school than you?* Yes, George. *Then if you and G. leave home at the same time in the morning and reach school at the same time, will you both have hurried the same?* Yes. *You're sure?* Yes. *G. will not be more out of breath than you?* No, we'll both be just as much out of breath.

Evidently then with one exception (Col) all these subjects begin by thinking that the speeds are equal, even while they recognize that the big circle constitutes a longer distance than the little one. Moreover, when they affirm this equality, for them it is as much a question of subjective impressions of speed, such as hurrying or being out of breath (see Chal, as late as 8; 11), as of actual objective speed. These initial statements are no longer surprising after the reactions observed in Sections I and II of this chapter. If in fact the earliest intuition of speed is overtaking, this estimate of equality is just what might be expected in this particular case since the two moving objects travel continuously neck and neck. Rou's case is quite clear on this point. The two dolls 'will both be just as much out of breath' since 'they always move together'. When Rou makes the little one overtake slightly he thinks that it goes 'a little faster, because it overtook the other one a little', and finally observing them reach the same points simultaneously concludes 'then they went at the same speed'.

But the problem arising is to understand why this intuition of overtaking seems rather more lasting (7 and 8 years!) in the case of concentric paths than with simple linear trajectories, especially straight lines. Should these subjects be credited with intuition of angular or rotational speed, which in effect remains constant? Certainly not, first because older children change their opinion (stages II and III) and in particular because these same subjects often come to consider the object travelling round the small circle as being faster, which is enough to indicate how primitive their conception of speed still is.

What then is the explanation of the slight time-lag in the ages for these reactions compared with responses regarding the speeds of movements in a straight line or in linear order? It is clear that in the latter case, the translation of the lengths of the trajectories in terms of overtaking is much easier with synchronous movements: even without visible overtaking in the actual movement, the superior length of one distance compared to the other suggests this overtaking in the displacements (Section I).

In the case of lengths having the same starting and stopping points (Section II) wavy lines have only to be straightened mentally and lines not already parallel have only to be made so, in order to imagine a longer distance in space and overtaking in movement. Two concentric circumferences on the contrary do not suggest two straight lines one of which is longer than the other and the similarity of the cyclic order of their points influences the intuition of speed far more than a relationship drawn from their lengths and the times taken. The present problem is therefore not exactly equivalent but only 'analogous' to the foregoing ones, whence the 'horizontal time-lag' observed between the ages for the initial reaction just discussed.

But, after affirming the speeds to be equal, many subjects in this first stage allow themselves to be influenced by the inequality of the paths (especially when, in the case of linear paths, they begin to dissociate the length of the path travelled from the order of the stopping points), and then they systematically and surprisingly conclude that the object travelling round the smaller circle is faster. The subject Nan even sets out to reconcile this second opinion with the first: the speeds are equal, he says, since 'they were both going at the same time', but 'the one on the outside went slower so as to go at the same time as the one on the inside'. As for Mat, Col, and Fau, they give us the key to the mystery: the object moving round the small circle goes faster 'because it has a shorter road to go or has less turns to do'. This curious dialectic helps us in fact to understand fully the nature of this new statement: the object moving round the small circumference goes faster than that moving round the big circle, because as its path is shorter it could finish, not ahead of the other one, but earlier than it. In this case then speed is temporal precedence and no longer spatial superiority, i.e. the reversal of the temporal order and no longer of the spatial order: the faster object is the one beginning later in time, but reaching its goal first. It is true that in this particular case both arrive at the same time, but the moving object in the little circle could reach its goal before the other one since 'it does not have so far to go' as Col says, and according to this child this is enough to show that 'it has more speed' one might almost say 'potential speed'. As for Nan, then, it must be recognized that he is thinking at one and the same time of space with the large track and of time with the little one, whence his paradoxical reconciliation of the two kinds of 'outstripping' in space and in time.

It is evident then why common speech, with its often childlike logic, uses 'quicker' equally well for 'arrived sooner' (overtaking in time) and for 'faster' (overtaking in space). In Swiss patois they even say 'doing a thing sooner' quite often in the sense of easier or more handily.

But then, if the child may thus define speed equally well as overtaking in space or in time, what is the explanation of the predominance of temporal precedence ('finished quicker') in the case of circular tracks, and of spatial overtaking with journeys in a straight line or in linear order? Let us begin by observing that even in this last case, it often happens that the child judges a short journey to be faster than a long journey made at the same time, due to the same schema of precedence in time, i.e. reaching the goal earlier (see Section II, § 4, case of Ros, etc.). But, in the case of the linear paths in Section II, the schema of spatial overtaking is suggested more readily although the starting and stopping points each coincide and each occur simultaneously—as soon as the child manages to dissociate the lengths from the arrangement of these points, he can imagine them as rectilinear and parallel, and thus intuitively visualize spatial overtaking. In the case of concentric circumferences, on the other hand, we have already seen that the translation of their lengths into straight lines is not easy, while they are easily translated into temporal order: shorter = finished first = travelled faster.

All things considered, it is easy to see that in the course of this first stage speed is not the result of correlating time and space travelled, any more than it was in the corresponding stage in Section I and II. Speed is still limited to intuition of overtaking, hence the original idea that the two speeds to be compared are equal. When the unequal lengths of the circuits are emphasized by us or possibly when this occurs to the child himself, their inequality is by no means translated in terms of spatial overtaking, since the circles are concentric and the moving objects travel continuously neck and neck: the child merely thinks that the moving object travelling along the smaller track might reach the same point first and then he either forgets they finished simultaneously and states that this object went faster, or else he remembers their synchronism but, thinking of a kind of speed in reserve, declares that the little one 'has more speed'.

8. The second stage: Intermediate reactions

In order to check the foregoing interpretations, it is necessary to examine carefully the intermediate responses which start off similarly, but reach the correct solution.

Bea (8; 2). *Does one of these two dogs hurry more than the other? The one on the inside hurries more.* Why? *Because its legs are not stretched so much.* How's that? *Because it has a shorter road; it's quicker.* But they finish at the same time? *Yes, because the one on the outside runs and the one on the inside does not run.* Then which one goes faster? *The little one.*

Dun (8; 2). *They both hurried the same.* Why? *They left at the same time and came back at the same time.* Are they both just as much out of breath or is one more so? *Both the same.* How do the tracks compare? *The one on the outside is longer.* Well then? *The one on the inside hurried more because it has a shorter road.* Then it has to hurry more? *It didn't hurry more, but it gets there quicker because it has a shorter road.* But they finish at the same time? *Yes, because the one on the outside hurried more, because it has a longer road.*

Pil (8; 5). *They both hurried the same, because they finish at the same time.* Same speed? *Yes.* Is one of them more out of breath than the other? *Yes, the one on the inside.* Does it hurry more? *Yes, because it has a shorter road.* Then it has to hurry more? *Oh, no, the big one has a longer road, so it has to hurry more to finish at the same time.*

PAL (8; 8). Same speeds and same want of breath. Are both tracks the same length? *No, the one on the inside is smaller.* Then how do they manage to finish at the same time? *Because both journeys are circles.* Well then? *It comes to the same thing.* So was the speed the same or did one hurry more than the other? *Oh, the one on the outside hurried more because it has a longer road.*

Iso (8; 11). The one on the little circle hurries more. Why? *Because it's on the smaller circle.* Then why does it have to hurry more? *Because it has to run and the one on the big circle can walk.* But why is that? *So as to finish first.* But don't they finish at the same time? *Oh, well, then the one on the big circle goes faster, since it has a bigger circle to go round.* Why did you say it was the little one? *Well they both travel together and they must go at the same speed.* Do they travel the same distance? *No, the one on the outside is longer.* Well, how do they compare then? *The one on the big circle will go faster, to finish at the same time as the other.* Why faster? *Because it has a longer way to go.*

CLE (9; 0). The one in the little circle hurried more because the circle is smaller. Are they going at the same speed or not? *Yes, because you made them go along at the same time.* Is one of them more out of breath than the other? *Yes, the one in the big circle because it has a longer road.* Has one of them got to hurry more? *Yes, the big one, otherwise the one in the little circle would finish before it.* In what way do they finish? *They both hurried the same, because they were going along at the same time.* But are the tracks the same? *The big one had to hurry more.* But they finish at the same time? *Then they both hurried the same.* But is one road longer than the other? *Then the big one hurried more . . . etc. etc.* Finally, after long reflection, Cle concludes: *The big one ran a bit more so as to finish with the one in the little circle.* Then does one go faster than the other? *Yes, the big one, but not much.*

BER (9; 5) likewise hesitates between two statements: *They both hurry the same because they finish at the same time.* Same speed? *Yes, since they move side by side all the time*

and *The big one will be more out of breath than the other
since it has a longer path*. Then he decides upon the latter
one.

In these intermediate reactions, there is the same time-
lag compared with the equivalent second stages in Sections
I and II, as was found between the first stages, for the
reasons already analysed, and they are of even greater
interest for the study of intuitive regulations since these
children are advanced enough to explain each answer
clearly. From this point of view, their attention, i.e. the
centration point of their perceptual or imaginative intuition, may be said to bear upon three distinct kinds of
given factor in turn: (1) The order (spatial or temporal) of
the starting and stopping points: the moving objects in fact
set off simultaneously from the same line and finish simultaneously at the conclusion of the race, which coincides
with their starting points (2) The disparity in length of
their trajectories, conceived in terms of precedence in
time: at equal speeds the moving object travelling round
the little circle would arrive before the other one. (3) This
same inequality conceived in terms of overtaking in space:
with equal durations, the movement effected on the larger
of the circles would outdistance the other if both were
simplified to movements in a straight line.

From the point of view of a synthesis of operations of
course these three kinds of given factors are easily recon-
cilable: it is enough for lengths and durations to be conceived as intervals situated between the sequence of starting and stopping points (in space and in time), for the
hypothetical relationships to be, not only compatible with
each other, but also implied by one another. However, for
this operational synthesis to be possible, the subject must
be able to translate cyclic movements into parallel linear
movements, without being misled by the cyclic order, and
this is the intuitive difficulty complicating the problem for
the child at this level.

Now, being unable to achieve this synthesis, the subjects plainly waver between the three possible points of

view, each corresponding to one of these three given factors considered in isolation: equal speeds, suggested by the fact that the two moving objects always travel neck and neck; greater speed on the little circle (precedence in time); or greater speed on the larger circle (overtaking in space with paths in a straight line). Hence subjects like Dun, Pil, Hei, Iso and particularly Cle may shift from the first solution to the second, from the first to the third, from the second to the first or from the second to the third, in an incoherent series of astounding volte-faces, until only the third point of view becomes practically stable (except in the case of Cle, and Ber who waver endlessly between the first solution and the third before deciding upon the latter). Three questions thus arise over this point: the reason for this indecision in general, the manner of arriving at the correct reply, and the reason for its greater stability.

On the first point, clearly if intuitive thinking means the use of visualization and mental experiment to evoke the process to be explained, this last has only to include several quite distinct aspects or relationships, for 'centrations' first on one and then on another to occur in exactly the same way as when perception is fixed on one or other point of a total configuration. And then, in the case of intuition as in that of perception, the point or the relationship centred on is over evaluated for that very reason and the others are under-estimated, which practically amounts to saying that each of the relationships considered successively causes immediate forgetting of the others. This forgetting is not in fact simply one manifestation of memory (we do not forget within a few seconds what we have just said) but a sudden devaluation of the reasons for the earlier statement: see e.g. the case of Cle. But these successive centrations do not follow one another at random: the child has only to be reminded of the point of view which he has just forgotten or underestimated, for this new intuitive centration to correct the earlier one through a kind of regulation, but reversing the positions as though on a see-saw.

It can now be understood how the discovery of the correct answer is made. This is not, or at least not often, through a sudden illumination co-ordinating the relationships in an operational or partly operational act of synthesis, but it is through gradual extension of the original regulation which led the subject to pass alternately from one centration to another. In other words, the solution is gradually achieved through decentration: while fixing his attention on one of the relationships, the subject manages to think of another and thus corrects the first one while differentiating it. Hence even while Bea says that the dog on the little circle 'hurries more', he already supposes that 'his legs are less stretched' and so manages to conclude that 'the one on the outside is running' but without entirely giving up his belief that the little one goes faster! Dun, in particular, after saying that the one in the little circle hurries more, later makes a correction when he thinks that 'he didn't hurry more, but he gets there quicker', in other words by dissociating the relations 'going faster' and 'stopping sooner', etc. Once these dissociations are made, the subject discovers the true solution by translating the lengths of the two circles into overtaking in space, i.e. by comparing them to straight lines. Now, here again, it is a question of intuitive regulation, but in the form of imaginative reconstructions and anticipations: circular lengths are simply adapted to the familiar lines which allow overtaking to be seen, even when perceptual observation of this is impossible in fact with the tracks in their concentric circular form. It must be noted however that such anticipations and reconstructions are already included in the earlier regulations, since decentration of one relation consists of remembering the existence of the others by reconstructing or anticipating them. This last manner of correcting intuition is therefore only an extension of decentration, the given (circular) path being as it were decentred a more familiar (linear) form and adapted to this.

The third problem is then spontaneously solved, if the third relation (overtaking in space) is actually the result of a progressive decentration due on the one hand to the fact that the various relations have been considered in succession, and resulting on the other hand from adaptation to the customary schema of displacement, it will naturally be more stable than the others. It is true that this relation implies the others since linear overtaking translated into circular trajectories implies the possibility of travelling neck and neck (first relation) and spatial overtaking at equal speeds (second relation). But the child does not begin with these suppositions: on the contrary he gradually achieves them by the painstaking reconciliation of the three points of view, but this reconciliation reaches equilibrium as soon as it is transformed into reciprocal implications. The level of operations, i.e. the next stage, is then reached.

9. The third stage: Operational solution of the problem

The average age of attaining stage III raises a curious problem. This is from 8 to 9 years, if the questions relating to the circular tracks are asked first, which therefore shows a perceptible time-lag compared to the third stage in Sections I and II (linear paths). But if we begin with the questions studied in those sections and in particular with that of the two tunnels (Section I) answers which are correct from the outset are frequently found in the region of 7 years, as if there were direct assimilation between relationships of speed on circular paths and overtaking on linear paths, where this has attained operational status. In fact, three of the subjects who have already been quoted in Section I (§ 3) will be recognized amongst the following:

PAS (6; 11). Does one of these go faster than the other? *That one* (outside circle), *because it goes round farther.* But they start off together? *Yes.* And they finish together? *Yes.* Then are they the same speed or not? *That one goes faster, because the circle is bigger.*

CLAN (7; 2). Do they start and stop together? Yes. Do they both travel at the same speed or is one of them faster? *That one goes faster.* Why? *Because the circle is longer and it has to run to catch up on the other one.*

LAUR (7; 4). Does one go faster than the other? *The one running round the big circle, because it has to go faster.* Why 'has to'? *To finish at the same time as the other one.*

NER (8; 11). *The one on the big circle runs harder.* Why? *Because it does a longer road in the same time.*

BUC (9; 2). *That one goes faster.* Why? *It has farther to go.* But it goes side by side with the other one? *Yes, but the circle is bigger.*

Obviously then, the relationships of distance and time immediately become factors of an operational whole, which would have seemed quite simple and scarcely analysable, if we had not seen the circuitous mental route painstakingly followed before it is achieved by conceiving lengths and durations as intervals between the sequences of points on which initial intuition concentrates almost exclusively.

10. The fourth stage: Circular paths of objects fixed to a rigid rod

The need remains to discuss the results obtained by means of the technique devised by Mr. Andre Rey: two dolls A and B, fixed to the same rod which pivots around one of its extremities, describe two 45° arcs of a circle, 'a' and 'b', of very disparate lengths (A is near the base of rotation and B near the other extremity: B thus describes more than double the path of A). Now, while finding exactly the same type of responses as before, Mr. Rey, in this case, only obtained the correct solution towards 11 years, and the reason for this must be sought. Here to begin with, by way of comparison, are some reactions from the first stage.

BAR (6; 0). Before experiment: Which one will finish first? *Both together.* Why? *They are on a thing which goes round at the same time.* After the experiment. Did one of them finish first? *No, both together: they are on the same rod.* But did one of them go faster than the other? *No, both at the same speed.*

MAD (6; 6). Before the test: Each of them moves on a separate path. Which one will finish first? *The little one, because it has a shorter road.* Does one of them go faster? *Both the same, because they are on the rod.* We do the experiment: *They stopped together.* Did one of them go faster? *The little one goes faster, because it has a shorter road.*

GEO (7; 0). Which one will finish first? *The one which has the shorter way to go.* (Experiment). Does one of them go faster? *Neither, because they are on the same rod.*

BEL (7; 0) forecasts that they will both stop together and that they will go at the same speed because they are fixed together. The experiment does not reveal his mistake. When the dolls are detached and made to go in a straight line, he sees perfectly well that one goes faster than the other *because that distance is longer* but when they are replaced on the rod and describe their arcs of a circle, they go at the same speed because of the rod.

CHAM (8; 0). *The little one will finish first because its path is shorter.* After the experiment: *the same speed.*

PER (9; 0). *The little one will finish first because it is not so far.* After the experiment, he recognizes that they finish at the same time, but concludes from this that *the little one goes faster because it has a shorter path.*

Thus the two solutions described in §7. reappear: greater speed of the doll covering the shorter distance, or equal speeds. In this case the first of these solutions is sometimes bound up with the fact that the child expects to see doll A finish first because he does not foresee the effects of the rotation accurately enough. But he usually expects the two moving objects to stop simultaneously, concluding from this that the speeds are equal, and this second solution is reinforced by the fact that both dolls are attached to the same rigid rod.

Here are some examples from stages II and III (II—Lint, and III, Alb, Bug).

LINT (9; 0). *They will both finish together and at the same speed.* After the experiment: *The same speed. Sure? The big one ought to be going faster all the same, but I'm not sure, because they're on the same stick.*

ALB (10; 0). Forecast: they will finish at the same time and at the same speed, because they are both on the same rod. But, after the experiment *The big one goes faster, because it goes a longer distance* and: *The rod goes a bit faster there* (b) *than here* (a), *because that's at the end.*

BUG (12; 0). Forecast: same speeds. After the experiment: *They finish at the same time and the big one* (B) *goes faster. That is because the spot where the small one* (A) *is attached is nearer the place where the rod is fixed* (centre of rotation) *and that is why it does not turn so fast. The other one is farther away, so the rod moves round faster, and so that one goes round faster than the other one: that's why they can both finish at the same time.*

Thus Lint (stage II) evidently gives an intermediate reaction like the subjects of §8 while Alb and Bug give the correct explanation of the phenomenon observed like the subjects of stage III. But unlike the subjects of §9 as far as the experiment of the two concentric tracks is concerned, they are not able to foresee this phenomenon and must analyse it 'de visu' to understand the ratio of the speeds. On the contrary, the subjects of stage IV (formal operations) manage this with no difficulty:

CHU (11; 0). Forecast: *They will finish at the same time. They are both on the same rod, so each one must go as fast as the other, no, the big one goes faster, because it's farther there, but it finishes at the same time as the other one.* After the experiment: *same speed, no, it's curved there* (A) *and it's nearly straight there* (B), *so the little one, no, the big one goes faster.*

Tur (12; 0). Forecast: *Same speeds, no, the big one goes faster, but I didn't say it right away because of the rod.*

As Tur himself quite rightly says, it is because of the rigid rod to which the dolls are fixed, that their respective speeds cannot be calculated 'right away'. Not until the appearance of hypothetico-deductive or formal operations is it possible to 'decompose' in advance these movements describing an arc of a circle, which theoretically resemble the experiment of the two circular race tracks but where in practice the unification of the moving objects makes the intuitive conditions much more complex.

CHAPTER SEVEN

Elaboration of Relations of Speed in Synchronous Movements

In the course of the previous chapter it was possible by studying three distinct kinds of test to observe that the intuition of speed was at first limited to visible overtaking. In this connection it is becoming clearer how the child in the course of the later stages proceeds from this perceptible overtaking to hidden overtaking (test of the tunnels), or from absence of overtaking, due to irregular or circular paths, to mental reconstruction of overtaking with the same paths made rectilinear in the imagination. But it has not yet been understood how the initial intuition of overtaking can be generalized to every possible case by virtue of operations translating overtaking in terms of relationships between time and space traversed. This is what will be investigated during the present chapter in the case of synchronous movements, and in Chapter Nine in the case of movements in succession.

It is now necessary therefore to see by means of which operations the conception of speed is actually constructed as a rational relationship, and we shall begin by studying pairs of rectilinear and synchronous movements in various intuitive situations: objects overtaking, catching up on one another (altogether or in part), moving towards one another from opposite directions, etc. The difficulty of the comparisons required is that the child is faced with two questions at the same time; a problem of speed and a problem of time. The space traversed gives little difficulty, in this particular case, since at nearly all ages considered in this work, the child will be able to distinguish the respective lengths of two rectilinear paths (at most there is some resistance where there is a time-lag in both starting and stopping points, but it is easy to avoid these obstacles which will in any case be dealt with separately when studying the geometry of the child). Conversely, it has been seen elsewhere (*Origins of the Child's Conception of Time*) that up to 7 or 8 years the child was not certain, in the case of dissimilar speeds, that objects started and stopped simultaneously nor, in particular, that synchronous durations were equal. Consequently it must be remembered that when solving the following problems the child must at the same time develop relations of time and relations of speed, as only spatial relations are given. From the point of view of theoretical analysis, there is no difficulty here, since all our research on time led us to consider this very relationship in space as a co-ordination of movements, and so the concepts of speed and duration are formed simultaneously and in close correlation with one another. But from the practical aspect of the actual interview it is difficult to conduct with each child, one conversation on times (simultaneousness and durations), and another on speeds at the same time. We therefore left in the background the question of durations and assisted perception of simultaneousness, by announcing beforehand that the moving objects would always start off and stop together, as well as each time indicating the starting and stopping times verbally (1,2,3 . . . off', and, 'stop!') or using sounds (striking the table with the two moving objects as they stop). Having agreed that the two moving objects start and stop together—whether the child understands this given factor or not—the judgement which he brings to bear on speeds will be that much more meaningful and will in turn illuminate the question of time.

Let us also note that from the vocabulary point of view the two expressions 'faster' and 'harder' must always be employed concurrently, as they are not always synonymous in the child's language nor even in everyday speech (for reasons noted in Chapter Six, § 7).

SECTION I. *Entirely synchronous movements over unequal distances*

The questions asked in this first section are four in number. Q_1: one object catches up on the other. One car, (e.g. red) starts off from a point placed some way behind the starting point of a second car (blue); both move off simultaneously and reach the same stopping point together. Thus the first car catches up with the second: 'Which one went faster or harder?' is our only question. $Q 2$: same apparatus but the first car does not quite reach the second (the gap remaining must be easily seen, and the colours changed in order to avoid any perseveration). $Q 3$: overtaking. Same apparatus, but the first colour (colours to be changed again in case of doubt) overtakes the second one. $Q 4$: moving towards one another from opposite directions and crossing over: each car sets off from a point facing the other and they meet at the same point (semi-crossing over, so to speak); or else each moves slightly beyond the other one (unequal journeys).

The results obtained are entirely in conformity with the stages established so far: during the first stage, overtaking alone produces correct judgements, and other arrangements are evaluated in terms of the placing of the finishing points; a second stage is characterized by intermediate reactions between this initial intuition, and logic, and in a third stage (7 to 8 years) operations of correlation are introduced.

1. *The first stage: Speed evaluated intuitively according to the arrangement of the stopping points*

The initial reactions equate speed with visible overtaking and are thus at a loss in situations where the objects move towards one another from opposite directions, or catch up on one another to some extent (or even altogether):

Eri (5; 0) Q 1 (blue catches up on red): Was one going harder? *Both the same.* How do you know? *Because one went as fast as the other.* Did one go a longer distance? *Yes, the blue one.* Then was one going harder than the other? *No.*

Q 3 (red overtakes blue): Was one going harder? *One of them was farther ahead, the red one.* Was that one going harder? *A bit more. It was not going fast, but it was farther ahead.* And the blue one? *Not so hard: it was away behind.*

Q 2 (red almost catches up with blue, travelling almost twice as far in the same time): *The blue one was farther ahead, the red one was away behind.* Was one of them going harder? *Blue.* Where did it start from? *From here.* Did one do a longer distance? *No, yes, red.* Can you tell if one was faster, going harder? *The red one was slower and the blue one faster.* Why? *Because I can see that it is ahead of the other one.* Which has the longer distance? *The red one.* Which one was faster? *The blue one.* Why? *Because it is ahead of the other one.*

Q 1: Did one of them travel for a longer time than the other? *Yes, no, both the same.* Why? *Because they stopped together.* Was one going harder? *No, the same.* Why? *Because I can see they are at the same place.*

Q 4: (meet from opposite directions: blue has a longer distance): What happened? *One of them came up beside the other one.* Did they start off at the same time? *Yes.* And stopped together too? *Yes.* Was one going harder? *No, both the same.* Neither one was faster? *No.* Why do you think that? *Because I can see that one of them started off from here and went up to there, and the other one went from here up to there, and that's the same thing.* Why the same thing? *Oh, no, I made a mistake, the blue one's road is longer.* Then was one of them going harder? *No, the same.* Why? *because they travelled at the same speed and stopped there.* Shut your eyes: the cars will set off on '3' and will stop at 'halt'. (We make the difference a big one in the ratio of 4 to 1 between the roads of blue and red). Was one going harder than the other? *It's the same thing again* (only looks at the stopping points). Wasn't one of them going harder? *The red one was slower because that's only a tiny bit, and the blue one did the biggest bit.* (We start with a difference of 2 to 1 again). Did one of them go farther? *Yes, blue.* Did it go harder? *No.* Faster? *No.*

Q 2: And this way (blue does half the distance covered by red, but stays ahead while red almost catches up with it). Was one of them going harder? *Yes, blue, because it is ahead*

and red is behind. Where did they start off from? *There
and here.* And you think blue went harder? *Yes.*

Q 1: Both the same thing. Why? *Because they both finish
here.*

PAN (5; 0) Q 1: Same speed or not? *Both the same.* Do they
do the same distance? *No, one starts here and the other
there.* The same length? *No, that blue one is shorter.* Were
they both going just as hard? *Yes.* One of them wasn't faster
than the other? *No.* Which one went a long way? *Red.* And
what if I said to you that one was going harder than the
other? *Well, I think they went at the same speed.*

Q 2: (red almost catches up with blue after a much longer
road): Same speed? *No.* Which one went harder? *Blue, because red is behind blue.* Same distances? *No, red is longer.*
Then which one was going harder? *Blue.*

Q 4: (meet from opposite directions: the blue one covers
twice the distance of the red one and they stop at the same
point): Did they go at the same speed or not? *Yes.* Same
roads? *No, blue longer.* Why do you think the speeds are the
same? *Because they stopped at the same time.* Shut your eyes
(same thing with ratio 4 to 1). *Blue went faster.* How can
you tell? *Because blue's garage* (= starting point marked
with a square standing for the garage) *is farther away.* Which
one did the longer road? *Blue.* Is that why it went faster?
Yes. (We start again with ratio 2 to 1 and with child watching). Same speed or not? *Yes.* Why? *Because one garage is
here and the other is over there. Same roads? No, blue is
farther.* Same speeds? *Yes.* Why? *They stop here.* And if I
say no, can you tell which one was faster? *The blue one because it goes a longer road.* Very good. Now watch (Q 1:
blue catches up on red with roads in ratio 2 to 1). Same
speeds or not? *Same thing.* Does one go faster than the other?
No. How do you know? *Because they both stopped at the
same time.* Do they travel the same distance? *No, blue is
longer.* Well then? . . .

Q 2: (blue almost catches up on red). Distances in ratio
2 to 1). Same speed? *No, one went harder, the red one.* Why?
It was farther ahead. Were they travelling at the same time?
Yes. Did they do the same distances? *No, blue was longer.*
Then which one went harder? *Red.*

MIC (5; 0). In connection with Q 1 and 2 this is an unusual
case of absence of differentiation between evaluation of speeds

and lengths. Q 1: Same speeds or not? Yes. Did one of them travel a longer distance than the other? Yes, no, because you see the blue one was there to begin with (blue caught up with red after a journey twice as long, but Mic indicates by 'there' red's starting point and not blue's) and then it was going alone for a bit at first (=before reaching red's starting point). We start again, and each time Mic recognizes that the speeds are equal, then refuses to recognize the given factors, as if both cars had set off from blue's starting point (earlier simply 'went by itself at first'). We then place two houses, as garages at the starting points: Did they start at the same time? Yes. Finished at the same time? Yes. Is one road longer than the other? Yes, blue, because its garage is a bit farther. And was one faster, did one go harder than the other? Yes, red, because it lives nearer, and blue is farther away.

Q 3: (same apparatus but blue overtakes red slightly). This time Mic replies right away that blue went harder than red, because it overtook the other one.

Q 2: (blue almost catches up with red after a path twice as long): And now, did one go harder than the other? Yes, red, because it lives nearer. How's that? You see, the man in the red car went full speed, so he was able to get there sooner, farther ahead. (Same thing in the ratio of 4 to 1). Was one of them going harder? Yes, red. Did one of them go a longer distance. Yes, blue. So was one of them going harder? Yes, red . . . Mic thus clearly sees the differences in lengths but pays no attention to them: the one which gets farther ahead goes quickest, and if they reach the same point, the one which left from the nearer point goes faster because placed farther ahead.

LIL (5; 0) Q 1: (blue catches up on red after twice the journey): Same speeds although blue did a longer road. We start again, increasing the difference (4 to 1): Blue was faster? Yes. Why? Because I can see it (perception of the speed itself). If you shut your eyes during its journey and you only saw the ends of the journeys, could you tell? No. (We do so). Why was blue faster than red? I just can't see why.

Q 3: Faster because it overtook the other one. And this way? (Q 1 as before 4 to 1)? Don't know.

EAN (5; 3) Q 1: (red is ahead when they set off, caught up by blue): *Red goes faster. Why? . . . Same roads? Red a bit shorter and blue a bit longer. Was one going harder? Yes, red.*

Q 2: (red almost catches up with blue after journeys of 2 to 1): *Blue goes faster because it started off farther forward.* Did they start at the same time? *Yes.* And stop at the same time? *No, that one (blue) in front, that one there (red) behind* (no differentiation of time and space): But did one of them go harder, faster? *Blue.*

Q 3: (blue overtakes red): *Blue goes faster, because red is behind and blue in front.* Did they begin at the same time? *One started quicker, blue, and the other began slower* (confusion of time and speed). And did they stop at the same time? *Blue ahead.* The colours are reversed: same reactions.

Q 4: (meet from opposite directions: ratios 4 to 1) *the same speed.* And this way (ratios 6 to 1)? *Blue goes quicker, because it is a long way from its garage and the other one is nearer.* (We begin again at 4 to 1). *Same speeds.* And the distances? *Red is longer.* And isn't one of them going harder than the other? *No.* Sure? *Yes.*

ELI (5; 9) Q 1: (blue catches up on red): *Blue goes harder.* Why? *It was first.* Did they stop at the same place? *Oh, yes, so they go at the same speed.*

Q 3: (overtaking): *That one faster because it was farther ahead.*

Q 2: same speed. Q 3: again correct. Q 4: (meet from opposite directions with distances of 2 to 1): *Same speeds.* Shut your eyes (exact repetition). Was one going harder? *Blue faster because it goes farther* (so in this case perception might be said to be an obstacle to reasoning). Thus at the end of the interview Eli reached stage II.

RAY (5; 5) Q 3: (blue very nearly catches up on red, after covering a longer distance): *Red goes quicker.* Why? *Because the distance is longer.* So Ray judges the actual lengths by the stopping points alone without taking the starting points into consideration.

These reactions are all of great interest for the analysis of the relations between intuition and logic. Let us also attempt then to see what they imply from this point of iew, as well as in connection with the development of the deas of speed and time.

The first observation is that at this earliest level only Q 3 is solved: it can therefore be said, as we have already een throughout Chapter Six, that the earliest intuition of speed is that expressing the action of overtaking. However, in view of the results of the other three questions, it an now be seen that this intuition of overtaking in fact ontains two distinct meanings. In the first place it might be said that any conception of speed is formed only in erms of situations where visible overtaking actually takes place: in that case, the child would simply answer Q 1, 2, and 4, by forming an analogy with overtaking and judging speed by the arrangement of the stopping points. But in he second place, the following statement might just as asily be maintained: just as movement itself is conceived t first simply as a change of order or position (displacement), the relationship of speed would also emerge at first from a comparison of two movements, and the movement judged to be faster would then be the one whose finishing point is located ahead of the other. Now, if this were the earliest theory it would of course give rise to correct evaluations in the case of overtaking, but not when one moving object catches up on the other, altogether or very nearly, or when they meet travelling in opposite directions. In short, the first solution would amount to saying that overtaking itself is the basis of the conception of speed, whereas the second solution would attribute the origins of this idea to comparison of the stopping points of movements generally, and so overtaking alone would be correctly evaluated.

In fact both interpretations are probably true to some extent in turn: at first the general question of the placing of the stopping points seems to dominate every judgment, but since the special case of overtaking is the most important and produces the most efficient estimates, this is the model which sooner or later influences judgements made in the other special cases and which in particular will explain, during the next stage, the articulation of the earliest intuitions of order.

Q 1 (one moving object catching up on another), for example, might also have led to a correct intuition: if two objects start moving with one placed ahead of the other, and the last one catches up on the first one, it would necessarily overtake it if it went on at the same speed. Now, it is very interesting to note that our subjects were unable to make this elementary composition of their own accord, or to anticipate it intuitively through immediate mental experiment as might justifiably have been expected. Eli's case is typical in this respect: he thinks he has seen the blue car overtake the red one and decides that the former's speed is greater, and then when he recognizes that they stopped at the same point, he immediately corrects himself, saying: 'Oh, yes, then they were at the same speed', as if speed depended only on the spatial arrangement of the stopping points. This is the general reaction in fact: 'both go at the same speed' says Eri, because I can see that they finished at the same place', or 'because they both finished at the same time'. (Pan) Yet all of them recognize that one of the moving objects travels a longer distance than the other. There are even some who momentarily conclude from this that the second one was going faster, because it is 'ahead' of the other (Ean), but the great majority decide that they are equal. Finally let us note that when the disparity in the distances travelled becomes too great, the child acquiesces and recognizes which of the cars goes faster. But in that case it is either simply a question of perceptual observation of the speed (Lil: 'because I can see it') without proving this statement by the greater distance travelled, or else it is a kind of unspecific intuition such that one maximum involves another without particular reference to the road followed as a distance. Moreover, as soon as the disproportion in lengths is reduced the subject returns to his original method of evaluation without concerning himself further about length.

Q 2. (where one almost catches up on the other) provides additional useful information, which clarifies the true significance of the intuition of overtaking: in fact, even while recognizing that the first car travels a longer distance than the one which it does not quite catch up with, the

very great majority of subjects think the latter goes faster
or 'harder', because it was 'farther ahead' and 'overtook it'
(Eri), because the first 'is behind the other' and the second
'was farther ahead' (Pan), 'because it lives nearer' (Mic),
'because it started off in front' and is 'farther ahead' (Ean)
etc. Only Eli thinks the speeds are the same, and none of
the subjects answers correctly, unless the disproportions in
the lengths covered are once again too great. But in this
last instance, it is only a question of a momentary and
essentially perceptual regulation, not affecting later judgements. According to these reactions as a whole, it is thus
the fact of being 'ahead' which indicates the greatest speed:
the child is unable to compare the movements involved by
their durations and their lengths at the same time, hence
the latter are meaningless by themselves, and comparison
is made by means of the placing of the finishing points
alone. At this level, therefore, the intuition of overtaking
is just a special case of these evaluations of order, though
they coincide in this case with the correct relationship of
the speeds.

Finally, Q 4 produces the same reactions: according to
every subject, the speeds are equal because the moving
objects finish at the same point, regardless of the distances
travelled. Here again, in the case of too great a disproportion (4 to 1 or more), the reply is momentarily correct
through perceptual regulation (perception of the speed as
such or centration upon too great a disparity in length,
hence upon one maximum which immediately involves
another, i.e. the greatest speed, without conscious reasoning), but even if subjects like Mic and Pan refer in this
connection to the longer distance travelled, they do not
draw any conclusion from this, when the ratio again becomes 2 to 1.

In short, all the replies tend towards the same result,
and towards a conclusion which entirely agrees with what
has been seen so far of the development of the concepts of
time (Origins of the Child's Conception of Time) and of
movement (Chapter Three of the present work). It is as if
the child judged speed by the finishing point alone, regardless of the distance travelled, and as if 'more quickly'

meant 'finishing in front of' or 'before', in a spatial and temporal sense at one and the same time (It will be recalled that at this level there is a relative lack of differentiation between succession in space and succession in time). Before and after, in the spatial sense, therefore require at the same time intuition of movement and speed as well as of time. Consequently 'quick' can mean 'in front of' or 'first' as well as indicating actual speed, hence the affirmations of equality or the inversions given in reply to Q 1, 2, and 4. As for overtaking, which is an inversion of order (the faster moving object being in the rear to begin with and later in front), certainly it produces correct answers, but this is because in this case, and in this case alone, finishing 'in front of' really does correspond to a greater speed.

One of the most important lessons emerging from these facts is that the intuition of speed is relative from the very start. There can be no absolute speeds if the judgement on which speed is based involves a comparison of order, since change of position alone is just displacement: speed therefore implies from the first a system of co-displacements. But what does this primary, intuitive or even perceptual relativity consist of? Clearly in the child's case as in our own, the very perception of a movement immediately provides some impression of speed: a moving car will thus appear faster than a horse, whether or not overtaking actually occurs. Then what is the rôle of previous experience and of 'potential' overtaking? Nothing is yet known about this. In this case of the differences of speed occurring in the present questions, the ratio is normally 2 to 1, and it is quite probable that the child perceives just as we do, at least qualitatively. But these given perceptual factors are either conceptualized differently or else ignored in favour of the order of succession of the finishing points. It is only in the case of overtaking that the sum of perceptual impressions coincides with the relation of order, and this is what leads to the primacy of overtaking as the 'prototype' intuition of speed. Therefore when the disproportion of the speeds or the distances covered is increased, e.g. up to 4 to 1, or 6 to 1, the child may momentarily give the correct answer because then this disproportion would be fitted briefly into the schema of overtaking. But, let us repeat, this is only a question of a momentary regulation, not affecting later evaluations, and it is not a change of equilibrium leading to a relatively lasting state, as it will be the case in stage II.

From the point of view of the psychology of intuitive thought these results are highly instructive. On the one hand they show that imaginative intuition differs from actual perception, since with Q 1, 2 and 4 two speeds can be considered conceptually equal although they are 'perceived to be unequal, or their ratio may be the reverse of that provided by direct perception.[1] But, on the other hand, they bring to light the existence of processes analogous to those of perception as such. In fact, intuitive thought does not reach a permanent equilibrium any more than does perception: the factors present (order of stopping points, order of starting points, lengths travelled durations, etc.) are as if charged with a quality which is not logical but causal, so that attention has only to be fixed on one or other of these elements, according to the value of the external given factors or their modifications, for this or that judgement to be reached straight away, or for this judgement to be reversed and taken up in another direction as if by a sudden change of equilibrium.

The dominant influence over intuitive thinking is undoubtedly perceptual in origin: e.g. the termination of two movements at the same stopping point is a perceptual given factor, the lengths of the paths being yet another, etc. However, it is as if these given factors instead of being considered together and correlated, were variable in value, some even being isolated and dissociated from the others, and the latter being as it were devalued or even ignored. Now, how is this dissociation achieved? Through a kind of 'centration', analogous to those of perception: the child momentarily fixes on one aspect of the phenomenon and

---

[1] It would also be useful to study whether intuitive criteria enter into actual perception, in cases where the speeds are greater, or simply closer to one another.

neglects the others, as if he over-estimated the former and underestimated the latter. The effect here is analogous to the relative over estimation produced by fixing one's gaze in visual perception, and which would be produced in this case by attention itself, conceived as an intuitive centration. This would therefore explain the striking 'see-saw' effect just recalled, e.g. in reactions to the text of concentric racetracks (Chapter Six, Section III).

If this mechanism of intuitive centration, distinct from but akin to perceptual centration, is allowed by way of hypothesis, then it is easy to explain that kind of logical absolute or non-relativity which characterizes the judgements of our subjects, and at the same time that intuitive relativity basically inherent in the conception of speed. As for the first of these two aspects of the phenomenon, it is quite evident why the stopping points immediately attract attention: they form the final point and goal of the movements. Now, when attention is fixed on the stopping points there could be no centration on the starting points at the same time: these are therefore neglected or regarded as if they were all alike. Thus the subject Mic actually goes so far as to correct the given factors, affirming against all the evidence that the blue car, which set off in the rear of the red one, 'was there first', i.e. at red's starting point. Likewise the distances travelled are ignored though the subject is not unaware of them, but the least advanced subjects go so far as to evaluate them in terms of their stopping points: Ray thus corrects the lengths in the same way as Mic the starting points. In short, centration on the stopping points as it were produces an underestimate of differences in starting points or distances travelled. With regard to 'before' and 'after' in time, on the other hand, they are not dissociated from the spatial order of succession, as if the speeds were all the same (see the case of Ean). In short, there is as it were an absolute implied in each intuitive centration: the very fact of centring the intuition on one given factor results in its exclusive valuation and consequently prevents its logical correlation with the others. It is this absolute, view, produced by the over estimation inherent in any centration which we have used so far to characterize the 'egocentricity' of intuitive thought, as opposed to the 'decentration' formed by logical grouping. But on the other hand it must be fully understood that these incorrect absolutes of intuitive judgement are always made up of overestimations and underestimations, and by that very fact they imply a kind of unconscious relativity, comparable to Weber's perceptions and thresholds, as opposed to logical relativity.

It will next be seen how in the course of stage II these early centrations are gradually 'decentred' by means of wider and more stable regulations than the sudden and very short-lived changes of equilibrium observed so far, at the level of stage I alone.

2. The second stage: Intermediate reactions between intuition centred on the stopping points and logical correlation

The subjects of stage II begin like the foregoing but gradually correct themselves in the course of the experiment, according to a continuous series of reactions extending between stages I and II. Here are some examples:

EDI (5; 1) Q 1: (blue catches up on red with simultaneous starting and stopping): Did they set off at the same time? *No, the red one before the other one* (=in front of!) Did they stop at the same time? *No, blue first* (wrong=caught up with). Did they go at the same speed? *Blue faster.* Why? *Because it was farther ahead* (he is therefore equating catching up and overtaking). Same distance? *Blue was longer.* Did one go quicker than the other? *Yes, blue.* Why? *Because it's farther ahead.*

Q 2: (blue almost catches up with red. Synchronous movements as always): Did they start at the same time? *No, red was quicker and blue slower.* Did they stop at the same time? *No, blue first* (=in the rear). Did one go faster than the other? *Yes, red.* Why? . . . Were the lengths the same? *No, blue was longer.* Did one go harder or both the same? *Red was faster.*

Q 3: (blue overtakes red): Did they set off at the same

time? *No, blue was faster and red slower.* Why? *It went like that* (mimes overtaking, using both hands). Were the lengths the same? *Blue was longer.*

Q 4: (meet from opposite directions, ratio 4 to 1; eyes shut): *Red was faster* (correct). Why? *No, both were fast. Both the same? Yes.* Were the distances the same? *No, red longer.* Same speeds? *No, red quicker.* Why? *Because it stops a long way from its garage* (repeat, changing ratios). *Blue faster.* Why? . . . Same lengths? *No, blue longer.* Why do you think it goes faster? *Because.* . . .

CLAV (6; 11) Q 1: (Red catches up on blue). Did they start off at the same time? *No.* Which one in front? *No, both at the same time. Red was a bit faster and it finished at the same time as blue.* How do you know? *Because I saw that blue was farther ahead than red.* And so? *So red went faster, since when it came up to the blue one, it kept up with it.*

Q 2: (red almost catches up on blue): Did they stop at the same time? *No, red went less slowly than blue.* But did they stop at the same moment? *Yes.* Did one go harder than the other? *Blue went harder than red.* (Repeat with greater differences). Did one go harder? *Yes, blue* (wrong), *but red came a bit closer.* Is one distance longer than the other? *Yes, blue.* Show me. *No, red.* Was one of them going harder? *Red, no blue.* What do you say? *Blue goes less slowly but red harder* (!) Then which went hardest? *Red.* And the slowest? *Blue.* And which went least hard? *Blue, it travelled slowest and red fastest.* Q 3 (Overtaking): correct.

Q 4: (meet from opposite directions: blue twice the length of red): Was one of them going harder? *No, both the same.* Why? *Because they both stopped here.* Is one of the roads longer? *Blue.* And if I told you that blue went faster, why would that be? *Because the road is longer.* What do you think is more correct, that blue went harder or that both went at the same speeds? *Both the same.* And now (travel past one another from opposite directions, with unequal distances, red's being longer)? *Red went harder because it went farther ahead.* And this way (meet from opposite directions, same ratios). *Red went harder because it travelled a longer distance.*

MAY (7; 0) Q 1: (red catches up on blue): Did they start off at the same time? *Yes.* And stopped together? *Yes.* Same speeds? *Red a bit harder.* Same distances? *Red is longer.*

Q 2: (red almost catches up on blue): Did one go faster? *Blue went harder.* Same lengths? *Blue shorter.* Then which one was quicker? *Blue.*

Q 3: correct. Problem 4 (eyes shut, red faster): Same speeds? *Same.* Same lengths? *Red longer* (we repeat the experiment twice with the child watching: he takes the cars, imitates their meeting from opposite directions, and says): *Red faster because it went farther ahead.* Why the greater speed? *So as to finish first.*

Dor (6; 7) Q 1: (red catches up with blue): Did they set off at the same time? *No, yes.* Is one going harder than the other? *Yes, red.* Why? (We start again). Why faster? . . . Which one does the longer road? *Red.* How do you know that it goes faster? . . . Red does a longer road and blue a shorter road, so why is it not blue which goes faster? *Because it goes slowly.* How do you know that? . . .

Q 4: (meet from opposite directions): Which one goes the longer distance? *Blue.* Which one went faster? *Blue.* Why? (Repeat with roads the same length). Which one faster? *Both the same.* And this way (moving red back)? *Red.* Why? *Because it was farther ahead.*

The problem raised by these cases is to understand how, beginning with evaluation of speeds according to the spatial order of succession of the stopping points, the child manages to establish that in equal times speeds are proportional to distances travelled. This is evidently achieved by progressive generalization of the schema of overtaking: by likening other situations to this schema, the subject manages to anticipate the continuation of each of the movements perceived or to reconstruct them from their point of origin, so that attention is decentred from the stopping point alone, and the latter is related to the starting point and consequently to the actual interval separating them; hence to the distance travelled.

So it is that Q 1 (one object catching up on another) is solved by all the subjects simply by equation with overtaking: in fact for overtaking to occur it is enough to have an anticipation extending the movement of that object which catches up on the other moving object. The subject Edi indicates this very plainly, although he confuses times and spaces: red set off 'before the other' (= in front of) and blue finishes 'before . . . because it was farther ahead', he says, as if he really did see inversion of order and over-taking. The subject Clav expresses the change of order more accurately without going as far as inversion: 'blue was farther ahead than red' on starting 'then red went faster, because when it came up to blue, it kept up with it'.

But this is only a question of intuitive anticipation, i.e. of a partial regulation due to decentration of initial intui-tion adapted to the schema of overtaking. So there is still only articulation of intuitions and no operational general-ization. The proof of this is that Q 2, although put after Q 1 and also involving the action of catching up, is by no means solved directly, and this is simply because the faster moving object does not completely catch up with the other at the close of the race. So it is that Edi fails, for want of prolonging the movement of the object which is in the rear: therefore the one in front goes faster, as in the first stage. Clav begins in the same way, but when we increase the differences in length, he extricates himself by saying that 'blue (in the rear) goes less slowly, and red goes harder', and only later removes the contradiction: so once more there is progressive decentration of attention direct-ed to the finishing points and regulation in terms of starting points and distances travelled.

In short, during this stage there is progressive decentra-tion of intuition fixed on the stopping point: the resulting intuitive regulations lead on through anticipated extension of movements perceived and reconstruction of journeys from their source, in due course, to the beginnings of generalization of the schema of overtaking, but without this adaptation reaching operational level.

3. The Third stage: Operational composition of relation-ships

Towards 7 to 8 years, three correlated constructions are observed: temporal order is dissociated from succession in space (*The Origins of the Conception of Time*, Chapter Three), distances travelled are conceived as lengths occupying the interval between the given starting and stopping points (Chapters Three to Four of this volume) and in the case of synchronous movements speed is defined in terms of these lengths covered in equal times:

Iac (7; 8) Q 1: *Did they set off at the same time?* Yes. *And finished together?* Yes. *Same speeds?* No, blue went faster, because it had a longer road to do.
Q 2: *Red goes quicker because it has a longer road.*
Q 3: (overtaking): *Same speeds?* No, red had a longer road to go, otherwise it would be there (pointing to its position if it were going less quickly). *Show me where it would be if it had gone at the same speed?* (He indicates a point too far ahead). *Sure?* No, here (correct). *And if red were not going so hard as blue where would it be?* Here (just about right).
Q 4: *Blue goes quicker because its path is longer* (same journeys). *And this way?* Same speeds.

It is clear (all our other examples are similar) that relations of speed are now expressed only in terms of lengths or distances and no longer of order, But, by connecting the new reactions with the foregoing ones, it can be seen how relations of length result from articulated intuitions as in stage II: intuitive adaptation of perceived movements into the schema of overtaking has been generalized to the extent that each pair of movements forms a potential overtaking: it can therefore be said that the stopping and starting points are related from the first due to immediate decentration which thus transforms progressive regulations into reversible operations.

Conversely, when it is necessary to depart from the given factors of the moment to calculate the positions in terms of hypothetical distances travelled in given times, hesitations reappear as if these were movements in succession: speeds in the latter case are in fact only constructed in a fourth stage, that of hypothetico-deductive operations (see Chapter Nine).

SECTION II. *Partly synchronous times (stopping
simultaneously) and equal distances*

Let us now examine the problem in reverse: if the distances travelled are equal but the movements begin in
succession (stopping simultaneously), how will the child
evaluate the speeds perceived? Let us call this first Q 1a,
and let us note that it is of no use to analyse successive
stopping points with simultaneous departures, because
then it is simply overtaking and the problem is reduced to
Q 3 of Section I. On the other hand, if both starting and
stopping take place in succession, and particularly if the
times and the distances vary at the same time, the problems then require formal operations (see Chapter Nine)
except in the especially easy case of a combination of
departures in succession with Q 2 of the previous section
(we shall therefore call this Q 2a).

4. *The first stage: Speeds evaluated intuitively in terms
of the order of the starting or stopping points*

The subjects of this stage either believe the speeds to be
equal because the objects reach the same point simultaneously or else that the speed of the moving object which
left first is greater, because it goes ahead of the other one:

Ios (5; 0) Q 1a: (the red car leaves after the blue one, but
from the same point and catches it up): Did they start off
at the same time? *No, blue first.* And did they finish at the
same time? *Yes.* Does one of them go faster than the other,
or both the same? *Blue goes faster.* (We start again). Same
speeds or not? *Yes, same speeds.* Did one go harder than the
other? *Blue.* Why did you think that? *Because it went there,
and then afterwards the red one did too* (=so it went ahead
of the other one).

Look (we start again, placing trees as points of reference
at either end, and a house half-way to mark the spot the blue
one had already reached when the red one set off from the
tree). Did one of them set off first? *Yes the blue one.* When
the blue one was at the house the red one set off from the

tree. How far had the blue one gone when the red one started off? *There* (correct). While blue was going along the road from the house how far had the red one gone? (points it out correctly). Then which one was going harder? *Blue.* (We start again). Did one of them go faster than the other? *Blue.*

We start again, moving the house forward a long way, i.e. adding to the difference in times and making red go very much faster: Did they stop at the same time? *No* (wrong). Did one of them stop first? *Blue* (wrong: confuses it with starting). Did they start off at the same time? *Blue first* (correct). Did one go harder than the other? *Red.* How did you know that? *I looked at it.*

Q 2a: (Blue starts first and red travelling faster almost catches up on it: so there is inequality in the parts of the distance covered as well as in the durations): *Blue went faster, no farther ahead* (!) Did they stop at the same time? *Yes.* Did one go harder? *Blue, then red for a bit.* Which one then? *Blue.*

MARL (5; 0) Q 1a: (Red catches up on blue which sets off first): *Blue goes harder.* Did one set off first? *Blue.* Did they finish at the same time? *Yes.* And this way (we add to the distance and the difference in durations)? *Red harder.* Why? *Because it wanted to catch up with blue.*

Q 2a: (blue starts off first and red almost catches up): Did one of them set off first? *Blue.* Did they stop at the same time? *No, blue ahead* (no differentiation between time and space). When red stopped was blue still going along? *Yes* (wrong: we start again). Which one was faster? *Don't know.* Which one went the longer distance? *Blue started first, then it went a longer distance* (again no differentiation between two relations, though each is true on its own). (We start again). Which one had the longer road? *Blue.* Did they stop at the same time? (Hesitates) *Yes.* Did one go harder than the other? *Same speed. Red a little bit slower.* (We begin again). Why? *Yes, I think I saw it.*

These facts are very interesting both from the point of view of the construction of speed and of time itself. As far as speed is concerned, it is clear that the reactions of Ios and Marl are of the same kind as those in § 1: when one of the moving objects sets off after the other to travel the same distance then the speeds are equal because the stopping points are the same, or else (and this is something new) it is the one starting first which is thought to go faster or harder, simply because it precedes the other. The disproportions in duration must be considerably increased for the child to attribute a greater speed to that object which catches up on the other, but it is then that he perceives the speed as such ('I looked at it'). When, on the other hand, inequality of departures is added to that of the journeys as in Q 2, the same theory is again found (as with the reactions in Section I)—according to which the moving object which moves ahead of the other necessarily goes faster. The subject Ios, it is true, shows the beginnings of differentiation between 'ahead' and 'fast' ('it was faster, no farther ahead') but afterwards returns to confusion between these two ideas.

Now, from the point of view of time, this want of differentiation is manifestly accompanied by the usual lack of dissociation between succession in space and succession in time: Ios thinks blue stops first, because it is ahead, and Marl confuses the types of relation twice over. Thus it is clear how far time actually is in fact a co-ordination of speeds, since the intuition of speed based on the spatial or temporal order of the stopping points is accompanied by a want of differentiation between spatial and temporal order, whilst later advances in the conception of speeds and times form a single whole, in which these two concepts remain closely united.

5. The second stage: Intermediate reactions

In the course of stage II the same reactions are again found as in §2.

IAQ (6; 0) Q 1a: (the red car catches up with the blue one which left before it): Did they set off at the same time? *Blue, first.* Did they finish together? *Yes.* Did one of them go harder? (Thinks, without replying. We start again). *Yes, red.* How did you know? *I looked at it.* (We start again). Did one go harder? *Blue.* Why? . . . How did you see it? . . . What distance did blue go? *The longer one* and red? *It was*

coming up behind. Was the length of its road the same?
Yes. Then why do you say that it was going faster?

Q 2a: (red almost catches up blue, setting off well after
it): Did one of them go harder? Red. How did you see that?
Because its wheels were going faster. But why does it go
harder? . . .

FRAN (6; 0) Q 1a: (red car catches up on blue after starting
later): Both the same speed. (We start again). Red faster?
Why? . . . How did you see it? . . . (Begin again, increasing
the disproportion in the times and making red go a longer
distance). Red faster. Yes. Why?

Q 2a: (red almost catches up with blue after longer distance and later start). Red goes faster. Why? . . . (Start
again). Blue. Why? (Start again). Red. Why? Which one
does the longer road? Red. Why did you say it went faster?
. . . Thus sometimes answers correctly, and sometimes not,
but without being able to formulate his reasons.

REN (6; 0) Q 1a: (equal distances, red catches up). Same
speeds. (Start again). Red faster. Why? . . . Did they go the
same distances? Yes. In the same time? No, red less. Where
was the blue one when the red one began to move? There
(correct). Why do you say that red goes faster? . . . If you
had your eyes shut, would you have known just the same?
Yes, it would be red, because it went all this way while blue
was doing this little bit here (=second half of common
path).

Red almost catches up with blue, with equal distances:
Which one is going faster? Blue. Why? No, slower. Why?
. . . (Start again). Blue etc., sometimes one, sometimes the
other, without explanations. Finally: It's red, because it
wants to catch up with the other one.

Q 2a: (same thing, with unequal paths): It was red, because it goes a longer distance, and it wanted to catch up
with the other one.

UL (6; 10) Q 1a: (red catches up with blue on equal paths):
Blue goes quicker. Does one of them go harder? Yes, blue,
so as to be first. And how does red move? Slowly at first,
then fast. Which one goes faster? Blue, so as to be first. But
is it first, at the end? Yes. And the red one? It was too, both
together. (Repeat). Red goes quicker, to catch up with blue.

Q 2a: Red almost catches up with blue after a longer distance, and a later start: *Blue left first. It went faster. Oh, no, both the same, because one is farther ahead.* Did one travel a longer distance? *Blue.* But look. Red longer, blue shorter. Did one of them go faster? *No, both the same, at the same speed all the time* (because blue is always in front and red goes a longer way!)

BLAI (7; 0) Q 1a: (blue catches up on red, equal distances: Same speeds?) *Perhaps one was farther ahead than the other.* (Repeat, increasing difference in durations). *I think it is red, because it was farther ahead than* (=before) *blue.* (Start again). *Same speeds, because they go the same distances, oh, no, blue faster, because it caught up on the other one.*

It is obvious how instructive these hesitant replies are. In the early cases, the child merely wavers between right and wrong answers without being able to justify the former (Iaq and Fran). In the more advanced cases, the reasons for these hesitations are more easily distinguished: the child begins by attributing the greater speed to the moving object which precedes the other in space (and consequently also in time): 'the blue one goes faster, says Ul, to be first'. Then when he decentres this initial intuition in the direction of the other given factors, he attributes to both objects 'the same speeds, because they do the same journeys' (Blai) and finally, he discovers that the two journeys are not made in the same time: 'it went all this way while blue travelled this little bit here', says Ren, pointing out the whole distance which red covers while blue travels along the second half. Now, how does the subject achieve this correlation when he is not helped to break down the factors? It is through the equating of 'making up on lost time' and 'catching up on space still to be covered', the latter schema being (as we saw in § 2) comparable in turn with overtaking. The right answers are obtained through decentration and progressive regulations and by no means through the grouping of operations at this stage. These short-lived regulations, alternating with one another, are particularly clear when a time-lag is included in question 2 of the previous section (one object very nearly catches up on the other moving object setting off in succession and covering unequal distances.) The precedence in space of the slower moving object then leads the subject to think it is faster, whilst the longer distance travelled by the other one makes judgement swing in the other direction, hence the alternation often observed (e.g. Ul ends up with a kind of compensation between the two inverse factors).

6. The third stage: Operational solution of the problem conclusion of both sections

Towards 7 to 8 years on average the child finally becomes able to solve the problem through immediate grouping of the relations involved.

VAC (7; 9) Q 1b: *It was red which went faster. Why? Because it caught up with blue. What does that mean? That it set off later and finished at the same time. And the distances? Same.* (Q 2a: red nearly catches up with blue after a longer journey). *It's red again. Why? It left after the other one and did a longer journey.*

Yet again it is impossible not to be amazed, in view of the apparent simplicity of these reactions, by the psychological complexity of the operations which they involve, and by the laborious constructions which have made them possible. It may therefore be of some interest now to try to reconstruct fully the mechanisms by which the child arrives at these operational reactions, both here and in § 3.

The intuitive starting point of the conception of speed seems, all things considered, to be based on a sensorimotor schema belonging to the subject's own activity: managing to be first in line, or in a word, ahead. Moreover, this 'unrefined' intuition of the early stages always proves correct in one particular case: overtaking, whence the special importance assumed by the schema of actions in which getting ahead is equivalent to overtaking. At any age, in fact, the child can tell that one moving object overtaking another is going faster or harder than it. When on the other hand he is shown two objects either covering two unequal lengths in the same time (Q 1) or the same distance in different times (Q 1a) it would seem to be easy for the child to adapt these new facts to the schema of overtaking, simply by mentally extending the movements perceived: catching up is in fact almost overtaking. Now, instead of beginning with this comparison, even in a purely intuitive form, the child actually begins by judging speed solely from the stopping points: he concludes that if the moving objects reach the same spot simultaneously (Q 1 and 1a) the speeds are equal regardless of distances covered and starting times (in any case these distances too are often evaluated according to their stopping points and these starting times according to their spatial order). It is therefore clear that the schema of overtaking must itself be interpreted in terms of getting ahead, i.e. an unrefined intuition of order, relating only to the stopping points. Hence the initial failure in Q 1 and 1a, 2 and 2a, and likewise in 4, with Q 3 alone being solved at once since it is based on simple overtaking, i.e. inversions of the arrangement of the 'forward' points of the movements, if such a childish expression may be permitted.

This fitting of perceived facts into the schema of the stopping point (precedence or overtaking), with the right or wrong answers produced in this way, therefore forms a distorting or egocentric assimilation. By this it must be understood—and this example is representative of all those to which this term is legitimately applied—that these given factors are in no way fitted into a system of operations which transforms them into composable and reversible relations, but merely into an action or system of actions which centre the relations involved at some particular point, chosen by reason of subjective activity. In particular, the goals or stopping points of movements centre the attention or intuition and this centration has the effect of over-evaluating the importance of this factor, as opposed to the others, which are underestimated or ignored.

This term of centration is borrowed from our attempted analysis of perception and seems to us to provide the key to intellectual egocentricity in general. In 'centring' one's gaze on any object (e.g. on one or two unequal lines which are being compared) this object is overestimated while the peripheral objects are under-estimated: this is what explains in particular the 'systematic error of standards' according to which every fixed measure is overevaluated in relation to the variable it measures. Centration is therefore a souce of illusion, (over-estimation attached to a transitory point of view) whilst decentration (or co-ordination of several successive or potential centrations) leads towards objectivity. It must also be recalled that in the perceptual totalities governed by the laws of centration and decentration, equilibrium is not achieved in a permanent form, but each external modification gives rise to a shift in equilibrium. These 'displacements', which testify to the irreversible character of perceptual transformations, are marked by 'non-compensated transformations', which, in the case of decentration, tend to diminish: there can then be said to be 'regulation' i.e. reaction in favour of compensation. Finally, if centration thus determines perceptual adaptation (the schema of which constitutes a total form or *Gestalt*), every displacement of equilibrium testifies to the existence of 'accommodation' serving to modify the schema of assimilation: the less accommodation and assimilation are in equilibrium, the greater are the displacements in equilibruim, while regulations testify to an advance in equilibrium between the two opposing processes. Operations must therefore be held to be the ultimate end of this mechanism: operational equilibrium is in fact permanent and is characterized by complete reversibility towards which regulations are directed when their mobility becomes sufficient.

With this in mind, the level of intuitive thinking may be considered exactly half-way between perception and operations, so that the laws of centration are again found though in an imaginative and no longer only in perceptual form. In the case of our experiments on speed, the question is in fact no longer simply one of perceptions: the child perfectly perceives the differences in speed of the movements performed in front of him, but he expresses these speeds through judgements which go beyond perception and incorporate schemas of thought. These schemas become operational in stage III because their reversible structure and their composition permit of objective interpretation of the perceptual data in a system of relationships co-ordinating all the elements involved. But in stages I and II these schemas remain pre-operational though more than perceptual, and it is this intermediate level that we call intuitive. Now, intuition, to the extent that it is still irreversible, gives rise in the same way as perception to centration and decentration, but centrations of the judgements and no longer of perceptual mechanisms, and it is this intellectual centration which characterizes what we have so far designated by the term of egocentricity. Hence the mechanisms of egocentric intuition are the continuation on the level of thinking, of the sensori-motor mechanisms belonging to perception and to 'motricity' which is closely allied to it.

To return to our present results, these show the fundamental fact, i.e. the one which is genetically the basis of the development extending between stages I and III, to be that the child begins evaluating speed solely by the stopping points of movements. Let us repeat that this is not purely perceptual fact: the subject can perfectly well see that the starting points are not the same, in space or in time. But when the various relationships have been perceived, instead of being translated into so many objective relations, each to be considered and 'composed' with the others, they seem to be influenced by separate co-efficients of importance so that the mere fact that thought is directed on to one of them devalues the rest: their organization is thus by no means formed by reversible composition (reversible because the increase in the resemblance or in the difference expressed by one of the relationships would ipso facto entail a corresponding diminution in the inverse relationships) but by an allocation of value governed by the element 'centred upon'. In other words, the order of the stopping points acquires a special importance while the order of the starting points and relationships of intervals (distances or durations) are under-estimated, not as perceptual given factors, but as elements contributing to a line of reasoning. This centration on the other hand forms an egocentric assimilation, since the order of the stopping points is overvalued to the same extent as the subject's activity is affected by these points as being the final points or goals of movements or actions.

To understand these things more clearly let us try to express this distorting assimilation in the terminology used for the analysis of perceptual activity. Transformations uncompensated by intuition will thus be translated into the symbols of reversible operations, which is the more legitimate because operations form, in fact, the final limit of intuitive compositions (while for perceptual compositions there is only an unreal boundary). Two objects moving for the same length of time cover two parallel trajectories equal in lengths (e.g. 3 cms.) with the same starting and the same finishing points. Di is the difference between the starting points (here Di$=$o) and Df the difference between the finishing points (here Df$=$o). Thus the difference in the speeds Dv may be expressed by subtraction as: $Dv = Di - Df$, in this case $Dv = o - o = o$. If the first moving object covers 3cms. while the second one does 2 cms. with 1 cm. separating them at the start, this will give $DV = 1 - o = 1$ (Q 1). If the first one travels 3 cms. with 2 cms. separating them at the start, while the second one moves 2 cms. going 1 cm. beyond the finishing point of the first one, we have $Dv = 2 - 1 = 1$ (Q 2). If the first one covers 3 cms. and the second one 2 cms., with 0.5 cms. separating them at either end and inversion of order, we have $DV = 0.5 - (-0.5) = 1$ (overtaking: Q 3). Finally, starting 5 cms. apart if the first one travels 3 cms. and the second moves 2 cms. in the opposite direction with o cms. separating them at the finishing point (meet from opposite directions): (Q 4) this will also give (when the movements are oriented in the same direction) $Dv = 1 - o = 1$ (or, taking into consideration the contrary directions) $Di = 3 - 2 = 1$ and $Df = o$, hence $Dv = 1 - o$). Now instead of proceeding in this way, or simply considering as he finally does the intervals or distances defined by the starting and finishing points (the paths traversed) it is as if the child were at first unable to consider both relationships, Di and Df, at the same time, and consequently even less so the interval or path traversed between starting and stopping points (i and f). Thus it is as if the fact of centring on one of these relationships (and we have seen why the child centres on the relationship Df rather than on Di) entailed devaluation of the other. There is no more in this hypothesis than the observation of the general mechanism of attention (which acts in this case as a centration of intuition): in fact attention illuminates the point on which it is focused and by that very fact neglects the rest. But attention guided by the operational need for correlation would alternately centre upon Di and Df, leading to compensation of the alternating values, whereas the child's attention, guided by his initial egocentric intuition, remains centred upon the relationships of the stopping points Df, because of his finalistic conception of movement. Consequently the relationship Di is neglected and its value becomes nil, not perceptually, but in relation to intuitive estimation of speeds by the order of finishing (or the end of the movements). Bearing in mind only Df, the child therefore infers at first that the differences in speed are $Dv=0$ in Q 1, $Dv=-1$ (the slower moving object being judged faster) in Q 2, $Dv=1$ (coinciding with the right answer) in Q 3, and $Dv=0$ in Q 4.

This method of presentation thus amounts to saying that initial intuition proceeds by means of centration which by its very mechanism rules out the operations or correlation $Di-Df$, since centration isolates Df from Di. But from this a procedure might almost be traced for measuring intuitive distortions by analogy with perceptual illusions. Considering situations 1 to 4 as the result of four objective modifications of elements moving at the same speed, the relation Dv being throughout $Dv=1$, each objective modification of the given factors may be said in fact to produce a displacement of equilibrium in intuitive relationships, since in each case the child judges the speed to be different: hence this displacement is characterized by an 'uncompensated transformation' P, defined as the difference between the speed the subject estimates and the operationally calculated speed $Dv=1$. This gives us, in Q 1 to 4, $P=1$; $P=2$; $P=0$ (since the reply to Q 3 is correct) and $P=1$. Hence these distortions P express the effect of centration on Df, i.e. the deforming or egocentric assimilation of speeds perceived by means of the stopping points alone. On the other hand, the fact that there is a displacement of equilibrium, and not a permanent equilibrium of judgement (defined as the operational composition $Dv=1$) indicates that so far there is no equilibrium between 'assimilation' to the schema of speed and accommodation to new situations, and this is natural since either assimilation distorts the given factors, or else accommodation to new given factors distorts the schema of assimilation: in either case there is a displacement of equilibrium, hence $P>0$.

Now let us considerably increase the value Di. E.g. in Q 1 the paths traversed would be 8: 2, i.e. $Di=6$, $Df=0$ and $Dv=6$. In this case, observation shows that the child can no longer ignore the difference in the starting points Di. It can then be said that the relationship Di is likewise 'centred'. But two possibilities might arise. The first would be forgetting the relationships of the stopping points Df. This does not often happen in the present instance, given the attraction of the end point of movements, but frequently in other situations where one of the relationships has taken precedence over the other, the reverse happens, subsequently when the second relationship is observed: another biased centration would then come about, i.e. a new distorting assimilation, and the previous phenomena would be repeated in another direction. On the other hand the new centration may not cancel out the preceding one and the subject may take both into consideration at the same time. In this eventuality, which corresponds in this case to the facts observed, there is no longer simply a central or distorting assimilation, but together with this (or perhaps independently) decentration, i.e. assimilation through correlation of the objects assimilated. The very fact of centring at the same time upon Di and Df, i.e. considering the relationship of the starting points and of the stopping points alternately, constitutes the beginnings of correlation since every decentration is made up of the correlation of two or more 'centrations'. Consequently, in considering the starting and finishing points of movements at the same time, the subject will only be able to relate them by starting to consider intervals, i.e. centring similarly on the paths traversed, which in the example chosen are 8 cms. and 2 cms. The fact of taking into consideration the starting points Di and the paths traversed, will thus lead to estimation of speed by the relation between Di and Df and no longer only by the stopping points Df alone. Hence the correlation of these will be directed towards the operation Di—Df which will be achieved as soon as the subject can co-ordinate the various relationships without distorting them any longer.

However 'decentration' only becomes operational from the time when the assimilating schema, uniting successively centred relationships into a single whole, achieves complete reversibility, i.e. allows of passing from one relationship to another and back with no further distortion due to biased centration. Now if centration on Df produces an uncompensated transformation P (to be called Pf) ultimately of course the two distortions will exactly compensate each other since each one tends to correct the other: hence at the finishing point there will in fact be complete reversibility $(Pf = -Pi)$, consequently, operations. But this is only at the final point, and before this is reached, compensations remain incomplete. 'Regulations' is the name we give to partial compensations due to decentrations which tend to diminish the distortions inherent in any centration. Regulation is thus an advance towards reversibility and properly forms the intermediary between distorting assimilation (centration) and operational assimilation.

It is obvious then how centration of intuition on the stopping points of movements involves systematic distortion in judging speeds, while decentration produced by comparison of starting and finishing points leads to regulation of these earliest judgements. As we saw in the course of stage I, regulations only appear when the difference between the two speeds is increased considerably, in other words, where the disproportion is great between Di and Df (relation of starting points and of finishing points). But on returning to slight differences, decentration diminishes again and the subject returns to his original errors: proof in itself that decentration is not at first operational, since at this first level there is evidently neither stable equilibrium nor reversibility so far. In the course of stage II on the contrary there is progressive regulation even in the case of slight differences, and the subject begins by centring his judgement on the placing of the stopping points Df, then notices the order of the starting points Di and gradually corrects his judgements by decentration with or without some alternation, but tending towards final equilibrium to the extent that decentration becomes complete.

Stage III, or the stage of operations properly so called, is thus easily explained by the fact that the regulations become immediate and by that very fact are transformed into reversible operations, and decentration or co-ordination of successively centred relations consequently forms an operational 'grouping'. In this particular case, it is even possible to follow in detail the transition between regulation and operation. The analysis of perception allows us in fact to distinguish two kinds of regulation: those due to relative decentration, i.e. simply to mutual compensation of the distortions P, without absolute diminution of their arithmetical sum, and those due to absolute decentration which diminish the total value of the distortions P because the interval between the points of centration is itself decentred. Now, in these cases of speed, a similar phenomenon is observed. When decentration concerns only the starting and finishing points it remains relative, whereas when the interval between centrations on Di and Df, i.e. the path traversed, is itself considered, then regulation acts on the total trajectories: so the static schema of speed judged simply by placing (Di and Df), is replaced by a mobile schema accommodated to the actual movement in its entirety, and regulation not only permits co-ordination of all the given relationships but also anticipation of the later course of displacements beyond the stopping points and reconstruction of their course prior to the starting points. Two interesting points consequently follow![1]

The first point is that in this case each of the various situations considered in Q 1 to 4 and 1a and 2a may be reduced to the same terms. Hence each of them can be likened to overtaking, at first by transposition of their intuitive schemas, but later through truly operational generalizations: situation 1 (catching up) is viewed as near-overtaking, situation 2 (almost catching up) as future or potential overtaking, situation 3 as actual overtaking, and situation 4 as overtaking in contrary directions (passing from opposite directions). Likewise situation 1a and 2a are viewed as precedence in time. In fact, overtaking is the intuitive format in which compensations are most easily made complete (through relative decentration) and consequently the easiest to employ for the representation of all differences of speed (through absolute decentration). It is in fact this progressively more generalized transposition that is observed in the course of stage II.

Consequently the second point is that, when displacements of equilibrium have been cancelled out, the system of relations involved becomes reversible. In fact, where the difference in speed between the two moving objects is constant ($Dv=1$) the four situations concerned in Q 1 to 4 can be derived from each other by moving the starting and stopping points forwards or backwards using the same relations or by reversing the direction of the journeys (4): this is just what the child understands when he equates with one another the various schemas of catching up (altogether or almost), of overtaking, and passing from opposite directions. Hence by that very fact he makes a new operational grouping which is no longer simply that of placements and displacements (Chapters One to Five) but co-displacements, i.e. a correspondence between the respective orders of two displacements, reduced to the

[1] These intuitive anticipations and reconstructions are functionally, though not structurally, comparable to perceptual anticipations and reconstructions.

format of overtaking. On the other hand, by that very fact he takes into consideration the intervals formed in space and in time by the arrangement of the starting and stopping points, i.e. the paths traversed, and the times taken: hence by translating intervals into the placing of starting and stopping points or vice versa, he grasps the fact that to increase the speed it is enough to increase the space covered in the same time, or to decrease the speed in relation to the same distance it is enough to increase the time. Thus all these modifications, which are reversible since they are no longer accompanied by displacements of equilibrium, result in the single ratio $V=S/T$, the mathematical expression of the qualitative grouping of co-displacements.

Now, this final grouping, like every other, results from the fact that assimilation, when it ceases to distort, reaches its point of equilibrium with accommodation. In fact it is clear that even if early displacements of equilibrium reveal successive clashes of accommodation with new given factors and clashes of assimilation with the schema of the stopping point, on the other hand regulations take a step nearer to the balancing of these two tendencies, since it is these endlessly renewed accommodations which differentiate the initial schema, and since the regulating assimilation serves to ensure a permanent accommodation to every new combination of the experiment. The equilibrium finally reached between assimilation and accommodation thus explains the reversibility of operational grouping, which is at the same time deduction or unlimited assimilations and constantly adaptable to new situations.

CHAPTER EIGHT

Relative Speeds

Before seeing how the grouping of co-displacements is generalized in the case of movements in succession, and in order to end this part of the present work devoted to the qualitative operations fundamental to the conception of speed, we thought it would be useful, in relation to Chapter Five (relative movements) to analyse a problem of relative speeds, i.e. of the co-ordination of two speeds into one single apparent speed. Whereas the operational conception of speed is acquired from the level of concrete operations (stage III) in correlation with the conception of time itself, the composition of two speeds, on the contrary, implies formal thinking, and it is in this way that its study completes those of the previous chapters.

1. Technique and general results

The children are shown a framework fitted with an endless movable belt on which are fixed eight cyclists made of card. A handle allows the speed to be regulated and in particular to be kept constant. Stretched parallel to this belt is a piece of string carrying a doll, representing the observer who counts the bicycles. This doll is stationary at first for fifteen seconds (enough time for the eight cyclists to file past him) and is subsequently set in motion by means of a second handle, which controls the strings: the doll moves for another fifteen seconds (the subjects are asked to check this according to their age), either in the same direction as the cyclists, or in the opposite direction and also at a constant speed, generally less than that of the cyclists.

The subject is asked beforehand to count aloud the line of cyclists passing in front of the doll. Each of them carries a serial number to avoid confusion. This established, the child is asked to forecast how many cyclists the doll will see in fifteen seconds again, when travelling in the same direction as they do. It is understood (this must be made explicit in the previous question) that this concerns only the cyclists passing in front of the doll, hence those passing the doll as it travels in the same direction as themselves, and not cyclists it may see coming from a distance along the road. The question is asked exactly as follows: 'Now the doll is going to travel along like this (direction of the cyclists) for fifteen seconds too. When it was standing still, it saw eight cyclists pass in front of it. When it is travelling along, how many cyclists will pass along beside it, like this (gestures to make this clear): eight again, or more, or less?' When the child has replied, he is asked the reason for his opinion, then the experiment is carried out and he is asked to explain what he has seen. Or we may go on directly to the next question, leaving both explanations to the end: the doll travels in the opposite direction from the cyclists, so how many will it see (once more in fifteen seconds) going past in the opposite direction?

Finally, and this is particularly intended for younger children, an additional question is introduced at a suitable moment to help understanding: a single cyclist sets off at the same time as the doll, and we ask whether it takes more time or less for the doll to reach the cyclist if the doll stands still, if it travels in the same direction as the cyclist or if they move towards each other from opposite directions. After asking this question we return to that of the eight cyclists.

Out of fifty children examined thirty-five boys and fifteen girls (between 5; 6 and 13 years), we were able to distinguish the following four stages. During stage I, the child cannot answer the question of the time needed for the doll and the single cyclist to meet, and gives random answers to the problems relating to the eight cyclists. During stage II (articulated intuition) the question of the single cyclist is solved, while that of the eight cyclists leads to a relatively uniform forecast: the doll will see just as many, whether it stands still, travels in the same direction as the cyclists, or they move towards each other from opposite directions. Hence there is no relativity of speeds (from 6 years to 7; 6 approximately on average 6; 6) In the course of stage III (concrete operations) the subject does not manage to deduce the results beforehand, but in retrospect he explains the relations involved quite correctly (which was not possible in the course of the first two stages, even after the experiment). This stage III extends from 8 years to 11; 4, with an average age of 9; 10. Finally, the fourth stage (from 10; 6 or 11 years: formal operations) produces correct deductions prior to the experiment and often excellent explanations of the relativity of speed.

It is of course possible to distinguish in addition two sub-stages in stage III, according to whether the correct answer is discovered earlier or later after some trial and error, and two sub-stages in stage IV according to the level of the hypothetico-deductive explanation.

2. The first and second stages: No relativity of speeds

Naturally at the level where absolute speeds are not yet understood operationally, but are conceived in terms of perceptual overtaking alone, and where time is not yet dissociated from spatial succession, there could be no understanding of the relativity of speeds. In the course of stage I the subject does not even solve the question of the single cyclist and the moving observer:

NAP (6; 0) counts six cyclists passing in front of the stationary doll: And if the doll goes in the same direction as they do, like that (gesture), how many cycles will go past it, more or less, or the same number? It will see more cycles, because sometimes you do see more, and sometimes less. Look at the doll here, the cyclist sets off from over here to come up to it. Did he take quite a little time? *Yes.* Now the doll starts to go towards him. Will it take more time than before, or less, for them to meet? *Same.* And now the doll is going the other way. You see, they're starting off and the cyclist will catch up with the doll. Will it take more time or less than when the doll stays there? *The same.* Why? . . . And now if the doll goes towards the cyclist? *Longer.* Why? *Because the doll is running.*

Mad (6; 6) eight cyclists: *The same.* Why? *Because that's how many there are.* Single cyclist: *The same.*

Responses to the problem of the eight cyclists are of little interest as long as the question of the single cyclist is not solved. As for this question, it is striking to see the difficulty in understanding that the times are modified when the speeds are not. In the course of stage II on the contrary, the latter question is solved, without the problem of the eight cyclists being any nearer a solution.

Ber (6; 8). The stationary spectator sees five cyclists passing. And if it goes in the same direction (gesture) at the same time? *It will see more of them, because it does not move as quickly as the cyclists.* And if they move towards each other, like that (gesture), will the doll see five cycles as before, or more or less? *About the same.*

Iac (7; 6). The doll standing still sees six cyclists: And if it goes in the same direction will it see more or less? *The same.* (Experiment 4). Was that the same? *No, less.* Why? *Because the doll was looking straight in front and didn't see those who were behind.* And now moving towards them: when it stood still, it saw six, and then four when it went that way, will it see more cycles or less if it goes to meet them? *It will see four.* Why? *Because it's back at the same place (=same starting point))and it's going along the same distance.* (Experiment 7). *It's because the cyclists were quicker.* Not at all. I was turning this at the same speed. *Then it's because the doll went slower.* No, no, it was the same. So why did it see more of them?

Watch, now the doll is waiting for the cyclist. How long

did it take for them to pass each other? *One minute.* Now,
the doll is going that way (same direction). Will the cyclist
take more time or less than before to catch up on it? *More
time because the cyclist has a longer distance to go.* And now
they're going towards each other. More time or less? *Less
because there's a shorter distance to go.* Very good. Now can
you explain to me why the doll sees more cycles when it goes
that way (to meet them) and less when it goes that way
(same direction)? *It's because there (same way) it can only
see the cycles which are in front (=with its back to those
who are coming) and there as well (=face to face).* Iac therefore does not see the relationship of speeds or movements
and explains the differences by the position of the doll.

PIE (7; 9). Stationary; 4: (Same direction)? *It will see the
same number.* (Experiment 3). Why one less? And if it goes
to meet them? *The same.* (Experiment 5). Perhaps the bit of
string is longer. (This is checked and we start again). *It will
be the same: 4.* (Experiment 5). Why? . . . The experiment
of the single cyclist is made and Pie answers like Iac. Returning to four cyclists he again expects the same thing in both
directions.

NEC (7; 10). In both directions: *It will see the same number as when it was standing still, because the cyclists are
going at the same speed.* No explanation after the experiment
nor after correctly forecasting in relation to the single cyclist.

It is clear that these subjects do not 'compose' the
movements involved or their speeds. One of the most
common answers is that of Iac and Pie: the doll will see
the same number of cyclists 'because it is going along the
same distance', hence Pie's explanation after observing
that it saw more: 'maybe the distance. . . . is longer'. Thus
the subject is concerned only with the absolute length of
the doll's path and not at all with its length relative to the
movement of the cyclists over the same period. Another
frequent response is that of Nec: if the cyclists' speed
remains the same, the doll will see the same number, as if
their speed were not to be composed with the doll's speed.
Ber seems to be thinking of composition when he says 'the
doll does not go so quickly as the cyclists' (in the same

direction), he does not reverse his reasoning when the doll travels towards the cycles, and so his intuition is merely articulated and not operational. Likewise Iac, after the experiment is made, cannot find any explanation other than to suppose an increase or a diminution in the absolute speeds, but once again without relative composition.

In short, as in the problem of relative movements (Chapter Five) of which the present problem is only a variation with the introduction of different speeds, the child only takes one of the movements or one of the points of view into consideration at a time: the observer covers the same distance in both directions or the cyclists go at the same speed in all three situations, so the same number of cyclists will pass by. The subject therefore does not understand that it is the addition or the subtraction of the movements and their speeds which alone decides the result. On the other hand, the child perfectly grasps that the single cyclist will meet the observer in a longer or shorter time, according to whether the doll goes farther away, stands still, or comes closer, because then the distance increases or diminishes. But simple intuitive anticipation of the displacements is enough for the solution of this problem. On the contrary, in the case of four to eight cyclists the question is not whether they will meet the observer in more or less time; what is required is the number of cyclists meeting or overtaking the doll, to be deduced from the times and distances, hence from a composition of the speeds. This is why, even after solving the temporal problem of the single cyclist the child of this level cannot apply the result to the problems of the speeds: Hence Iac, directly after saying of the single cyclist 'he has a longer (or shorter) road to go' merely repeats this in the case of the group of cyclists.

Now, this egocentric non-relativity will continue to some extent during the following stage, with the difference that the experiments conducted in front of the child will lead him to discover the explanation of the phenomenon more or less completely.

3. The third stage: Concrete operations: Relations under-stood after experiment, which is gradually anticipated

Concrete operations are not enough to solve the problem of relative speeds any more than for that discussed in Chapter Five. Nonetheless the child does sometimes antic-ipate certain of the relationships involved, from the age of 8 to 9 years, in particular with movements in the same direction rather than with movements in contrary direc-tions. But he is not able to foresee everything. On the other hand, after the experiment, and often just after the questions asked about the single cyclist, the subject man-ages to understand the whole thing. Here are some exam-ples, starting with an intermediate case between stages II and III:

SIM (8; 10). *Same direction. It will not see many of them. Why? Because it moves just a short way.* (Experiment). *Yes, because it moved this little distance, and some of them are still behind it.* (Opposite directions). *It will see the same number as before (as in the same directions), because it travels the same distance* (he measures with his hand) *it's the same length.* (Experiment). *It's difficult. I don't understand why it sees more of them.* (Single cyclist in opposite direc-tion). *Less time to reach other because they have a shorter way to go.* Then tell me why the doll sees more of them when there are a lot of cyclists and it moves towards them? . . .

REG (9; 1). Standing still: *Six.* Same direction: *It will see less cyclists than before, because it is travelling along with them and it goes more slowly.* (Experiment). *Yes, if it goes forwards it sees less of them. Why? . . .* (Opposite direc-tions). *It will see the same number, no less. Why? Because it's going in this direction.* (Experiment). *It sees more of them! Why? Because it is going this way.*

Single cyclist. Same direction: *It will take longer for them to meet.* (Opposite directions). *Less time. And when it goes towards all the cyclists? It sees more cyclists because they go faster. Am I turning the handle any quicker? No, but they take a shorter time.*

LEO (9; 3). Same direction: More, no, less, because if it goes forwards along with the cyclists, it will always see the same ones (Experiment). Yes, it was going over that way: it cannot see them all (Experiment with one only). Oh, yes, the cyclist has a longer distance to go. Well, can you tell me why now? So long as the doll is going forwards, there are some of them who stay behind. (Opposite directions). It will see the same number: when it is going forwards it sees the same as when it stands still. Sure? No, it will see more of them, because they are going the same distance, but it sees more of them because it always sees more coming. Before (standing still) it saw them coming gradually (hence difference in the apparent speeds) (Experiment with one only). Less time, because there is a shorter way to go. Well then? The doll travelled a longer distance because it goes towards them and there are always more coming.

CHOT (10; 2). Same direction: It will see the same number passing, since it is going in the same direction as they are. (Experiment). Oh, it sees less of them because it only sees those who pass in front of it. And now if it goes towards them? (Long hesitation). I don't know. (Experiment). It sees more of them because it goes to meet them, because they are coming along (while it is moving forwards).

LIN (10; 9). Same direction: Same thing. (Experiment). No, it sees fewer of them, because it goes forward slowly, and as the doll is the starting point, the others will not be able to make a complete circuit (=come back to it). (Opposite directions). It will see more of them. Why? . . . (Experiment with one only). At the end of one minute, it will not have reached the doll again, because it is already farther on (= same direction). In the opposite direction, it'll be less than one minute and the distance will be shorter. And with all the others? Yes, it's the same thing.

SOUR (11; 0). Same direction: It will see more of them. Sure? Yes. (Experiment). No, two less than before. That's because the cyclists are not going past so quickly: it sees fewer cyclists ahead because it is moving too. (Single cyclist). The doll is moving forwards, so that cyclist takes longer to catch up with it. (Opposite directions with all the cyclists, before the experiment). It will see more of them because they will take less time to come up to him.

From these few examples representing the different steps in stage III (from 8 to 10 years on average) two facts emerge clearly. The first is that none of these subjects manages to foresee what will happen and above all none finds the correct explanation before being questioned on the problem of the times or distances needed for a single cyclist to meet the observer, or before there has been an opportunity for experimental observation of one of the results which have to be forecast in the case of the eight cyclists. There is no doubt that some, like Sim, Reg, and to some extent Leo, foresee, but it is an intuitive anticipation, with no generalization in relation to travelling in contrary directions. This difficulty over explanation, and even over general anticipation of the relations involved, in the case of children who, otherwise, have an operational conception of simple speeds, is enough to show that the problem of relative speeds implies the appearance of a formal mechanism, and the reason will emerge when studying stage IV.

Conversely, a clear indication of the progress of this stage III beyond stage II is that these same children can construct the correct explanation and even accurately forecast the results of the remaining experiments as soon as they have actually observed the result of one of the earlier experiments or have answered the question of the single cyclist. In both cases, the impression is given that a latent operational mechanism is released on contact with the concrete given factors. More accurately, the results of the finished experiment are organized by means of concrete operations which are then generalized to the point where they imitate formal operations, which could not be used in advance. Only Sim (intermediate case between stages II and III) does not achieve this generalization. Conversely, all the rest adopt the correct explanation: movements in opposite directions lead to a greater number of encounters 'because there are always more coming' (Leo, Chot, etc.) and even 'because they will take less time to reach to him', says Sour. This last subject, after predicting an incorrect result, reaches the fourth stage in explanations, even saying, in the case of travel in the same direction 'the cyclists are not going by so quickly: it sees fewer of them going past, because it is moving along as well', which is the expression of relativity as such.

In short, this stage III reveals the gradual discovery of the correct answer by trial and error and a succession of approximations, but still without direct deduction. Finally, in some exceptional cases (even amongst the youngest subjects of this stage) it is interesting to observe a kind of rational intuition which anticipates what this deduction will be, though explanation is not possible. Thus they forsee the results, but without being able to give any explanation for them.

Ios (7; 6). Same direction: *It will see fewer of them.* Why? ... (Experiment). *That's right.* Why? ... (Opposite directions). *It will see more of them.* Why? ...

Mon (8; 0). Same direction: *Fewer.* Why? ... (Opposite directions). *It will see more of them.* Why? *Because the cycles come along.* So why does it see more of them then? ...

Reactions of this kind, too numerous to be a matter of chance, provide a new example of the time-lag sometimes existing between prediction of phenomena and their explanation, thus introducing stage IV.

4. The fourth stage: General solution of the problem by formal operations

The special feature of reactions in stage IV is not only that the facts lead to correct prediction, but they are also fully explained before the experiment. Here are some examples, beginning with an intermediate case interesting because of the release of the formal mechanism:

Net (11; 6). (Same way): *It will see fewer of them, because the cyclists go fast and it is going forward as well.* (Experiment). *Yes, it goes slower than they do, and because it is going forwards at the same time as they are it goes quite a long way.* (Opposite directions). *It will see less of them as well, it's the same thing as before* (=same direction) *but just* the opposite way. Oh, no, it should be 'more' that it sees because it is going in the other direction. There's something going forwards there and something moving back there: the cyclists don't have so far to go.

PAN (9; 8). (Same way): It will see less of them, because it will be following them, and will not see so many of them pass. (Opposite way). It will see more of them. It's going twice as fast because the cyclists are going the opposite way. It sees them passing more quickly. Why? Because when a car comes towards us, we see it going past more quickly. The doll and the cyclists are each doing part of the distance, so it goes faster.

TER (10; 4). (Same way). It will see fewer of them. The cyclists take longer to catch up on the doll. (Opposite way). It will see more than at first. When it stands still, the cyclists take longer to come up. When it is moving, they take less time, because they have to come up. When it is moving, they take less time because they have a shorter way to go. Why? The doll does that distance instead of them.

POL (10; 3). Same way: It will see fewer of them, because it goes forward at the same time. If it goes at the same speed as the cyclists it will only see one of them. It depends on the speed of the doll. And with opposite directions: It will see more of them. When it goes towards them, the cyclists can go past quicker: they have a shorter way to go to catch up with him.

CHAP (11; 0). Same way: Less. Since it is moving forwards, the cyclists will not catch up with him so quickly. Opposite way: It will see more than when it stood still, because it is going towards them. It's the same as if the cyclists were going faster. Do they really go faster? No, just the same speed, but they only seem to go faster.

SAUT (12; 5). Same way: Fewer: it goes forwards and the cyclists will not catch up on it so quickly. Other way: More. It's as if the cyclists were going faster: they take less time to reach it.

NAR (12; 7). Same way: It will not see so many: the cyclists will take longer to reach it. Other way: It will see more than *before: it will be the opposite. It is nearer the cyclists: when the doll moves, the cyclists come along faster.*

BAI (13; 0). Same way: *Fewer, because they have to catch up on it, and it is going forwards.* Other way: *More, because the cyclists will pass more quickly in front of him. In fact they are going at the same speed, but they gain more ground.*

We were careful to quote quite a number of these replies from children between 9; 8 and 13; 0 years, to show that the facts are by no means exaggerated in speaking of a spontaneous qualitative composition of movements at the age when formal operations begin, and of a very keen understanding of the relativity of speeds composed in this way.

This composition is already emerging in Net's intermediate response: after predicting that movement of observer and cyclists in contrary directions gives the same results as movements in the same direction, Net cries: 'Oh, no, there's something going forwards there, and something moving back there'. . . . i.e. growing awareness of a reversible operational mechanism. In Pan's case operations are already clarified: 'the doll goes twice as fast, because, the cyclists go the opposite way' from the observer, hence the speeds are added.

And to make it quite clear that this additive composition by no means alters the absolute speeds composed with one another, Pan states that this result is relative to the observer's point of view: 'he sees them passing quicker. When a car passes us in the opposite direction we see it going by quicker.' Ter also summarizes this relative composition by saying that the cyclists take less time to meet the doll moving towards them because the 'doll does that distance instead of them'. Pol generalizes from the hypothesis 'it depends on the speed of the doll': moving at the same speed and in the same direction as the cyclists it will see only one etc., and in the opposite direction it will see more cyclists in that they will have a shorter way to go. Chap formulates this relativity in a striking way by saying that if 'the doll moves towards them, it is the same as if the cyclists were going faster', and he states that the speed in this case is an apparent one ('they only seem to go faster') overlaying the absolute speed ('they travel at the same speed all the time'). Saut continues with this formulation 'It's the same as if the cyclists were going faster: they take less time . . . etc'., and Nar too ('when the doll moves, the cyclists reach it faster . . .') as well as Bai ('they will travel past quicker: in fact they are going at the same speed, but they gain more ground').

The problems raised by responses in this last stage are thus as follows: what constitutes this new operation of composition of speeds overlaid by these subjects upon the operations which at about 8 years of age form the whole concept of speed (Co-displacement, with generalization of overtaking and correlation of time with distances covered) and why does it emerge only at the formal level?

The second point is clear: just as with relative movements, from which the present experiment differs only by the introduction of dissimilar speeds, solution of the problem implies co-ordination of two distinct systems into a single simultaneous whole. Of the two speeds involved, that of the doll and that of the cyclists, each one in fact forms a separate system. If it were only necessary to compare these two speeds in order to conclude that the cyclists go quicker than the moving doll, there would not be two systems to consider, but only one, characterized by synchronous times and unequal distances: hence the problem would simply require concrete operations. But on the contrary while being kept quite distinct the two speeds have to be composed to make a third such that the number of cyclists overtaking the doll or moving past it from the opposite direction is diminished or increased. Now, this composition implies the ability to think separately of each of the two speeds as though of two different systems, instead of merging them into a single comparison, and yet to co-ordinate them into a simultaneous whole. This co-ordination acting upon two systems simultaneously, i.e. this operation performed upon other operations, is what defines formal thinking, as has already been seen in Chapters Four and Five (see Chapter Four, end of §5). From this very fact the form of the new operation achieved by subjects of stage IV becomes clear as compared with the achievement at stage III. If the observer is stationary, the cyclists file past at a given speed V_1 defined as the number of encounters, X, in the time T_1. If the doll moves towards the cyclists, the same number X will go past in a shorter time T_2 (hence $T_2 < T_1$) and the faster the doll moves the shorter it is. Consequently in the time T_1, $X + N$ cyclists will go past, i.e. it will see them pass at a greater speed. It may also be said that if D is the distance covered by the X cyclists in the time T_1 when the observer is stationary, the speed of the cyclists if then D/T_1 while if the doll goes towards them it becomes D/T_2, where $T_2 < T_1$. Conversely if the doll goes in the same direction as the cyclists at a speed less than theirs, a time $T_3 > T_1$ will be needed for X cyclists to pass. Hence in T_1 it will only see $X - N$ cyclists and their speed will appear less to him: it is only D/T_3. The new operation thus rests on the distinction between the absolute speed (i.e. in relation to a stationary observer) D/T_1, and the relative speeds (i.e. seen by a mobile observer) D/T_2 or D/T_3 or, in terms of overtaking, on the distinction between the absolute speed X in T_1 and the relative speeds $X - N$ in T_1.

PART 4

The Quantification of Speed

The operations constituting speed are of a qualitative nature: if movement is above all a change of order (displacement as opposed to placing), speed results from a comparison between two movements (co-displacements) and the basic intuition of overtaking is thus translated operationally by a reversal of the order of the two moving objects being compared.

But just as the intervals between the starting and finishing points of movements can be quantified, in space and in time, in the form of distances covered and durations, so also the qualitative relationships of co-displacements may be translated in the quantitative form $V = D/T$. This quantification in turn may appear in a purely extensive form (proportions between two distances covered and two durations), or in a metrical form. It is these two kinds of operation, each now mathematical and not merely logical or infra-logical, which still have to be examined in this fourth and final part.

CHAPTER NINE

Speeds of Movements in Succession Travelling Unequal Distances in Unequal Times

In the course of Chapter Seven it was shown how, towards 7 to 8 years, an accurate conception was formed of speed to the extent that concrete operations were involved: different distances travelled in equal times or equal lengths in unequal times, the movements to be compared being always wholly or partly perceived at the same time. But two questions remain to be discussed, which immediately follow on from the foregoing ones. What happens when, instead of perceiving both movements at the same time, the child can then only see them one after the other (except of course by recording the given factors in drawing or writing): will the need for this comparison in succession which is no longer directly perceptual simply delay the solution, by requiring more work of the child, or will it cause the reappearance of methods of reasoning already outgrown on the preceding level? On the other hand, how skilful will the child be in comparing unequal distances covered in unequal times? In other words what will be the structure of the extensive operations (proportion) and the metrical operations necessary in solving these new problems?

The technique adopted is extremely simple. A moving object starting off at right angles to a base line is made to travel along a rectilinear path and the journey is timed with a stop watch. The path followed is then sketched and beside this straight line is recorded the number of seconds read off by the child, e.g. 2. This is repeated with another moving object, travelling along a parallel straight line, e.g. in four seconds, and the subject is simply asked whether these two objects travelled at the same speed or if one went harder than the other.

The results obtained were very clear. In the course of stage III, which as we saw (in Chapter Seven) is characterized by understanding of speed on the level of concrete operations, the child is still, at least during sub-stage IIIa, unable to compare the speeds of movements in succession, and this is so even when their times are equal (though no longer synchronous) over unequal distances, or their distances are equal in unequal times: and then the subject returns to, or rather persists in, difficulties which are completely overcome when the movements to be compared are perceived entirely or partly at the same time. Then of course he also fails to understand differences of speed where times and spaces are unequal, even with ratios as simple as 2 to 1. It is only where the disproportion is great that he momentarily gives the correct answer, due simply to intuitive regulations. In the course of sub-stage IIIb conversely, the subject succeeds in questions on equal times and unequal spaces (or vice versa) but still fails where both times and spaces are unequal. More accurately, a continuous series of cases is found each slightly more advanced than the last, and the most advanced of these finally understand the ratio of 2 to 1 though failing to generalize to every ratio, even while they already possess an implicit feeling for proportion. In the course of sub-stage IVa, the child manages to solve the problems by trial and error though formal operations are already implied, and in sub-stage IVb all problems asked are solved systematically, apart from mistakes in calculation.

1. Difficulties with equal distances and unequal times or vice versa, when movements are in succession, and inability to establish proportions where times and distances are both unequal.

Sub-stage IIIa

The operational conception of speed is acquired in stage III, even in the mathematical form of a ratio between time and distance covered provided the movements compared are wholly or partly simultaneous. When movements are in succession, the most basic mistakes reappear regularly:

GUED (7; 11). *Journeys in succession, 4 cms. in four seconds and 5 cms. in four seconds: Did they take the same time?* Yes. *And did they cover the same ground?* No, the second one went farther. *Did they go at the same speed or did one go quicker than the other?* Both the same. *But why did that one get farther ahead?* Because it took bigger steps.

Same distances (4 cms.) in four and three seconds: The second one (three seconds) goes more slowly than the other. *And the distances?* They are the same. *And did they take the same time?* No, the second one took less. *So then which one goes faster?* The one taking four seconds. *Why?* Because it travelled faster. *Which one gets there in the shorter time?* The one that took three seconds. *And which one was going harder?* The one that took four seconds. *Is what I'm asking you easy or hard?* Easy.

Same times (two seconds) with paths of 3 and 5 cms. Do they go the same distance? No, the second goes farther. *Do they take the same time?* Yes. *Does one of them go faster?* Yes (hesitates) . . . the one which got farther ahead. *Why was it faster?* Maybe that's the reason why. *Two cms. in one second and 4 cms. in two seconds:* The one taking two seconds goes faster because it went a longer distance. *Sure?* That one (one second) goes faster because it only goes a little way (and takes less time).

Two cms. in one second and 7 cms. in two seconds: The one taking one second goes faster. *Did one of them go harder than the other?* No, both the same. *Same response with 4 cms. in one second and 5 cms. in two seconds.* Both the same speed. *And there (differences in times)?* Same thing again.

GEO (7; 9). *Same distances in two seconds and three seconds: Same distances?* Yes. *Same times?* No, two seconds and three seconds. *Does one of them go faster than the other?* The one in three seconds. *Why is it faster?* Because it took more seconds. *How long does it take you to come here from home?* Quarter of an hour. *And if you run, does it take more time, or less?* Less. *And there, does one of them go faster?* The one doing three seconds. *Why?* It ran.

Four cms. and 7 cms. in four seconds: The second one

goes faster, it hurried and ran. Two cms. in one second and
4 cms. in two seconds: *The second one went faster*. Why? *It
went a longer distance*. Sure? *Not so quick*. Why? *Because it
took two seconds*. It takes longer? *Yes, and it goes farther*.
What can you say about 1 and 2? *It's double*. And their
paths, look and see if they're double. *Yes*. Then does one of
them go faster than the other or not? *Yes, the one in two
seconds goes faster*. Why? *Because it took longer and went
farther*. Watch (they are made to set off together and when
the first one stops the other continues at the same speed).
They were side by side. When they were travelling together
did one go faster than the other? *No*. And altogether then
did one go quicker than the other? *Yes, the one which went
farther went faster*. We then return to movements in succession. Two cms. in one second and 3 cms. in two seconds:
The second goes faster. Why? . . . Are you sure or not? *Not
very*.

Four cms. in one second and 5 cms. in two seconds: *The
first one goes faster*. Why? *Because it almost caught up with
the second one, and it did that in one second*. (4 cms. in one
second and 7 cms. in two seconds) *The second one goes
faster because it goes farther* (2 cms. in one second and 6
cms. in two seconds) *The first one goes faster, no, the second*. Why? *Because it did a long distance and the first one
went a short way*. And if the second one does that (5 cms.
in three seconds) and the first one that (2 cms. in one second)? *The second one goes faster again*.

And like that (3 cms. in one second and 6 cms. in two
seconds)? *One of them does go quicker, but I don't know
which one*. Is it not possible that they were both going at
the same speed? *No, it's the second one that goes faster, because it goes farther. Oh, no, it's the first one because it
takes less time*. Which one goes farther? *It's the second one
which goes faster*. Which one takes longer? *No, it's the first
one which goes harder*.

STU (8; 7). Four cms. in five seconds and 4 cms. in four
seconds: *The second one goes faster. No, both the same*.

(Five cms. in four seconds and 6 cms. in four seconds)?
The second one went a long way. So? *It took longer*. How
much? *Four seconds*. And the other one? *Same*. Which one
goes quicker? *The first one, because it goes a shorter distance*.
But the time? *The second one took a longer time*. Why? *No,
the same time*. So then? *The second one goes quicker because*

*it travels a longer road. Why did you get mixed up? I thought
the first one went quicker. And now what do you think?
Both the same speed.*

Proportions: complete lack of understanding,

JACK (8; 8). Six cms. in five seconds and 6 cms. in three seconds: *The second one goes slower. Why? Shorter time. So
then? It is not going so hard.* How long does it take you to
go home from here? *Ten minutes.* And when you run? *Less
time.* And there (new attempt). Which one takes less time?
The second one. And which one goes faster? *The first one*
(simultaneousness test, which becomes Q 1a as in Chapter
Seven, but Jack is only allowed to see the starting and finishing points). *The second one is quicker. Why? Because it
takes less time.*

Four cms. in one second and 5 cms. in two seconds: Which
one went farther? *The second one.* And which took less time?
The first one. Which one travelled faster? *The second one.
Why? It went farther.* But in a longer or a shorter time? *In
a longer time.* Then was it faster or slower. *It was faster because it went farther.*

FLAC (9; 0). Five cms. in five seconds and 5 cms. in 5½
seconds: *The one in 5½ seconds goes faster, because that's
more than five.* And like this (4 cms. in six seconds and 4
cms. in five seconds)? *The one in six seconds was faster because six is more than five.* And now (5 cms. in ten seconds
and five seconds)? *The one in ten seconds is quicker.*

Watch: 6 cms. in five seconds and 7 cms. in five seconds?
The second one goes faster because it is farther.

And like this (2 cms. in two seconds and 4 cms. in four
seconds)? *The first one goes quicker. Why? It's less time.*
And the distance? *Short.* Does one of the two go harder?
*Yes, the second one went harder, because it went a long dis-
tance.*

We return to the first question: 5 cms. in five seconds and
ten seconds: *The first one was faster. Why? It was less time.*
And this? (5 cms. in five seconds and six seconds) *The one
in five seconds again.*

Returning to proportions: 2 cms. in two seconds and 3
cms. in three seconds: *The first one was faster, because it was
a shorter time.* And like this (3 cms. in one second and 4
cms. in two seconds)? *The first one goes faster.* (3 cms. in
one second and 8 cms. in two seconds)? *The first one goes*

*faster. (3 cms. in one second and 12 cms. in two seconds)?
The second one goes harder because it goes farther.*

BER (9; 6). Five cms. in five seconds and in six seconds:
*This one in five seconds goes quicker because it takes less
time.* Fine, and (5 and 6 cms in five seconds)? *They both
go at the same speed, because both took five seconds.* Does
one of them go farther? *Yes, the second one.* Then does one
of them go faster? *No, both the same.* Which of them does
not go so far? *The first one.* Which one goes harder? *Both
the same.* And like this (5 cms. and 15 cms. in five seconds)?
The second one goes quicker, because it goes a long distance.
(5 cms. and 7 cms. in five seconds)? *Both go at the same
speed, because both do five seconds.*

(Two cms. in two seconds and 4 cms. in four seconds)?
*The second one went farther: it was faster, and went harder
because it took more seconds. The one in two seconds was
not going so hard because it took only two seconds.* Where
would it get to if it did another two seconds? (Ber draws a
line like the one for the first two seconds and notes that the
end coincides with the end of the line 4 cms. long). Well?
Both went at the same speed and did the same distance. And
before? *Before, it was the one going four seconds which was
going faster.*

(Four cms. in two seconds and 5 cms. in six seconds)?
*The one doing six seconds goes quicker because it took six
seconds.* Which one travelled hardest? *The second one.*

Reading these answers the impression given is that these
are reactions typical of the first stage studied in Chapter
Seven, or stage II in some cases, but particularly of stage
I, in the course of which time, space and speed are still
completely intermingled. And, in actual fact, these are the
same responses, with only one difference, in addition to
the contrasting ages (7 to 9 years, instead of 5 to 7 years),
which is that the movements involved are no longer perceived simultaneously, but in succession. In fact, when
these same subjects are asked Q 1 to 4, 1a and 2a, from
Chapter Seven, they solve them with no difficulty (see, e.g.
Jack on problem 1a), because it is then simply a question
of constructing a single 'field' by means of 'concrete operations', making the given perceptual factors reversible and

logical. But when the same movement (equal times and unequal distances, or vice versa) are made in succession, there is no longer any question of organizing given movements actually within one single field of perception, (even if the ends alone are visible, cf. Chapter Six, Section I), but movements which have been perceived and structured separately and which are subsequently represented only by symbols consisting of lines for the paths covered and figures for the times taken. By that very fact, a new sphere of operations is now introduced: the co-ordination of two systems or fields, which in reality were in succession, into a single whole, which is sumultaneous only in the mind's eye. And this new sphere requires the construction of new operations: formal or hypothetico-deductive operations. Now in their structure these formal operations are nothing other than concrete operations transposed in terms of propositions, i.e. integrating concrete classes and relations into a system of implications and incompatibilities expressed by propositions. Formal operations are thus concrete operations transformed into hypotheses or assumptions and related to each other simply by an interplay of implications. Consequently it is natural that there should be a time-lag between the same operations, or what seem to be the same operations, some being concrete, in the case of simultaneous movements, and the others hypothetico-deductive in the case of movements in succession: these are indeed the same movements, but evaluated in retrospect they imply a reconstruction of the relationships of time and space, which can therefore only be formal, and no longer concrete or real. Hence the time-lag (horizontal or belonging to the understanding) of one to two years or even more, which has just been observed in the facts.

A time-lag of this kind is so surprising, at first sight, that we were anxious to verify it. In addition to the usual subjects, about twenty subjects from 7 to 8 years old were selectively questioned on certain of the foregoing problems, which in each instance were asked in two ways, (1) on seeing simultaneous movements, and the other (2) on seeing movements in succession. The great majority of these cases (more than three-quarters) are successful with questions of type I and fail with questions of type II (the order must of course be varied I to II, and II to I):

Erd (7; 8). II: (4 cms. in five seconds and in six seconds)? *The one in six seconds went faster. Why? Because it took six seconds.* I: (Same distance setting off in succession)? *That one went faster.* (correct) Why? *Because the other one went slower, it took a longer time.*

Mar (7; 2). II: paths 5 cms. in five seconds and in four seconds: *The one in five seconds was faster. Why? Because it went a longer distance. Is that true? No, the same path. Then? They went at the same speed. But in the same time? No. Well? It makes no difference.*

I: Same problem: One object sets off after the other on a path of 5 cms.: *That one is quicker, because it set off after the other one and caught it up* (correct).

II: Same problem: Did one of them go faster than the other? *Yes, the first one* (five seconds) *because it took a longer time. Then did it go quicker than the other? No, because they went the same distance. But did one take a longer time? Yes. Well? Both the same speed.*

II: (Unequal distances both in five seconds). Did one go quicker? *No, neither one was faster because they both finished in the same time.* (=movements in succession but each of five seconds) (I): And like this? (Same problem but simultaneous movements). Does one go faster? *Yes, the one beginning last: it went faster to catch the other one up.* And like this (II: same problem)? *Both at the same speed because they took the same time.* And like that (I: same problem). *That one goes faster: it catches up.*

Gui (7; 6). II: (5 cms. and 6 cms. in five seconds): *The second one goes faster* (correct) *because it goes a longer distance. And this* (5 cms. in four seconds and in five seconds)? *Both the same speed.*

I: Unequal distances in the same time: correct. And this (5 cms. setting off in succession and finished at the same time (correct).

Bac (7; 6). II: Unequal paths in five seconds: *Both the same speed, because they took the same time as well. And that* (5 cms. in four seconds and five seconds)? *The first one was quicker because it took less time* (right).

I: Unequal paths in the same time: *That one was quicker because it finished farther ahead.* (Equal paths in unequal times?) *That one was quicker, because it took less time.*

In the case of other subjects, though less frequently, the solutions of questions relating to movements in succession are influenced, through transfer or generalization, by the propositions stated in regard to simultaneous movements, but in that case the subjects involved are ready to pass from sub-stage IIIa to sub-stage IIIb. Here is an example of this:

Col (7; 2). II: Wrong at first with the same distance travelled first in four seconds then in five seconds: *Same speeds because they are the same distances.* And like that (4 cms. and 5 cms. in five seconds)? *Same speeds.* Why? *They take the same time.*

I: Same problems: correct estimates *because it caught the other one up and? because it went a longer distance.*

II: Now, when we return to II he answers correctly: (Unequal paths in four seconds)? *That one goes quicker, because it goes a longer distance.* And (same road with four and five seconds)? *That one goes harder, because it takes less time.*

Finally, but even more rarely (an exceptional case) one finds children who, while still in stage II for synchronous movements, are successful on some point in the questions on movements in succession and subsequently apply their discovery to simultaneous displacements:

Ande (7; 10). II: Unequal distances in five seconds: *That one goes faster, because the line is longer* (correct). And like that (same distance in four and five seconds)? *The second one went faster because it took five seconds* (wrong).

I: Unequal distances in the same time: *They both go at the same speed* (wrong). And like this (II in succession)? *The first one is faster because it goes a longer distance.* And like that (I: simultaneous)? *Oh, that one there goes faster!*

Ande thus gave one right and one wrong answer at first with movements in succession. Then in I he answered wrongly just where he had been right in II, then, through generalization from the problem of movement in succession, II, he finds the right answer to I.

All things considered it may therefore be said that in the great majority of reactions there is a clear time-lag: the same problem which is easily solved when the movements to be compared are given simultaneously (stage III) gives rise to systematic difficulties when the same movements (with the same distances covered and the same time ratios) are presented in succession. It is therefore clear that the retrospective organization of movements implies other (formal or hypothetico-deductive) operations than does their direct organization (concrete operations). However, proof that these two kinds of operation do in fact have a common structure, is that on this new level one does not find mistakes of an unforeseen type, but exactly the same kind of mistake which occurred in stages I and II on the concrete level.

E.g. with equal distances travelled unequal times, the idea is regularly found that the relation 'more quickly' is equivalent to 'more time' (Gued, Geo, Stu, Jack, Flac, etc.). Yet again the idea is found that two unequal distances may be travelled at the same speed if they are covered in the same times, (Gued, and particularly Stu and Ber). However, it is no longer the fact that the finishing points coincide which misleads these subjects but that the times taken, expressed formally, coincide. Nevertheless, Mar, who no longer makes this mistake on the concrete level, still says of objects moving in succession that they move at the same speed 'because they both finished in the same time'! In short, no differentiation of time and space, of time and speed, and of speed and space, this is the very same confusion as in stages I and II, merely retained on the hypothetico-deductive level in the course of stage III, in the absence of a formal structure permitting extension of concrete operations.

As for the proportions or disproportions between different spaces and different times, children of this level must not, of course, be expected to succeed in solving these problems, since even the simplest questions, in which only one of the factors varies, are still insoluble. It is worth noting however that large disproportions, such as 8 cms. in two seconds, and 2 cms. in one second, give rise to some intuitive success (e.g. Geo) and curiously enough, with less difficulty than simple proportions such as 2 to 1. Conversely, when the disproportions are slight and even, let us repeat, when times and spaces are directly proportional (e.g. 2 cms. in two seconds and 4 cms. in four seconds), the subject does not manage to understand either the equality or the inequality of the speeds: Sometimes he thinks of the time and forgets the distances, sometimes the other way about. Ber's case is very unusual in this respect. This child judges that 4 cms. in four seconds gives a greater speed than 2 cms. in two seconds. However, he manages perfectly well to draw the path of the object which stopped at 2 cms. as if it were to continue to 4 cms.: he then infers equality, but only in the case of 4 and 4, and continues to believe as before that 2 cms. in two seconds is less than 4 cms. in 4 seconds!

2. Immediate success with speeds over equal distances in unequal times, or vice versa, and progressively with times and spaces both unequal

Sub-stage IIIb

The subjects of this second sub-stage no longer experience difficulty in comparing speeds when either times or distances are equal, but are at first unsuccessful, then gradually succeed, when both factors are unequal (more easily in the case of larger disproportions). Here are a few examples, which we shall try to arrange according to the sequence of their development.

Mos (8; 10) 5 cms. in five seconds and in four seconds: *The second one goes faster. Why? Because it takes less time* (5 cms. and 6 cms in five seconds)? *The second one went harder. The times? Equal. How do you know which one is faster? You can see that from the line.*

Two cms. in three seconds and 4 cms. in six seconds: *The*

second one goes faster. *Why? Because it goes a longer distance.* And the times? *The first one took less time, but it went a shorter distance.* So then? *The first one goes quicker because it took less time.* And if you made it go on at the same speed, how much time would it need to reach the second one? *six seconds.* So? . . . For the bit left over, how much time would it need? *Another three seconds.* So is one of them going faster? *The one doing six seconds goes faster than the other.* Why? *Because it goes farther.*

We start again: 2 cms. in one second and 4 cms. in two seconds: Does one go quicker? *The one which took four seconds.* Why? *Because it goes farther.* (2 cms. in one second for both)? *Both the same.* (We add 2 cms. in one second to the former). *Still the same.* And all this (full drawings again: 2 cms in one second and 4 cms. in two seconds)? *The second one goes quicker.*

MAF (9; 7): 5 cms. and 6 cms. in four seconds: *The second one goes quicker because it went a longer distance and they travelled for the same times.* If the first one had gone up to there (6 cms.)? *They would have gone at the same speed.* And if that one had taken five seconds (for 6 cms. in both cases)? *It would have gone slower.*

4 cms. in four seconds and 8 cms. in eight seconds: *The first one was quicker, because it took less time.* And the distances? *The second one did more.* Did one of the two go harder? *The first one because it took less time.* And the path? *Shorter.*

Watch here on the table (repeating the foregoing problem, but with simultaneous journeys): the first one stops at 4 cms. the other one continues. *They were going at the same speed.* And when you don't see them can you still tell? *Yes.* How do you do it? Would you like to measure with these things (papers, ruler, etc.?) Watch (in succession 1 cm. in one second and 2 cms. in two seconds) . . . Was one of them quicker? *The first one.* Why? *It took one second and the other one took two.* And the path? *The second one did twice the distance.* And the times? *2 and 1.* What is 2 and 1? *That's twice as well.* Does one of them go quicker? *It's the same.* When that one (I) was there (1 cm.) where was the other one after one second? *There* (1 cm.). And at the end of two seconds? *There* (2 cm.). Did it travel quicker there (1 cm.) than there (2 cms)? *The same.* Then do you understand why they both go at the same speed? *I am not very* sure. Then we'll start again on the table (1 cm. in one second and 2 cms. in two seconds, both journeys starting simultaneously). Now? *I saw them together: they went at the same speed.* And like this (same thing but with movements in succession)? *I am not very sure.*

Watch then (a single accelerating movement: 2 cms. in one second, then 4 cms. in one second, then 8 cms. in one second, then 4 cms. in one second, then 8 cms. in one second). Did it go at the same speed? *No, it went faster there (4 cms.) and it was even faster there (8 cms.).* Fine, and now this (2 cms. in one second and 2 cms. following this again in one second). Did it travel at the same speed on both sections? *Yes.* And if we put the other one at the side (hence two paths each of 2 cms. in one second)? *It's the same.* Are you sure? *Yes, sure.* Now, look. Suppose that there's a third one which doesn't stop and does this (4 cms. in two seconds). Is it the same speed as (2 cms. in one second)? *No, that one was quicker.* Why? *It did a longer road!* Maf thus understands as soon as it is broken up, but ceases to understand when it comes to the whole (Cf. Ber in §1).

CHAL (11; 7) finds out by trial and error the solution of ratios 2 to 1, but not of any others: (4 cms. in two seconds and 8 cms. in four seconds)? *The long journey was quicker.* Why? *Because it is longer. And the first one? Shorter, oh, and a shorter time too: they're both the same.* Why? *That's half of that.*

(Six cms. in two seconds and 12 cms. in four seconds)? *The second a bit faster.* Why? *Because it was farther . . . Oh, no, it's the same again.*

(Twelve cms. in three seconds and 11 cms. in two seconds)? *The first one goes faster.* Why? *Because it goes a little bit further than the other. And the times? One minute more.* Well then? *The first one goes faster.*

(Fourteen cms. in three seconds and 13.8 cms. in two seconds)? *Still the first one. But it takes a longer time? Yes, but it goes a longer distance.* And this way (14 cms. in three seconds, and 14 cms. in two seconds)? *The second one went faster, because it took less time.* And this (14 cms. in three seconds and 13.8 cms. in two seconds)? *The second one went faster, because it took less time.* And this (14 cms. in three seconds and 13.8 cms. in two seconds)? *The second one was faster!* Why? *It's practically the same thing.*

(Seven cms. in two seconds and 12 cms. in three seconds)?

It's the one traveling 7 cms. which goes quicker, because that's more than half. Are two seconds half of three seconds? You have to get half of that (12 cms.). So it's the first one which goes faster.

RIC (9; 10) is further advanced than the others for in the question of ratios he immediately relates time and space instead of considering them separately, but without achieving precise relationships: (4 cms. in four seconds and 6 cms. in five seconds)? *Both at the same speed. Why? The difference is one second and the second one was farther. But can you tell which one was quicker? Neither one was, they're both the same.*

And this way (4 cms. in one second and 8 cms. in two seconds)? *The second one was quicker. Why? If you double this little distance, you do not get this length.* And (5 cms. in one second and 8 cms. in two seconds)? *The first one was faster. Why? (Same reasoning).* And (4 cms. in four seconds and 6 cms. in five seconds). *Same speed. Why? Oh, no, the first one was quicker, because if you add the same bit (4 cms. in four seconds), you get a bigger bit than 6 cms.* (So wrong again as at the beginning of the interview).

And this (3 cms. in two seconds and 4 cms. in three seconds)? *The first one goes quicker because if you add a length like that (3 cms. added to 3), that makes . . . Oh, no, same speed!* He thus constantly makes mistakes, but yet with an incipient feeling for proportionality.

FAT (9; 9) 4 cms. in one second and 8 cms. in two seconds: *It's the same speed. This road is double that one.* And this (7 cms. in one second and 8 cms. in two seconds)? *The first one goes faster, because twice this length comes to more than that one.* And now (4 cms. in two seconds and 6 cms. in three)? *Same speed.*

And that (4 cms. in two seconds and 5 cms. in three)? *Twice this length comes to more than that (5 cms.). It's the second one that's faster. But how long? Oh, three seconds. Well then? I don't understand at all.*

And this way (9 cms. in four seconds and 13 cms. in five seconds)? *Equal as well.*

MAT (10; 9) finally, is an instance of the subjects who reach the threshold of stage IV, with a lively feeling for proportions, but without reaching their exact ratio: (4 cms. in two

seconds and 8 cms. in four seconds)? *Same speed, because
the first one is half the other.* And if (>8 cms. in four seconds)? *It would have been quicker.* And if (>4 cms. in two
seconds)? *Again, it would be quicker.*

(Seven cms. in four seconds and 10 cms. in six seconds)?
The second one goes faster because it goes farther. But it
takes longer? *Yes, but it goes farther.* Well then? *Wait a bit,
the first one goes faster, no, the second one.* Why? *Because
it goes quicker in proportion.* How can you be sure? *By doing
it again* (he repeats the journeys and tries to compare the
movements in succession). *No, by measuring* (he records 7
cms. on one bit of paper and 10 cms. on another without
knowing what to do next). And now? *In any case it's right.*
Where did you hear the word 'proportion'? *Everywhere.* At
school? *No* (true: has not yet begun the subject).

And this (4 cms. in two seconds and 5 cms. in three seconds)? *The first one is quicker.* Why? *You can see it* (looks
at the drawings of the paths).

The gradual construction of proportions which may be
observed in subjects at this stage is very instructive.

The first observation is that provided the times are
equal and distances unequal, or vice versa, there is no
longer any difficulty for the child: hence after the time-lag
characterizing sub-stage IIIa, they have managed to transfer the operations of Chapter Seven on to the formal level.
But this is only a first step, due to the fact that the content
of these operations is already familiar, thanks to the un-
derlying concrete constructions. On the other hand, as
soon as unequal times and spaces are involved, even if the
ratios remain fixed and maintain a constant speed
$v=d^1/t_1=d_2/t_2 \ldots$ etc., the problem becomes more complicated. The child is unsuccessful at the very outset of the
new construction, because he thinks either of the times, or
of the distances, in a kind of alternating intellectual centration, without being able to unite them in a single ratio.
The cases of Mos and Maf are especially instructive in this
respect: these subjects succeed in understanding the equality of the speeds as soon as the double trajectory is halved,
but they are wrong again when the two halves are re-
united, as if total values possessed special qualities from
the viewpoint of attention of centration of judgment. Chal

begins similarly, but finally discovers their synthesis, while in the case of disproportions he is still quite unable to grasp the dual relationship. Ric and Fat are successful from the first with ratios of 2 to 1 but not with any others, though they do show a kind of implicit feeling for proportionality. Finally, Mat formulates this feeling explicitly, but still without discovering the correct relationships though achieving intuitions which are broadly correct. Each of these steps, as well as this final discovery of proportion, raises interesting problems, which will be discussed at the end of this chapter.

3. The fourth stage: The construction of accurate proportions

In stage IV extensive construction and even measurement of proportional ratios are finally reached. However two sub-stages must be distinguished: sub-stage IVa, during which this construction is still accompanied by mistakes and uncertainties, and sub-stage IVb, in the course of which a systematic method is found. Sub-stage IVa, however, already shows understanding of proportions to the extent that they are operations: it is the technique followed which is not yet developed. Here are some examples beginning with an intermediate case between IIIb and IVa:

BURG (9; 7) (4 cms. in two seconds and 8 cms. in four seconds)? *Both the same speed. Why? Because this distance is half of that one.* And this third one (12 cms. in six seconds)? *It was slower, because this is not half of that one: it is not double the distance* (8 cms.) *and double the time* (four seconds). Where was it at two seconds? *Here* (right). And at four seconds? *Oh, yes, it is the same speed.*

(Two cms. in four seconds and 6 cms. in 8 seconds)? *The second one is faster because it is not a half* (2 cms. and 6 cms.). And that (2 cms. in two seconds and 3½ cms. in three seconds)? *The first one goes more slowly and that* (2 cms. in one second and 7½ cms. in four seconds)? *Same, no, the first one is quicker, because the second one did not reach there* (2 cms.) *in one second* (points to it without measuring).

Flei (9; 0) (very gifted, son of a well-known intellectual): (4 cms. in four seconds, and 4 cms. in five seconds)? *They went the same distance, but the second one took longer: it's the first one which goes quicker.* And (4 cms. in two seconds and 8 cms. in four seconds)? *Same speeds, because the second length is twice the first one and the time of the first one is half the second time.*

(Four cms. in four seconds and 6 cms. in six seconds)? *Same speeds. Did you guess? No, but the extra bit* (the 2 cms. difference), *is half the length of the first one. And it's the same thing with the times.*

(Four cms. in three seconds and 12 cms. in four seconds)? *The second one is faster. You have one second more for the second one, and it did three times the distance of the first one!* (6 cms. in four seconds and 5 cms. in three seconds)? *The first one goes faster . . . no, the second, because it took three seconds and moved too far ahead in that three seconds.* Where was the first one at the end of three seconds? (correctly indicated). And the second one at the same time? *Farther on.*

Same thing with 7 and 10 etc. So he understands proportions, but cannot measure beyond the ratios of 2 (or 4) to 1, and 3 to 1.

Por (9; 10) (4 cms. in four seconds and 8 cms. in eight seconds)? *Same speeds, because that's half of that.* And now? (3 and 9 cms in three and nine seconds)? *Same speed, because in that one there is three times this length.*

(Five cms. in five seconds and 7 cms. in six seconds)? (He measures the difference in lengths, but gives up and says): *The second one did more in six seconds than the first one in five seconds.* How did you know that? *Because it travelled farther in six seconds* (he shows the difference) *than this one would have done.*

(Three cms. in three seconds and 4.5 cms. in four seconds)? *The second one goes faster because it went a greater distance in one second than that.* Why? *You can see it.*

Men (10; 6) succeeds right away with ratio 2 to 1. With 3 to 1 (3 cms. in three seconds and 9 cms. in nine seconds) he starts like Burg by halving, then carries forward the 3 cms.

twice: *The same speed, because it also took three seconds to travel that length. And that* (3 cms. in three seconds and 5 cms. in four seconds)? *The second one goes quicker because it went a longer way in one second. Can you work it out?* (he adds three and four seconds, compares 3 cms. to 5 cms. then gives up and says:) *That one takes three seconds to go that distance, this one takes one second longer to do this length: so it goes faster.*

All these subjects have therefore some feeling for proportion. They can formulate this with ratios of 1 to 2, 1 to 4 and 1 to 3. As for other ratios, they try either to find out where the moving object which travelled longest was when the other stopped, or else they compare the difference in the two lengths with the difference in times, and compare this relationship with the relation of the time and path of the object which stopped first. In both cases therefore these are correct operations, limited only by difficulties in calculation.

As for reactions in sub-stage IVb, they employ a systematic method:

DIZ (12; 0) (4 cms. in two seconds and 8 cms. in four seconds)? *The same speed because that's half the distance of the other one. And this* (8 cms. in six seconds and 5 cms. in five seconds)? *It's the first one that goes faster, because if the second one had been the same distance, it would have taken a longer time: it went a short distance, and even so it took five seconds.*

(Sixteen cms. in six seconds, 15 cms. in five seconds, and 13 cms. in five seconds)? *In any case, the second one goes quicker than the first one, because the rest of the way is less than one second (i.e. less than one second's journey). Fine, and the first one and the third one? You'd have to measure them* (he measures and finds 16 and 13 cms.). *You have to divide 16 by 6 and 13 by 5.*

MARG (12; 5) (14 cms. in four seconds and 21 cms. in seven seconds)? (he takes a ruler and measures the cms.). Tell me what you are looking for? *I am working out the distance between 21 and 14 so as to know how many seconds it took to do it. It was the first one that was quicker, because if it had done 21 cms. it would have taken less time than the other.*

How long? *It would have taken six seconds. How's that?*
The difference is 7 cms. and it took four seconds for 14 cms.
(Fifteen cms. in five seconds and 18 cms. in nine seconds)?
*It was the first one that went faster because the piece left over
is too short for four seconds.* And (10 cms. in five seconds
and 20 cms. in ten seconds)? *It's the same—it's half.*

PAH (12; 6) (5 cms. in six seconds and 8 cms. in seven seconds)? *I take half there and if that's added on, it would take
nine seconds.* (So he sees the 7.5 cm. <8 cm.). *The second
one was faster, because if it took seven seconds up to there,
in two seconds it would go a long way, since it went all that
distance in seven seconds.*
(Seven cms. in five seconds and 10 cms. in eight seconds)?
It's the first one that goes faster. (He adds on half, hence
10.5 cms. in 7.5 seconds and notes that this is more than 10
cms. done in eight seconds).

Hence two methods already used in sub-stage IVa are
seen again with these subjects: finding where the objects
were after an equal length of time, and comparison of the
difference in the distances travelled with the shortest trajectory. However instead of adhering rigidly to the operational framework of these solutions, the children of sub-
stage IVb use measurement from the first and so reach a
simpler construction, showing that they have greater mastery over the deductive schema discovered at the beginning of this stage.

4. Conclusions: The discovery of proportional rela-
tions

The facts set forth in the course of this chapter allow us to
return to and develop the discussion broached at the end
of Chapter Seven, on the passage from intuitive regulations to logical operations.
It will be recalled that where unequal distances are
covered in equal times or vice versa, and both movements
are perceived wholly or partly at the same time, there is at
first centration of the intuitive judgement only on the

stopping points (relationship Df), i.e. on the actual results of movement, then there is decentration regarding differences in the starting points (Di) and finally decentration in terms of the path traversed conceived as the interval between i and f. Correct operations are thus achieved when these regulations become completely reversible.

When movements are no longer perceived simultaneously, and it is necessary to reason from drawings symbolizing in retrospect journeys made in succession, this special rôle of the stopping points tends to diminish and the problem simply becomes comparison of lengths in relation to times taken. However, what happens then is that the child reverts to two types of error already outgrown on the level of concrete operations: for some, two unequal paths travelled in the same time involve the same speed because the times are equal (the moving objects finish 'in the same time'), and for others, where two equal distances are covered in different times, it is the object taking the longer time which must be said to go faster. In this second case, speed is conceived as directly proportional to the time taken as if this last, in itself, were the index of a path travelled. But how is it that the child continues to hold such assumptions, vestiges of the earliest ideas of time undifferentiated from space, when they lead to interpretations in plain contradiction to the given factors themselves? This new-found distorting assimilation has to be explained, since we have come up against it throughout this chapter, at a level where concrete operations are already constructed.

This can only be interpreted as a new process of centration of judgements, otherwise it would be impossible to see why given factors as obvious as the distances covered could be ignored in favour of times taken represented only by a number of seconds: instead of correlating time and distance covered the child of sub-stage IIIa simply centres his judgement on one of these terms, as though totally neglecting or underestimating the other. This biased centration recalls that of Df which led to undervaluation of Di, but in this case is the difference in times, i.e. Dt, which is overestimated as opposed to the difference in distances

Dd, which is neglected. In the course of sub-stage IIIb on the other hand, the two relationships Dt and Dd are centred equally, i.e. a regulatory decentration leads to their correlation. Let us remember that the question of equal times and unequal distances is solved more quickly than that of equal distances and unequal times, and it can now be seen why this is the case: the inequality of the distances attracts the attention more, and thus forms a more powerful centration than on Dt, when they are equal, i.e. where Dt=O. (See e.g. Geo's case, etc.).

The mechanism remains the same when moving on to questions in which times and distances are both unequal. In the example of the ratio 1t to 2t, and 1d to 2d, the child begins by thinking either of the distances and neglecting the times (hence the idea that the object travelling 2d is faster than the one travelling 1d), or of the times and neglecting the distances. In this second case, time is either inversely proportional to speed (and then the moving object taking 1t is quicker than that taking 2t) or else it is still conceived as directly proportional to speed (hence once more 2t=2d=faster). In the course of sub-stage IIIa, one of these centrations on Dt or Dd still takes precedence over the other, or each alternately, by relative decentration though not by the absolute decentration which would lead to progressive regulation. Even in Ber's case, when for a moment the two movements are shown simultaneously, the correct solution discovered on the level of concrete operations does not produce decentration on returning to movements in succession: he still thinks that 4 cms. in four seconds is faster than 2 cms. in two seconds. This is a good example of short-lived relative decentrations which do not lead to absolute decentration for want of additive composition and reversibility, with each new situation giving rise to a new displacement of equilibrium in the absence of permanent relationships.

On the other hand large disproportions (e.g. Geo with 5 cms. in two seconds against 4cms. in one second) sometimes lead to absolute decentration but this is not generalized and remains bound to these particular cases. This is easy to explain. The first moving object goes faster, 'because it almost catches up on the other one, and does so in one second', says the child, correlating the relationships of time (Dt) and distance (Dd): though he achieves this correct reasoning, the fact is that here the relative difference in distances covered is slight (4 to 5 cms.) while that between the times is great. On the contrary, in case of equal proportions $(d_1/t_1=d_2/t_2)$ both have the same value. This it is as though when Dt and Dd are in an analogous relationship, one of the terms alone were considered, and as if, when Dt differs considerable from Dd, the subjects were forced to consider them both because of their very disparity. This rule is in any case not absolute, being only statistically true. Its relative frequency however illuminates the facts and especially the process of the later regulations.

Going on to sub-stage IIIb, it is evident in fact that the advances made during this next period consist of gradual correlation of Dt and Dd according to the laws of decentration and regulation, which are now to be demonstrated.

At the beginning of the stage, there is still (with Mos and Maf) an inability to understand equality of speeds even with spatio-temporal ratios of 1 to 2. The subject can understand as soon as the distances are split up but can no longer do so when the path traversed and the time are again doubled: so once again there is centration on either Dt and Dd (with relative but not absolute decentration), in other words, the thinking of these children remains too irreversible, on the formal level, to travel simultaneously over times and spaces in either direction and to observe in this way that the speeds are equal. On the other hand, the rather more advanced subjects (e.g. Chal) reach the correct solution by overestimating first Dd then Dt, and then by making a synthesis immediately afterwards. But it is noteworthy that they go on to discover metrical proportion ('it's half') in retrospect by way of a result and not as a hypothesis controlling a line of reasoning: it is when observing that judgments centred on Dt and on Dd give contradictory conclusions that they begin to compensate and only then discover the answer. So it is the feeling for compensation which leads the child to discover proportion and not the metrical ratio, however simple, which leads to compensation. The subject Maf to whom this metrical relationship was pointed out before he had begun to sense the compensation of Dt and Dd, did understand it for a moment, but with no stability ('I am not very sure') and he later reverts to his error, while the subject Chal, who felt the compensation before seeing the metrical relationship, did reach a final understanding of this last and even generalized it to the case of 2/6=4/12. Hence there is again among the following subjects that the feeling for proportion or disproportion is formed before any systematic measurement or altogether independently of it, and that this is a necessary condition of understanding the latter. Now, this feeling is quite simply the result of decentration of the relations of time and space (absolute decentration of Dt and Dd, with progressive regulation). Moreover, as soon as these regulations lead to complete compensation, the ensuing correlation attains its operational form, as the final form of equilibrium of decentration.

It is interesting to note that the first correct judgements sometimes refer to simple proportions (1 to 2) as has just been seen, and sometimes to large disproportions as was seen earlier. It might therefore be said that where Dd and Dt are equal, or are greatly dissimilar, decentration is easier than with moderate differences: in this last case there is biased centration of the greater relation, at the expense of the lesser, while with great inequalities the very contrast compels the examination of both with the same attention.[1]

But how does decentration work, and more particularly, in the case of moderate differences, what is this mechanism of progressive regulation whose final goal will be the operation of proportionality itself. In the course of sub-stage IIIb, therefore, what is involved is above all a feeling for compensation, which does, in spite of their rough measurement, (by simple dichotomy) lead these subjects to an ever more precise awareness of the dual

[1] This is a mechanism governed by a law analogous to the one we named 'law of relative centration' in the field of perception.

relationship which Mat expresses by saying: 'It's quicker by proportion'. Nevertheless this child cannot justify himself by any measurement: he gives up measuring after a brief attempt, and merely ends up: 'at all events, it is true'. Where does this conviction come from, in advance of any definite operation and any system of measurement?

In point of fact, the intuition of proportions results from a dual decentration, hence from a dual regulation, and this is what explains its delayed appearance in comparison with simple and simultaneous comparisons. When the two movements to be compared are perceived simultaneously, the subject has only to think of the differences in starting points Di, and in finishing points Df, at the same time, in order to be able to compare the times and distances covered. In the case of movements in succession, on the other hand, he not only has to compare the absolute differences Dd and Dt with each other, but also to make them relative, i.e. to compare Dd and d and Dt with t, hence the differences in the distances with the actual distances. This in fact is what the subjects of level IIIb do, when they start to compare the difference in distances Dd with the shorter of the two paths travelled d and subsequently compare the difference in times Dt with the time required to travel over it. But at the beginning of stage IIIb this dual decentration still comes into play only with simple proportions and with large disproportions. On the contrary at the end of this sub-stage IIIb (Mat's case) and above all at the beginning of stage IVa, the mechanism is generalized and leads to systematic regulations, developing from those described in Chapter Seven.

It has already been seen, in fact, (Chapter Seven, §6.) that when the child is trying to compare Df with Di, he traces the path in both directions and so starts to take the intervals into consideration after having centred only on Df (relationship of the stopping points) and shown bias towards it due to the one-way movement of the actual journey. Now, in stage III, the child begins by alternately centring the differences in space and time Dd and Dt, which is an advance from stage II since this dual centration directly bears upon the intervals but is not enough as long as these relations are conceived as absolute. Complete regulation, on the other hand, begins at the point where in his reconstruction of the earlier perceptual given factors, the child begins to reverse the direction of travel so as to recall the position of the moving object making the longer journey when the other object was at the end of its path. As for the subjects who directly compare the differences in the distances travelled Dd with the smaller of the paths proceeding similarly, though by a shorter method. In short, in both cases, the dual decentration of Dd in relation to Dt and of Dd in relation to d as well as Dt in relation to t really amounts to a reconstruction of both movements concurrently, i.e. to the determination of either the order of the moving objects (overtaking etc.) or of the dual relationships of space and time (of the given relation between the two relationships d/t).

All things considered, it can therefore be said that intuitive regulation is an extension of perceptual regulation. Perceptual decentration results from the regulation of movements made by the subject himself in order to attain the object (focusing of the sense organs, i.e. centration or co-ordination of centrations, i.e. decentration). Intuitive decentration on the contrary results from the regulation of the configurations of the complete action (in this case action of overtaking and its variations, and especially reconstruction or anticipation of co-displacements over the whole of their trajectories). When the two movements to be compared are simultaneous, there is first of all centration on the stopping points, and then decentration allows the two displacements to be grasped in their entirety, and so their speeds may be judged by assimilation into the schema of overtaking. When on the other hand the two movements are in succession, intuitive centration bears at first upon the difference in distances (Dd) or in times (Dt); then decentration first of all associates these two relationships Dd and Dt with one another and finally each of these with the trajectories d and the durations t as a whole. Hence the intuition of proportion is to be conceived as the transposition of a relationship, and this intuition becomes correct when there is dual decentration:

that which bears on the actual relationship to be transposed and that which bears on the transposition itself to the extent that it is a new relationship. Thus it is that proportion or the ratio of relationships differs from a simple relation while being an extension of its original mechanisms.

This being said, what is the explanation of the passage from the intuition of proportions belonging to stage III (IIIb) over to the actual operations of proportionality characteristic of stage IV? Of course, when regulations are complete, the exact reversibility then achieved transforms them *ipso facto* into operations. But this simply defines the general process of which ample evidence has been found in all areas. The problem in this case is to find out what indicates that regulation has become complete (or reversible) and what forms the operation which is an extension of it.

Let there be a distance d_1 traversed by a first moving object in the time t_1 and a distance d_2 traversed in t_2 by the second moving object. If $d_2 > d_1$ and $t_2 > t_1$, we shall also give the name d^1_1 to the difference Dd between d_1 and d_2 (hence $d_1 + d^1_1 = d_2$) and t^1_1 to the difference Dt between t_1 and t_2 (hence $t_1 + t^1_1 = t_2$). There will, therefore, be operations (and no longer simply regulations bearing on Dt and Dd) when the subject is able actually to construct, and no longer simply to discover, these proportions correctly, $d_1/t_1 = d^1_1/t^1_1 = d_2/t_2$. How does he manage to do so? In other words what do the operations leading to this result consist of? This has been observed already: the subject either tries to find out the position of the second moving object when the first one reached its finishing point d_1, or else, and this comes to the same thing, he compares d^1_1 with d_1 and t^1_1 with t_1 to establish whether d_2 and t_2 are in the same ratio as d_1 and t_1. Now this dual operation (or rather this same operation under its two different aspects) goes beyond the purely qualitative operational framework envisaged in Chapters Six to Eight. Throughout that part, in fact, the judgements found stated only that one speed was greater or less than another, one distance travelled was longer or shorter than another, and one duration longer or shorter than another—hence in every case there is nesting of the part within the whole and use of intensive quantity defined by the relationship (whole $>$ the part). Now in the case of proportions the child does not merely say: 'the distance d_1 is smaller than d_2 and the time t_1 is smaller than the time t_2'. He goes further and is led to state that the part distance d_1 is the same size in relation to d_2 as the partial time t_1 in relation to t_2. Consequently, he now has not only to compare the part with the whole, but one given part with the other part composing the same whole, i.e. d_1 with d^1_1 within d_2. The operation forming proportion is none other than this relation of the two parts: $d_1/d^1_1 = t_1/t^1_1$, and it is this extensive and no longer intensive relationship which allows the inference $d_1/d_2 = t_1/t_2$.

In itself the operational structure of proportion is doubtless no more difficult than nesting the part within the whole, of which it is only a generalization. Certainly this is a particularly important generalization since it marks the passage from the logical or infra-logical to the mathematical. However this generalization might have been immediate in the same way that, after the construction of the seriation of asymmetrical relations and inclusions of classes, fully developed number emerges directly as the operational synthesis of the two. (See *Origins of Number*). It is thus possible, that in the purely spatial or geometrical sphere, certain propositions emerge from stage III by way of operations. In the particular case of speeds, this appears even in connection with some simple relationships as will be seen in the following chapter when studying conservation of speed. But when it is a question of quite distinct movements in succession as during the present chapter, operational proportionality requires formal deduction, since the problem then involves operations bearing on other operations (see Chapter Four, end of § 5.) and this is why it appears so late.

Finally, as soon as extensive proportions are constructed, metrical proportions are derived from them by that very fact. Indeed, the part d^1_1 may be conceived in relation to the part d_1 either as one segment associated with another segment in the same way as the segments t_1 and t^1_1 by a simple geometrical construction (so called qualitative, i.e. extensive theory of proportion), or else as a unit such that $d_1 = d^1_1$ and $d^1_1 + d_1 = 2d_1$ (or as a fraction of a unit) and then the proportion becomes numerical or metrical. The psychological facts described in this chapter provide evidence that the two conceptions of proportion are quite distinct, since the intuition of proportions is formed and becomes reversible independently of any system of measurement, and at the same time correlated, since measurement is the completion of extensive proportion as soon as this last is achieved.

CHAPTER TEN

Conservation of Uniform Speeds and their Relationships

Having studied how the speeds of simultaneous movements are constructed (Chapter Seven) and then movements in succession (Chapter Nine) we can now investigate the child's conception of conservation of uniform speeds.

The questionnaire adopted for this is extremely simple and allows us to follow the reactions of subjects from 5 to 11 years of age. Two parallel straight lines are drawn on a sheet of paper. A car (or rather a lorry) moves along the first line travelling a certain distance, e.g. 2 cms., between the first morning and the first evening. During the same time a doll setting off simultaneously from the same point cycles only half the distance (of course this word is not used, the vehicle's stopping point being simply marked at 2 cms. and the doll's at 1 cm.). The child is then asked the following questions:

Q 0. (preliminary): starting and finishing simultaneously, synchronous travelling times equal.

Q 1. How far will the car go on the second day and in the third, etc. if it always starts and stops at the same times and travels at the same speed? i.e.: to discover the equality of the distances (conservation of a uniform speed) at equal speeds and times.

Q 2. What distance will the doll cover if it continues to travel at its own speed for equal periods of time (conservation of the difference between uniform speeds).

Q 3. On the last day, the car only travels half a day. Hence the time is halved but the speed is the same (emphasis on the same speed). Where will it stop?

Q 4. To find out the distance the doll travels during the same time (half of the last day) at its own speed.

Q 5. Given the car's position (e.g. on the seventh day) and the doll's position (e.g. on the same day or on the third day etc.), how many days will the doll take to catch up on the stationary car. Hence the question is simply to find out whether the child manages to answer: twice the number of days taken by the car, or twice the units (daily journeys) marked along the line.

Q 6. Does the (absolute) distance between the stopping points of the car and the doll stay the same at the end of each day or does it increase regularly?

The reactions observed among some sixty subjects of 5 to 10 years of age were found to be extremely interesting, both in their agreement with previous results and for the individual light thrown on the problem of speed.

From the point of view of time, first of all, confirmation is found of what has already been seen in other work: simultaneousness of finishing points (or even starting points) is acquired at the age of 5 years by only 25% of subjects; at 6 years by 50%, and at 7 years by 75%. As for the equality of synchronous durations, this is on average slightly delayed: 33% at 5 years, 25% at 6 years, 70% at 7 years, and 75% only at 8 years.

Concerning speed itself, a first stage is found (age limits of subjects examined: 5; 0 to 6; 11), during which the child does not understand conservation of speed: in the question of the car alone (Q 1) he cannot even bring forward equal distances from one day to the next, as if the equality of the speed, which he had been told of, were not necessarily reflected in equality of the distances travelled (when the stopping points do not coincide). As for the doll's journeys, in the course of this same stage I, two types of reaction may be distinguished: the first consists simply of marking a slight difference (at random) in the stopping points of the doll and the car as if the doll travelled the same distances but simply remained slightly in the rear. The second reaction begins with the same theory but is applied to keeping a constant absolute difference between the two moving objects, e.g. if the car (according to the arbitrary estimates of subjects of this stage) travels (2) +3+1.5+2 cms. in the first four days, then the doll will travel (1) +2+.05+1 cms., with a difference of 1 cm. in the distances each time. Hence evaluation of speeds as a function of the finishing points (cf. Chapter Six and Seven: stage I) is again found in this case.

In the course of a stage II (average age 6 to 7 years, with a few subjects from 5½ years) the child manages, by trial and error and intuitive regulations to solve the first question empirically by carrying forward the same distance each day. But he is only successful in using this procedure with one speed at a time. Concerning the doll, the subject would naturally conserve its particular speed as well, if it alone were under consideration; but as its speed is different from the car's, and the conservation of this difference would consist of keeping a ratio and not an absolute distance constant, the child does not manage to conserve the doll's speed: he simply carries forward the original distance between the finishing points of the doll and the car each time, believing he will mark the difference in the speeds in this way, whereas this procedure amounts to attributing to the doll the same speed as the car.

From stage III (beginning on average at 7 to 8 years) the child succeeds by means of concrete operations in constructing the respective paths of the car and the doll, while conserving their separate speeds at the same time. On the other hand he does not manage to anticipate this construction deductively, i.e. to foresee 'in abstracto' that the distances between the finishing points of the car and the doll increase continuously, nor does he even discover the number of days the doll needs to catch up on the car.

In the course of stage IV finally (towards 10 to 11

years, with some examples of exceptionally early reactions from 9 or even 8 years) these last questions are solved by formal deduction.

1. The first stage: No conservation of speed

Observing that the car covers a certain distance on the first day, the child of stage I does not even manage to establish that on the second day when travelling for the same length of time at the 'same speed' the car will cover an equal distance in continuation of the first. In fact, it is necessary to help him find the path travelled during the second day, following on from the length done on the first day, and this is where the whole trouble lies. If the two daily journeys were not continuous and the subject were simply shown a second route parallel to the first, he would have no difficulty in reproducing the same distance; he would make the starting points coincide by placing them side by side and so would find the stopping place at the end of the second day, by putting a point exactly above that which marked the end of the previous day's journey. But it is not possible to infer from this intuitive behaviour that the child has understood that a movement made at the same speed for the same length of time corresponds to an equal length: the child would simply have expressed equal speeds by identical stopping points and there was evidence in Chapter Seven of the kind of systematic error produced by such a criterion. Now on the contrary the problem put to the subject is to bring forward the same length in continuation of the distance travelled during the first day, and this moreover entirely corresponds with the concrete given factors, since the car is considered to continue its route and not to cover it again. Now, this question of continuation, which for us is directly equivalent to duplication of the first journey, on the contrary presents greater difficulty for the child, or rather two complementary difficulties, which may usefully be recalled in order to construe the following facts to advantage. The first depends on the conception of time: to carry forward the same time is still meaningless for the subject, for two successive durations cannot be compared at the intuitive level, in the absence of operational reversibility. Two synchronous durations are even held to be unequal when the simultaneous movements to which they correspond do not have the same starting and finishing points. More especially, in the second place, it was observed in Chapter Three that distances travelled are evaluated, at first, according to their stopping points, and in Chapter Seven that during stage I, speeds, as such, are estimated according to this same criterion. Under these conditions of course the carrying forward of an equal distance constitutes a real difficulty and conservation of speed would as yet have no meaning in the absence of an operational structure allowing correlation of the factors in question.

Here are some examples of a sub-stage Ia, i.e. among the least advanced cases observed.

GER (5; 4). Car and doll are set in motion: Which one goes quicker? *The car.* When do you get up in the morning? *At seven.* Then watch: the doll and the car here both start off together at seven o'clock in the morning and they both stop at seven o'clock at night (journeys made). Did they set off at the same time? *No.* Which one set off first? *The car.* Did they stop at the same time? *No.* Which one first? *The car.* Did they travel for the same length of time? *No, the car was moving longer.* Why? *Because it got farther ahead.* (Repeat with audible starting signals: Ger then agrees that they were simultaneous and even that the times were equal, but with prompting from us). Then where would the car finish on the second day. *It starts again at seven in the morning and stops again at seven in the evening.* Will it travel for the same length of time and at the same speed? *Here* (indicating shorter journey than the first one). Does it travel the same distance, the same length on the second day? *The second day, it moves farther on* (distance thus immediately translated into the arrangement of the stopping points). But this (indicating the second journey) is this distance longer than that (first journey)? (does not understand) Why did you make it shorter? . . . And the third day, if it goes at the same speed again from seven in the morning to seven at night? *That* (arbitrary distance, again too short). Watch, you can measure it with this paper (he copies our actions). Well now where will it stop on the second day (repeating the given factors)? *Up to here* (distance indicated much too long). Why does it go a longer way? *Because the car went as far as that—I think it stopped here* (pointing out a distance equal to the first one). Who is right? *I am* (firmly). Impossible to proceed any farther.

Do (5; 2) says he gets up at eight o'clock and goes to bed at 10 p.m.: Then watch. The car sets off at eight and stops at ten, and so does the doll (experiment). Which one went faster? *The car.* Did they set off at the same time? *Yes, but the car goes on farther, and the doll doesn't.* Did they stop at the same time? *No, the car goes faster.* Did they travel along for the same length of time? *No.* And the second day (same data) where will the car stop? *I don't know.* But if it travelled again at the same speed from eight in the morning to ten at night? (Indicates an arbitrary point). Could you use this paper to help you measure? *No.* And where will the doll stop? *Not so far as the car* (again arbitrary).

Drr (5; 6) says he gets up at 9 a.m. and goes to bed at 10 p.m. After explanation experiment is made: Did they set off at the same time? *No, the car goes faster.* And did they stop at the same time? *No.* But did they not stop at the same moment? *No.* And the second day, if ,etc. . . . (exact repetition of data)? (He indicates a distance nearly twice as long as on the first day, doubtless wishing to show that it goes something like twice as far on the second day: in fact, the result is therefore approximately three units). But it goes at the same speed as on the first day and it travels again from 9 a.m. to 10 p.m.: if it goes at the same speed, will it go the same distance on the second day, just as far as it does on the first day? *No, not the same.* Why? *Shorter* (this time he points to an arbitrary point shorter than the first length). Watch (bringing forward the same distance using paper strip). And the third day? (He traces a shorter journey) etc.
    And the doll on the second day (repeating the data)? (He points to a distance slightly different from the car's, but gives it a longer journey than the first day). Is that the same length that it went the first day? *No.* Well then? (Repeat, etc.).

Mic (6; 1) thinks that 'the car took longer' between 8 a.m. and 9 p.m. because it stopped 'farther ahead': And the second day, if it starts again at 8 a.m. and stops again at 9 p.m. and travels at the same speed? *It stops here, maybe* (pointing too far ahead). Why have you made it longer than the first day? *Because it did all this much. It has to be longer because it stops farther ahead* (confusion of plus loin—farther ahead—and plus long—longer—as in Dit's case). Was the speed the same as the first day? *Yes.* And it was moving for the same length of time? *No, one hour longer.* But didn't it set off at 8 a.m. and stop again at 9 p.m.? *Yes.* Then why one hour longer? . . . (same confusion as for speed). And how much does the doll do the second day? *Up to here because it does less than the car* (too long). But does it do a longer or a shorter distance than the first day? *A bit longer.* Why? *Because it travelled half an hour longer.*

And where does the car stop on the third day (repeat data)? *Up to here* (again distance too long). Why? *Because it travels three hours longer.* And if the car on the last day only travels half a day up to twelve o'clock? *Like that* (indicates an even longer distance)?

Gis (6; 2) nine o'clock to eight: *The car stopped farther ahead because it moves faster.* (Second day). *Here* (much too long) *because it travels farther on.* Why have you made the second day's journey longer than the first? *Because it wasn't far the first day.*

These are the earliest reactions to the questions of conservation of speed. The child obviously does not question the statement that the speeds are equal on the first and second days, and is able to repeat this verbal formula freely. Nevertheless his inference from this is by no means that the successive journeys are equal and to some extent the reason for this has already been seen at the beginning of this section.

In fact, if the intuition of speed is basically overtaking and the only criterion the subject can use to evaluate speeds is the spatial order of succession of stopping points, then of course he will not be able to translate equal speeds of two movements in succession as equal paths, hence as equal distances covered: to do this, speed would have to be conceived as a relationship between distances and times and this is precisely what is absent in the intuition of

overtaking. It was observed in Chapter Nine that, even at
the beginning of the stage of concrete operations (stage
III) subjects who can judge the speed of simultaneous
movements correctly in this way are confused as soon as
the movements are in succession: in spite of perceiving the
movements in succession, in spite of the drawings and
measurement of the times, they do not understand that the
distance A travelled in n seconds is equal in speed to the
distance 2A travelled in 2n seconds. It is thus perfectly
natural that in stage I, i.e. well before the concrete operational construction of the spatio-temporal relationship of
speed, the child is unable to carry forward the same
distance in order to express the conservation of a speed,
since distances covered in succession by the same moving
object correspond to successive and not simultaneous
movements.

But in the absence of precise operations, could the
subject not guess from our statement, that the car's speeds
during its daily trips and also the times during which it
travels are equal, that the lengths covered are also equal?
This actually is what happens in the course of stage II
during which the correct solution is anticipated intuitively
though it still cannot be achieved logically. However, at
the level of stage I the subject still seems to be unable
either to carry forward an equal distance or to imagine the
equality of two successive durations.

As regards the distance travelled, the results of Chapter
Three are confirmed by Ger, Mic, and Gis explicitly and
implicitly by the others, given that the distances travelled
as well as the speeds themselves are measured at first only
by their stopping points, and not by the relationship between starting and finishing points, these subjects have the
greatest difficulty in carrying forward the distance done on
the first day, since the starting point of the second day's
journey coincides not with the first day's starting point but
in fact with its stopping point. So the child simply states
that the car goes 'farther' on the second day, and like Ger
and Do, gives it an arbitrary stopping point for the second
and third days, in the absence of correspondence with the
first day. It is true that the subjects Dit and particularly

Mic and Gis try to break away from arbitrary selection and discover a distance corresponding to the same speed, for the second day. But then given that the moving object stops farther ahead on the second evening than on the first evening (farther: in the absolute sense), they conclude from this that it travelled a greater distance on the second day than the first (greater, in the relative sense, i.e. the second day in isolation compared to the first day in isolation, and not both days together compared to the first one). The car 'went all that way' says, e.g. Mic, 'it has to be longer since it stops farther on'. And Gis, it's longer, because 'it goes farther on', because the distance 'was not very long the first day'. Dit goes so far as to calculate a journey for the second day nearly twice that of the first day, without seeing that he thus obtains three units, equal to three and not two days. This last example, by the way, shows that it is not the technical difficulties of evaluating the lengths which hold up these children (since their visual awareness is fully adequate for correct estimation) but the theoretical difficulties relating to movements in succession.

Now it is interesting that this estimation of length by means of stopping points, hence this want of differentiation of the interval (distance) from the arrangement of the finishing points, is found again in these same subjects where the problem concerns the other kind of interval, i.e. the duration, and the other order of succession, which is in fact temporal order. Understanding, that if the car maintains its speed on the second day it will cover the same distance in the same time, implies besides bringing forward the same distance, also bringing forward the same duration, conceived as the temporal interval contained between the moment of starting and the moment of stopping. Is the child of this level able to grasp such an idea? In other words, will he see that the duration comprised between 8 a.m. and 10 p.m. on the first day is equivalent to the duration comprised between 8 a.m. and 10 p.m. on the second day, particularly as, to make things easier, the times adopted are always those indicated by the child himself as being his times for getting up and going to bed (whether they are right or not is unimportant)? It should first of all be noted that none of these subjects has even the concept of the equality of synchronous durations: when they see the car and the doll start together and stop together on the first day they deny that the objects stopped simultaneously and often even that they started simultaneously, precisely because the car goes faster and farther than the doll. If they do not understand this elementary synchronization, then how could they accept their isochronism, i.e. equality of successive durations? For this it would have to be possible for a temporal interval, removed from its starting and stopping times, to be the same between new starting and stopping points, equivalent to the first: now this equation of two successive intervals, detached from the events which set their limits, undoubtedly implies the operational construction of time as a whole, qualitative and metrical. Thus our youngest subjects (Ger, Do, and Dit) do not even understand the question. As for Mic and Gis, they grasp it to some extent, but give a solution exactly analogous to the one they found for spatial distance: the size of intervals is proportional to the absolute order of succession of their stopping points, i.e. n hours elapsing after a first n hours amount to a longer duration than the first precisely because it comes afterwards. This is why Mic, though having no difficulty in recognizing that the car and the doll start at the same times and stop at the same times on the second day, and on the first, still state that the car travelled one hour longer on the second day and three hours more on the third day, or that the doll travelled half an hour on the second day (half an hour because it doesn't go as far as the car): he simply means by this that the durations on the second and third days are not equivalent to the first, because they come after it, and likewise that the journeys performed during these subsequent days are longer than the first days's journey because the moving object stops farther ahead. (See *Origins of the Child's Conception of Time*, Chapter Two). There is nothing surprising about this, in any case, since at this level time is undifferentiated from space and from speed itself, and all three are evaluated in terms of finishing points.

In short, since neither an equal distance nor an equal duration may be carried forward, following the linear sequence of the trajectory in space or in time, the idea of the conservation of speed could obviously have no spatio-temporal meaning for the child. This idea may be understood intuitively thanks to the experience of movements of one's own body: the car and the doll maintain their respective speeds if their journey is neither accelerated nor slowed down. But it still could not be operationally constructed because this would then imply a constant ratio between successive equal distances travelled in successive times which are also equal. So it is evident in this case of speed, as in all other examples of the development of the idea of conservation, that in the absence of 'groupment' no conservation is at first possible: because neither successive distances nor successive durations may be combined in an additive, associative, or reversible way, at the level where speed is conceived in terms of a simple intuition of order, incomplete and often even incorrect, as with all intuitions.

It is thus clear that the question of the half day (Q 3) could not be solved nor even understood, in the absence of any consideration of the distances. Mic goes so far as to forecast, in the case of the half-day, a much longer journey than on the third day, taking into consideration only the order of the stopping points and quite unaware of proportionality.

As for the difference in speed between the doll and the car, (Q 2) obviously if speed were thus judged only by the arrangement of the stopping points, this difference would be more easily conserved than the speeds themselves, but absolutely and by no means relatively: in other words, the child will place the doll's finishing point a little way behind the car's, whatever the latter's position might be. But, at the level Ia now being considered the subject neglects the distances so completely that he does not even try to conserve the (absolute) difference between these two stopping points correctly, and indicates the doll's position arbitrarily, provided it stays behind the car's.

In the course of a sub-stage Ib, on the contrary, this question of the differences in stopping points between the

doll and the car gives rise to a slight advance, the other
reactions remaining exactly similar to those of sub-stage
Ia. This step simply consists of keeping the absolute difference in the stopping points of the two moving objects
constant wherever the child places the car's stopping
point, which continues to be arbitrary in every case:

CHEL (5; 10) for the second day of the car's journey, carries
forward a distance similar to the first, and for the third day,
a much longer journey: Why do you go on making it longer?
It did all this distance here. Why? . . . And the following
day if it goes at the same speed, will the distance be longer,
shorter or the same? *Don't know.*
    And where will the doll stop on the second day? *Here*
(bringing forward the same difference) *because the car goes
quicker.* And the third day? *Here* (same difference). But look,
if the doll did this on the first day, and goes at the same
speed all the time, will it get as far as this? . . . And on the
next day? *You can't tell yet.*

LIL (6; 11) accepts simultaneousness of the starting points
but not of the finishing points, nor equality of synchronous
durations. For the second day, Lil make the car's journey
longer than the first day, and the doll's longer too, while
carefully keeping the difference constant: Which one goes
faster? *The car.* How far did it go the second day? (Indicates
this). And the doll? (Indicates this). But did they both go
at the same distance on the second day? *No.* Is one of these
distances you have just shown me shorter than the other?
Yes, the doll's (he thinks it is shorter simply because it is in
the rear). But aren't these the same length, there, and here
(actions indicating the two lengths)? *No.* Did they travel for
the same length of time? *Don't know.* Start again with the
third day but same reactions again.

JAN (7; 0) accepts simultaneousness of starting times, but not
of stopping times, nor equality of durations: And where will
the car stop on the second day? *Here* (shorter path). Did it
travel the same distance? *No.* Well then, show me . . . Watch
(we indicate it). Which is the more correct, my way or yours?
Yours. Why? *Because you know best.* And the doll? (He
transfers the absolute difference). And the third day (repeating explanations), what will the car do? *A longer distance*

(he points it out). And the doll? *Shorter* (an equal journey, keeping the absolute difference constant).

These cases of sub-stage Ib show interesting indications of the earliest way of evaluating lengths travelled and speeds themselves. From this second point of view they fully confirm the reactions of sub-stage Ia: if their speeds are really evaluated only in terms of the stopping points of movements then, of course, it follows that the difference between the points of arrival of the cyclist and the lorry, at the end of the first day, will remain absolute. For, in order to see it as relative, it would be necessary for the child to understand speeds as being relationships between distances and times: then only, would he understand that the distance between the stopping points of two objects moving at different speeds could not be thought of as absolute, but that it was in the form of a constant relationship. Hence the fact that these subjects, being slightly more advanced than those of substage Ia, keep this absolute difference exactly constant, simply confirms with paradoxical precision that speeds are measured by finishing points. And in fact with Q 1 these children reason like those of sub-stage Ia.

However, the result is that by carrying forward the absolute difference between the stopping points of the car and the doll each time, the child of sub-stage Ib unintentionally and even unsuspectingly makes their journeys exactly equal each day. Hence from the operational point of view they give them equal speeds from the second day on, with just a time-lag in starting and stopping. Now not only does the child think he is keeping the speeds very different, since the stopping points do not coincide, but he even believes that the paths travelled are unequal, not seeing that they are equivalent but just one slightly behind the other. More accurately, he thinks the distance travelled each day by the car is longer than the doll's on the same day, because the former is in advance of the other, and he is not concerned with the disparity in starting points. This is why Lil energetically refuses to accept this equality suggested by us, etc.

Now this reaction entirely agrees with what has gone before. From the point of view of the length of the paths travelled, it confirms the conclusions of Chapters Three and Six: the actual length of a movement is seen at first only in terms of the stopping point alone. From the point of view of speed, it verifies the conclusions of Chapter Seven. According to an unexpected schema (amounting simply to a variation upon Q 2 of this Chapter Seven): if an object travels along the straight line AB and another moves along the straight line $A_1 B_1$ equal to AB but some distance behind it, the moving object which stops farther ahead is thought to go faster (just as in Q 2 where one moving object setting off from a point farther back almost catches up on another one, the slower one is considered to be faster because it always remains in front.)

2. The second stage: Progressive intuitive discovery of conservation of speed in a single moving object, but no understanding of the relation between dissimilar constant speeds

The child of this level manages progressively to understand that if the car maintains its speed on the second and third days, stopping and starting at the same times each day, it will cover paths of equal lengths. As for the doll, obviously the subject would reason similarly if the doll were considered in isolation, but when its speed is compared with the car's they cannot be correctly correlated: so the subject, as in stage I, carefully keeps the absolute difference in the stopping points from day to day without considering the relative difference in the distances travelled compared with the durations. Conversely, as a step forward from stage I, the subject will accept the correct solution if he compares the two series of journeys constructed separately, and will understand the experimenter's explanations when relative differences are suggested. Here are some examples:

BERN (6; 3) accepts simultaneousness of starting and stopping points but denies equality of synchonous durations. For the second day, he indicates too long a journey for the car at first: *And the doll? Here* (keeps the difference absolute). Does the car do a longer journey on the second day, or a shorter one, or the same length as the first day? *The same length.*—No, it did a longer journey . . . Why? (We show him two equal paths). *No, that's too little, because the distance gets bigger all the time* (confusing the intervening distances with the total length, i.e., with the arrangement of the stopping points). And the third day? *Oh, it's the same distance* (he measures and corrects earlier replies).

And where does the doll stop on the third day? (Indicates the same absolute difference as for the second day). How far did it go the first day? (Indicates correctly). And the second day? (He brings forward nearly the same distance because he is no longer thinking about the car now standing still at the end of its third journey). Why there? *Because it does not go as fast as the car.* And the third day? (He is about to carry forward the same short distance but, seeing the car, he then places the doll near it, conserving the original absolute difference). Why did you put it there? *It always does the same road.* Look at what you have done: does the doll always go at the same speed? (He looks at the distances). *It goes slower at first and faster at the end* (hesitation). *Oh, no, it always goes at the same speed.* (Bern corrects the last distance).

What is half a day? *It's only from early morning to midday.* Right, now look: the fourth day the car stops at midday. It only goes for half a day. So where will it stop? (He indicates a full unit's length and says proudly, seeing all the paths equal including the half day's journey). *I've found out how it works. And now it's going to travel two whole days without stopping. Where will it finish?* (Wrong again: points out the equivalent of three to four trips).

Dor (7; 2) accepts simultaneousness of stopping and starting points but not equality of synchronous durations. At first he adds the journeys not in a continuous line but one below the other: hence strictly equal journeys both for doll and for car. We tell him to begin with the previous evening's stopping place: he then gives the car a slightly longer journey than the day before, then too short, then right. Third day, right straight away.

With the doll Dor indicates more or less correctly for the second day, but for the third day, reverts to the absolute difference: Do you think that the doll goes farther on the third day than on the second day? *Oh no, the same.* And the fourth day? (Moves the car forward a distance equal to the earlier ones, but in the doll's case again reverts to the absolute difference).

CLAU (7; 11). Did they set off at the same time? *Yes.* Did they stop at the same time? *Yes. The doll travels 10 hours. And the car? 11 hours, because it is farther ahead.* But don't they both set off at 6 a.m.? *Yes.* And when do they both stop? At 6 p.m. If you like. So how many hours does the doll travel? *11 hours, no, 12 hours.* Right. And the car? *12 hours, too, no, 13 hours, because it is ahead.*

We repeat the given factors for the second day: Where does the car stop? (Too far, then corrected). And the doll? (Indicates the absolute difference). Why does it not stop there (car's stopping place)? *Because it goes more slowly.* But why did it go all this way, and not such a long way the first day? *I thought it moved a bit faster than before.—No, no, because it's still the same speed.* Well then (repeat)? (He places the car correctly, and the doll as before!) Did they travel exactly as on the first day? *The car did, yes, the doll was a bit faster.* But it goes at the same speed as before! (Clau moves the doll back a little, compares with the distances of the first day, moves it forward reproducing the absolute difference and finally moves it back to the right point). Why there? *Because it went the same distance as the first day.* If you travel at the same speed for a whole day, and take as many hours as you did the day before, do you cover the same distance, or longer or shorter? *It could be longer or shorter.* A car travels one hour and stops, and then travels again for one hour at the same speed: what distance will it do? *It can be longer or shorter.* Do you know what a minute is? *A little while.* In one hour, do you know how many minutes there are? *Sixty.* Does every hour have sixty minutes, or more, or less? *It can be more or sometimes less.*

For half a day for the car, Clau marks a journey slightly less than a unit. Look (experiment: he marks a point halfway) And the doll? (Indicates nearly the same length). Show me the distance the doll went on the second day (he does). And while the car was going that far (half) what was the doll doing? (He indicates a complete unit for the doll).

Mon (8; 1) does not immediately accept simultaneousness of stopping points. As for the durations? *The day is shorter for the doll than for the car.* From 1 p.m. to 2 p.m. today, is that the same time as from 1 p.m. to 2 p.m. yesterday? *Yes.* And tomorrow. *Same.* If the car travels from 7 a.m. to 8 p.m. and the doll does too, do they not travel for the same length of time? *The doll moves for a longer time.*

Second and third day: places the car too far ahead, then gradually reduces this length, and finishes with the correct point. With the doll, begins with the absolute difference, then progressively corrects this.

Half day: car's journey too long, and doll's nearly the same as the car's. Finally, Mon thinks that the doll will catch up on the car in three days, over a distance requiring six.

Cla (8; 1) accepts simultaneousness and synchronization. Carries forward too short a distance for the car's second day and too long for the doll's (absolute difference): Did one of them travel farther than the other? *Yes.* (he notices that the journey he gave the doll is longer than the car's). *Oh, no, that's wrong.* Does the car move at the same speed on the second day? *Yes.* And the doll? *Same.* So? *Up to there* (too short a distance for the car). And if it were like that (shorter still)? *No, because that doesn't make a whole day's journey.* And like this (too long)? *No. If it were to be longer it would be all day and part of the night as well.* Well then? (Trial and error, finally measuring with a piece of paper). And if it went that far (half-way? *That would be half a day.*

And the doll on the second day? (Too long: absolute difference). And the car the third day? (Correct). And the doll? (Again too long). And if it were travelling by itself? (Removing the car)? (Correct). And with the car? (He reverts to the absolute difference).

And if the car only went for half a day? (Too long). And the doll? (Again too long).

A boy is walking along a road for one hour. Later on he walks for another hour. What would the lengths be like? *Both the same.* Why? *Because he walked for the same time.* Are all hours the same length of time? *Yes.*

The first problem raised by these cases is that of how the child arrives empirically at reproducing equal paths for the car alone and whether intuition, as seems to be the case in view of the general context of these interviews, is enough for the discovery of the right answer.

The subject Bern, e.g. begins as in stage I by thinking that the 'distance gets bigger all the time' (no differentiation between arrangement of stopping points and distances): in fact, he denies the equal distance we suggest, finding it 'too short'. But for the third day, when he is about to increase the difference again, he changes his mind in retrospect, and discovers 'Oh, it's the same distance'. Dor follows exactly the same process. Thus in the case of these two subjects, there is at first centration of the intuitive judgment on the stopping points and not on the intervals, hence the idea that as the car moves forward farther each day it must make a longer daily journey each time. But on the third day the increased distance becomes too great, hence there is regulation by a sudden decentration in favour of the interval (Oh, etc.). In Cla's case, the same initial centration simply leads to the idea that the car goes farther ahead, leading to an arbitrary path which is too short but this smallness has only to be exaggerated slightly for Cla to answer 'no, because that wouldn't be enough for a whole day', or else to increase the length a little, for him to say 'no, if it were longer, that would be all day, and part of the night as well': the hesitation provoked between these two exaggerations then releases a decentration on the interval, leading to exact equality. So this is a good case of solution by 'intuitive regulation'.

As for the doll's journeys, the regulating mechanism is even clearer here. In the first place it can be observed that by assimilation to what the child has just acquired the conservation of the doll's speed and the equality of its successive journeys give no further difficulty when the second moving object is not placed too close to the car, i.e. is not too closely connected with it visually: when the car is already in its position at the end of the third or fourth day, reconstruction of the doll's earlier journeys is no longer influenced by the car's position and, in fact, results in correct answers. Conversely, as soon as the doll approaches the car and the doll's movement is correlated with the car's, i.e. as soon as they have to reconstruct the distances covered by the doll while the car is making its journeys, then the subjects of this level, like those of stage I (even when they have already understood that the car's daily journeys are equal) all begin by placing the doll's stopping point in the same relation to the car's stopping point at an absolute (and not relative) difference, as at the very start of the journey: in other words, they simply conserve the original absolute difference, without seeing that it increases each day. There is therefore, in the doll's case far more than in the car's, centration of the intuition on the stopping points, without decentration on the intervals traversed, since the child does not even suspect, at first, that he is thus giving the doll longer and longer journeys each day. However, starting with this initial intuitive centration there subsequently appears in these subjects of stage II, a decentration, which is often quite spontaneous or arises in the course of discussion: when the distances attributed to the doll are equal or particularly when they exceed those of the car, there appears a regulation, which is sometimes immediate in fact, to 'moderate' the error. E.g. Bern begins by adding a distance (second day) which is nearly correct for the doll (the car being farther ahead) and by explaining his actions correctly: but on the third day he bases himself on the absolute difference thinking he has hit upon the right way ('I always make it the same distance'), the contradiction resulting from this then leading him to the solution. Dor, on the contrary, alternates endlessly between centration on the stopping points (absolute difference) and centration on the intervals, without managing to make up his mind. Clau's case is analogous to Bern's.

The intuitive (or regulatory) and not as yet logical (or operational) nature of these various reactions is likewise observed in the co-ordination of ideas of time with estimation of distance travelled. Firstly, all these subjects, except the most advanced (Cla), either dispute the simultaneousness of the stopping points, or the equality of the synchronous durations, or both together. (Particularly to be noted is Clau for whom 6 a.m. to 6 p.m. makes twelve hours when you go slowly and thirteen hours when you go quickly, and Mon: 'the doll's day is shorter than the car's'). Even when they reach the correct solution of equal journeys intuitively, they cannot translate it into complete spatio-temporal relations. The subject Clau (e.g. he is right in stating that on the second day the doll 'does the same distance as the first day') denies that at equal speeds and in equal times you always get equal distances; 'It could be longer or shorter', which we can easily understand when we see how he conceives of an hour in time, since an hour does not always have sixty minutes, but 'it can be more, or sometimes less', according to the events which occupy it. Conversely, in Cla's case intuitive, regulation finally reaches the level of operational reversibility: for the first time the child understands and explicitly formulates that at the same speeds the distances travelled during two different hours will 'both be the same', because the moving object 'did the same hours'. What is new in this reasoning is that the expression 'the same hours' is applied to hours in succession, hence considered as equivalent: now, it is precisely this qualitative permutability (interchangeability) of durations in succession, which by generalization will lead to the conception of units of duration, equal to each other because being permutable, and by that very fact, to two correlative ideas of the uniform elapsing of time itself and the conservation of uniform speeds. In fact it is when the conservation speed rests on the idea of the uniform elapsing of time (and vice versa) that it attains the operational level and outgrows the level of simple intuitive regulations: it is through this that Cla reaches the threshold of stage III.

But before passing on to the analysis of this third stage let us just go on to consider why the child of stage II is still unable to solve the problems of the half day, and the number of days required for the doll to catch up on the car in any given position. On the first point, after Bern has correctly defined half a day, he is seen to add one complete journey without suspecting his mistake ('I've found out how it works') while for two days he adds three to four units! Clau makes a journey of eight tenths of a day for the half day; so do Mon and Cla. As for the problem of the number of days needed, their failure is again due to intuitive centration. But the drawings made by the subjects, in order to help with their calculations and to represent the correspondence of the paths remaining to be done, are of great interest and form a sort of graphic representation of the preoperational regulations peculiar to this stage II. Amongst these one begins by observing, with regard to the car's journeys, drawings representing unequal daily journeys, some of which are too long but which are then followed by a definite decrease in the subsequent journeys. Others are too short and are followed by a longer journey. The equality of the daily journeys is thus the result of regulations alternating in one direction and the other, and progressively tending towards this equality, without operational measurements transferring the unit. As for the doll's journeys, every extreme between the following two types are found to be equally represented (it will be recalled that this question of the number of days comes at the end of the interview, hence after all the preceding questions have been solved. See Mon's case). In the first case, the child begins correctly by placing the doll's stopping point half-way along the car's path, but, with the later journeys, the subject is obsessed by the memory of the original difference between the stopping points and, no longer considering the distances covered, unconsciously, but to a greater extent each time, brings the doll's stopping point closer to the car's he thus tends to return to the conservation of an absolute difference and even, in extreme cases, unites the two points. Hence the random forecasts on the number of days the doll would need to catch up with the car. In the second case, the child begins on the contrary by conserving the absolute difference, then gradually decentres his attention in favour of the distances, and finally arrives at the relative difference: however, here again the result is wrong because the series began according to another principle. Between these two extreme cases, every kind of fluctuation may be seen.

All things considered, the reactions of this stage II constitute a good example of intuitive regulations finally, through their progressive equilibrium, attaining operational reversibility (Cla's case towards the end). Starting off by denying simultaneousness and synchronism the child cannot, in fact, immediately arrive at the idea of conservation of speed based on the relation of the time and the distance travelled. Therefore, proceeding first of all by intuitions centred on the finishing points, the subject does however gradually decentre his judgement in favour of the actual spatial and temporal intervals, after the absurdities resulting from his original point of view. The regulations which follow, by gradually equalizing the paths anticipated or constructed, thus lead the subject at the same time to progressive structuring of durations, leading in the direction of reversible relations between successive moments of time, and through this very fact to the spatio-temporal conception of speed, making possible the conservation of uniform speeds. Thus, yet again, time and speed appear to be unified from the point of view of the operations which genetically constitute them.

3. *The third stage: Operational conservation of speed, but no understanding of formal proportionality: determination of the distances done in half a day by the car (IIIa) then by the doll (IIIb)*

The subjects of stage III are able unaided to add on equal distances at equal speeds and times, for the doll as for the car, i.e. for two different speeds at the same time. Consequently they master the ideas of simultaneousness and synchronism, and from sub-stage IIIa, they even manage (sometimes without any transition), to find the simple ratio 2 to 1 in the example of the half day's journey by the car. On the other hand, during substage IIIa, they do not succeed in solving this question for the doll, which itself already covers half the distance of the car (hence the dual relationship $\frac{1}{2} \times \frac{1}{2} = \frac{1}{4}$.) In sub-stage IIIb this last problem is solved. But, neither in IIIb nor in IIIa do the subjects manage to forecast how many days journey for the doll correspond to a number of days' travel for the car.

Here are some characteristic examples from sub-stage IIIa, beginning with an intermediate case:

PIE (6; 6). Simultaneousness and synchronism correct. For the second day the paths of the car and the doll are correct. The path of the car, for the third day is too short, but Pie corrects himself saying: (*Journey has to be the same*) because *this day was the same length as the other one*. He gives the doll one complete unit on the third day, but seeing the inequality with the foregoing days, he adds: *That must be wrong* and corrects himself saying: *I looked at the length*. The questions of the half day are successful neither for the car nor the doll.

SER (7; 9) accepts the simultaneousness and the synchronism. On the second day, they set off at the same speeds and for the same times as the first day. Where will they stop? (Rather too long for the car, then corrects himself): *Oh! yes, the same distance as before*. And the doll? (A little too long as well, then measures). *Oh! No, it's the same thing*. And the third day? (Carries forward the correct distances). And if the car only does half a day? (Right). How much does the doll do in one day? (Points). And in two days? (Indicates correctly). And in half a day? (Wrong: indicates one unit). And to go as far as the car (half) how long would the doll need? *Two days*. Hence everything is understood except the last two questions.

NIC (8; 7). Simultaneousness and synchronism correct. At once marks the two paths for the second and third days correctly, measuring accurately and without hesitation for the doll: How far does the car go in half a day? (Too long, then makes it less). And the doll? *As before: it does one day's length*. Why? *Since it does half*. And in one day what does it do? (Right). In two? In three? (Right). And in half a day? *Oh, it only travels a little way* (makes it less, but without precision).

As for the days needed for the doll to catch up on the car, Nic makes a drawing which marks an increasing difference between the corresponding finishing points but he does not comprehend this sufficiently to understand the matter deductively: If the car goes three days, like this, and then four days, five days, etc. will the distance the doll must do to catch up on it always be the same or will it grow longer all the time, or shorter all the time? *It will always be the same.*

REN (8; 10) accepts simultaneousness and synchronism. Second day: right for the car: *because it has to go the same distance as the day before, if it goes at the same speed. And if it does that (slightly longer journey) in the same times? Then it would have been faster, if it travelled the same length of time both days.* And the doll? (The path he indicates is too long but he corrects it at once). *No, it has to do the same road as before. Both of them go at the same speed all the time* (=conserve their respective speeds). And the following days? (Quite right).

A child walks one hour and goes 1 km. If he walks another hour at the same speed? *He will do the same distance.* Could he possibly go a longer distance? *Perhaps a bit longer if he went a bit faster.* But it is exactly the same speed? *Then he does the same distance.*

And if the car goes for half a day? (Gives a visual estimate, then measures accurately). *That comes to the same distance as the doll.* And how far does the doll go in half a day? (Indicates the unit). Why? *Oh, no, that's not right, because it has to go a shorter distance* (but he hardly makes it any smaller). As for the days needed to catch up on the car, he becomes confused in spite of his drawing and makes three days for the car correspond to four and four to five days for the doll.

GEO (9; 10) begins by getting the paths correct, for the car and the doll: he finds the half journey for the car in half a day, but he is not successful with the doll: And how far did the doll go while the car did its half day journey? . . . . . . Can you tell? *No.* How much faster does the car go than the doll? . . . . . . In five days how far would the car go? (Drawing correct). And the doll? (Draws correctly). So how many times faster does the car travel? . . . . . .

The new fact, as compared with stages I and II, is that each of these children has understood the relationship: for equal times and equal speeds, the distances covered are necessarily equal. The prior condition for this operation is naturally that equal times and equal spaces have some meaning for the subject, i.e. that simultaneousness of starting and stopping as well as the equality of synchronous durations should be accepted without discussion and that the paths traversed should be conceived as intervals capable of measurement from their starting points. Now, all of these subjects have mastered these ideas. It follows that from the beginning of the interviews the emphasis is placed on the length of the journeys, instead of developing in this direction in the course of discussion as is still the case in stage II. In the transitional case of the subject Pie, this is already clear: 'I looked at the length' says the child in explanation of his method, and 'it's because this day was the same length as the other', he declares to express the principle behind it. In the indisputable cases of this stage, there is no longer any question of an empirical method, but definitely of a deductive operation: 'the car must travel the same distance as the day before, if it goes at the same speed' says Ren. It follows that Q 1 and 2 relating to the respective journeys of the car and the doll no longer present any difficulties at this stage III: from now on there is conservation of uniform speeds and their ratios.

Now, what is the operational nature of this conservation. In other words, by what mechanism of thought did the subjects of stage III come to establish this, beginning with the intuitive regulations of stage II? The essential fact is the possibility of understanding the equality of two units of time when the durations involved are in succession and not synchronous: in fact, the construction of equal units of time implies, at one and the same time, the uniform elapsing of time and the conservation of uniform speeds, just as this conservation implies the idea of successive equal durations (isochronism) and consequently the uniform elapsing of time. It has been seen elsewhere how the concept of successive and uniform units of time are formed.[1] On the one hand, simultaneousness and the equality of synchronous durations are elaborated in terms of additive, associative, and reversible operations, whose composition, which is still entirely qualitative (seriation and 'nesting' or inclusion) permits construction of homo-

[1] *Genesis of Child's Conception of Time.*

geneous time, common to a number of movements perceived simultaneously. On the other hand, the very fact that reversibility is necessary for the construction of synchronous, equal times, means that as soon as this first construction is completed, it may be extended by the conception of two successive durations as if they were synchronous; it is in fact the property of operational reversibility of thought that the order of events and the course of time may be reversed, hence the possibility of passing from the synchronous to the successive, and vice versa: operational synchronism is thus immediately extended into isochronism.[2] However, this passage (from the synchronous to the successive) involves the mind in using as a basis some given external movement capable of duplication and involving the necessary repetition of an equal duration. If synchronization results from a qualitative groupment, then isochronism requires the construction of a repeatable unit, resulting from generalization of the original qualitative operations (and of the fusion of 'nesting' subdivisions and changes of position). This is why, if homogeneous time (=common to all given phenomena simultaneously) is basically of a qualitative nature, then uniform time (=possible equation of successive durations) is necessarily metrical. But it is immediately evident that, in addition to the foregoing, isochronism implies conservation since it involves repetition of any given movement or equivalent distances within one uniform movement. So naturally conservation of uniform speeds appears closely connected genetically to the construction of successive units of duration, i.e. of uniform time: the conservation of a uniform speed and the construction of successive units of time in fact form the two inseparable aspects of a single process, and this is perfectly natural since time itself is simply co-ordination of movements and their speeds.

So, when Pie, at the beginning of the replies in stage III, stages the fundamental truth that 'this day was the

[2] In stage II the subject Dor cannot pass from intuitive synchronization to isochronization (creation of equal units of time) in the absence of the operational mechanism.

same length as the other' the isochronism which he discovers potentially contains the operational conservation of uniform speed, and this is what Ren deduces, when he concludes from the equality of the daily duration that if the moving object travels at equal speeds 'it must cover the same distance'.

But this is nothing less than a circle: the equation of successive durations implies a speed which is conserved, and verification of this conservation implies a measurement of time founded on isochronism. It must therefore be agreed that between these two kinds of metrical operation there appears, as a result of groupment of purely qualitative operations, the conclusion that a movement which travels a certain distance in a given time will cover the same distance in the same time if none of the conditions is changed.[1] It is only when these spaces and these times have to be repeated that the operations becomes metrical.

It is therefore by extending to successive duration distances an equality which has been established qualitatively that the child is prepared for ideas of uniform times and speeds, but this extension, formed by a dual qualitative reversibility (one concerning time and the other space) thus necessarily becomes a metrical system.

But if the subjects at this level achieve the operations which constitute the conservation of speed in this way, the operations involved are still only concrete and not formal. It is in fact striking to observe that these subjects, even while they can indicate the point the car will reach in half a day, cannot manage to do the same right away in the doll's case, as if it were not easy to halve the doll's path after halving the car's journey. On the other hand these subjects observe empirically that the distance separating the doll from the car, at the end of each day, increases from one day to the next. They still cannot make up their minds to anticipate that it will continue to increase (Q 3):

[1] There is no need to stress the fact that the ability to see the possibility of duplicating a movement with its speed, by no means implies that the subject can conceive of the conservation of uniform movement in general, as with the theory of inertia.

the distance to be made up 'will be the same all the time' says Nic. Finally, in spite of repetition of the tests, the child does not succeed in formulating the law according to which the doll travels half the distance of the car in the same times (Q 5). These three difficulties or at least the last two, which thus separate concrete operations from formal operations, raise an interesting question, which will be found again after examining the reactions of sub-stage IIIb.

The only step forward accomplished by the subjects of sub-stage IIIb is in fact, that they manage to generalize the question of the distances travelled in half a day to the doll's journeys:

GIL (8; 1) Q 1 and 2 correct: *And if they both travel for a week, will the doll be able to catch up on the car? The car is a long way in front, the doll cannot catch up on it.* Does it do the same distance every day? *If it goes quicker, it does a longer distance; at the same speed, it does the same distance.* And in half a day how far will the car go? (Correct). And what does the doll do meantime? (Correct). So how many days does the doll have to travel to catch up on the car at this point (one and a half units for the car)? *One and a half days* (i.e. wrong). At the end of the third day, we ask him: You see this distance between the doll and the car which still has to be done. Will there still be the same distance between them the next day, or will it be longer or shorter? *It will be the same.* Why? *Because they always do the same distance.* Show me where they are on the fourth day? (Right). Is the difference the same? *It is bigger.* Why? *The car goes faster.* And on the fifth day what will the difference be? *Just a little bit smaller.* Why? (He makes a drawing). *No, bigger.* And the following day? *It will be the same.* Why? *No, just a little bit farther, because the car goes faster than the doll, and the difference will be a little bit bigger, because it goes quicker.* How long will the doll have to travel to do the distance that the car does in four days? *It will go six days.* And for one day? *Two days.* And for two days? *Three, no, four days.* For three days? *Six days.* And for four? *It will travel for ten days.*

IEA (8; 7) also answers correctly for the half days. You see the difference between the doll and the car (we show him the one on the third day), will it stay the same the next day, or will it be bigger or smaller? *It will be the same.* Why? *They travel at the same speed the next day as on the day before.* Look at where they are on the fourth day? (he indicates this correctly). So the difference? *It's the same thing. Oh, no, it is bigger.*

ED (9; 1) after a slight initial hesitation replies correctly for the first four days (Q 1 and 2). And will the distance between the doll and the car always be the same, or will it be bigger or smaller, on the following days? *The same thing.* Why? *Because they both travel for one day.* Look at what happened on those four days? *Oh, no, it is bigger because the car goes faster. It gets bigger all the time, because the car draws ahead all the time, and the doll stays farther behind.* And the fourth day, what will the difference be? *The same.* Look. *Oh, no, longer still.* And the sixth day? *Longer.*

Half days correct, for the doll as well as for the car. And now if the car does this extra distance (two days) how far will the doll get? *One day* (=a day's journey) *and a little bit.* And when the car is here (eight days) where will the doll be? (Has to draw it and find it empirically day by day).

TEL (9; 6). Journeys correct: Look (third day): is there a big distance between them? *Yes.* And the next day will it be bigger, smaller, or the same? *It always stays the same.* Why? *They do the same distance every day.* Look. *Oh, it is longer, because the car went faster and the doll slower.* And the fifth day, will it be longer again or not? *Perhaps.* Look. *It's bigger, because the doll went half the distance.* So he seems to be formulating the law but when we ask him how many days the doll will need to catch up with the car four days ahead, or ten days ahead, etc. he is unable to do so, without an empirical construction, and forgets the ratio of 2 to 1.

MAR (10; 7). Same reactions. Finds out empirically that the doll needs six days to do the car's journeys for three days, but he cannot generalize to five or to ten. Moreover he believes the difference is constant in spite of the observations made.

Thus we can see that these subjects, just like those of sub-stage IIIa conserve the speed operationally, by deduc-

ing the equality of the successive journeys from that of the
speeds and the times: 'At the same speed, it does the same
distance' says Gil. In addition, and this is their innovation, they are immediately able to determine the distance
performed in one half day by the doll and no longer just
that of the car. But they do not manage, any more than
those at level IIIa, either to forecast that the differences in
distance between the car's and the doll's stopping points
increase regularly (Q 6) or to formulate the proportion of
1 to 2 which links their respective journeys (Q 5).

As regards Q 6 (and this is interesting from the viewpoint of the theory of time-lags) it is evident that these
subjects from 8 to 10 years reproduce exactly these mistakes which they now no longer make when they are
actually constructing the successive paths of the doll in
relation to those of the car, but which they regularly made
in the course of stages I and II. They believe that the
absolute difference in the stopping points is maintained,
and only manage empirically, after much trial and error,
to forecast that it will increase (see in particular Gil and
Ed). As for the ratio of 2 to 1 between the distances
traversed by the car and the doll, it is extraordinary to
see these subjects, who can correctly deduce one by one
the respective daily journeys of the two moving objects,
as well as their journeys for half a day, unable to formulate the law according to which the car goes twice as far
as the doll in the same time. And yet, in each particular
case, they see this ratio perfectly well, since Tel, in referring to the distance between two simultaneous stopping
points says 'it's bigger because the doll went just half
the distance'. But, when we return to the general problem
of forecasting how many days the doll will need to make
a journey performed in n days by the car, they are unable to give the answer 2n simply by doubling the suggested figure and have to proceed empirically at the risk of
gross errors (see Gil, Ed and Tel).

These reactions are easily explained. In order to solve
the problem of the conservation of speed, concrete operations alone are required: bringing forward equal distances
from equal times, i.e. no longer only considering the stop-

ping points alone, but also considering starting points and intervening intervals (distances and durations). But in order to solve the three problems; (i) of the distance covered in half a day by the doll, going half as fast as the car; (ii) of the absolute distance between the stopping points, which will continually increase beyond the limits of the construction already carried out; (iii) and of the ratio of 1 to 2 between the journeys to come, more is needed than a simple concrete construction: in fact a hypothetico-deductive one, i.e. formal, construction, analogous to that necessitated by the concept of the extensive or metrical propositions analysed in Chapter Nine.

In the case of the half-day journeys, which is the easiest case in half a day a doll does one half of its own distance, just as the car does half of its own distance, the problem may be solved either by reasoning (the journey of the car=1, that of the doll=½, hence ½×½=¼) or empirically. The best proof that the child proceeds by the empirical method of simple dichotomy, not by deduction from the proportions is that this problem of the half days is solved in two stages: for the car in substage IIIa and for the doll in IIIb. As for Q 5 and 6 (ratio 1 to 2, and increase in the absolute difference), it is clear that their solution is only possible by a formal method. It is only in retrospect, and once the constructions are completed, that their solution is possible by concrete operations, while if it is a question of forecasting (and this is what is asked), reasoning has to manipulate future journeys, hence hypothetical ones, related to one another purely by proportion. Thus we find again the results of Chapter Nine as compared with those of Chapter Seven: just as comparison of the speeds of successive movements defined by unequal times and spaces went beyond the framework of concrete operations (adequate for the case of simultaneous movements), so it can now be seen that forecasting the ratio of two future movements implies hypothetico-deductive operations, while forecasting the continuation of each of these two movements may be ensured by concrete operations. Simple continuation of the given movements (conservation of speed discovered in this stage III) in fact only constitutes a problem relating to a single system, while the ratio of future movements, each of which must be constructed mentally and not in practice, raises a problem of formal proportion because it is a case of relating to one another two distinct systems: $D_1/D_2 = \frac{1}{2}$ and $(2D_2 - 2D_1) > (D_2 - D_1)$, where D_2 is the distance travelled by the car, and D_1 that travelled by the doll in the same time.

4. The fourth stage: Deduction of the ratio of uniform speeds and formal operations of proportionality. Conclusions

Just as the subjects of stage III manage by means of concrete operations to deduce the equality of successive journeys from that of the durations and the speeds, and hence to construct the respective movements of the two moving objects with their different speeds, by coordinating the stopping points progressively drawing apart from one another, in the case of each journey; so the children of stage IV manage by means of formal operations to anticipate this regular increase in the distance between the finishing points as well as the constant ratio between the paths traversed before completing their construction. The average age for the commencement of this stage IV is from 10 to 11 years, but as in each of these problems of proportionality, some exceptionally early reactions may be found from 9 and even from 8½ years.

RAY (8; 6). Simultaneousness and synchronism correct. Journeys of the second day correct: The third day the car only travels up to midday? *Then it will do half the distance.* And the doll as well just up to midday? *I'm taking the measuring card for the doll and I'm looking for where half of it comes.* Now see how long the car will need to do what the doll does in three days? *One and a half days.* And for this (six days) or this (eight), can you tell me? *One half less.* Why? *The car travels this distance, so you have to measure half of that for the doll.* What is the distance between the two of them on the third day? *That.* And the days following that?

It will stay . . . oh, no, it isn't the same because the car goes faster. The distance gets longer all the time.

LAN (9; 6). All the journeys, including the halves are correct. The difference between the car and the doll will be the same on the next day? It will be bigger. Why? The car goes faster, and it always goes the same distance, and the doll goes slowly, and it always does the same distance as well. What is the difference between their two paths? It's half. The car goes ten days and travels this distance, so how long will it take the doll to do so? Twenty days. And for this distance here (half the previous one)? Ten days etc. No mistakes.

NIN (10; 10). Journeys correct. Does the difference between the two of them always stay the same? No, longer all the time. For this distance here how many days will the car need? Two. And the doll (without looking)? It will go for four days. How did you find that out? I worked it out: the doll always does half.

LAUR (11; 4). Journeys correct. And the distance between the two will it increase the third day or stay the same? The same. Oh, no, not at all: it will increase every day because the car goes quicker. How long would the doll need to do this distance (six days for the car)? (He starts to count on the drawing, but from the second day, says): Twelve days, because the doll does half the distance each day.

This is the only way in which this evolution of the ideas of conservation of speed and the constant ratio between two distinct uniform speeds is completed. Before trying to interpret the whole of this development, it is important to recall how much it converges with the results of Chapters Seven and Nine.

Two obstacles in fact hold back the children of stages I and II (hence up to 7 to 8 years) in solving the questions asked. Firstly as regards the greater speed (that of the car) they confuse the distance covered each day—which remains constant—with the total distance, which increases in terms of the arrangement of the stopping points, and either simply conclude that the object will move farther ahead each day, or even that it will do a longer journey each day. There is, then, no differentiation between the order of the stopping points and the length of the intervals. Secondly, as regards the difference in speed between the two moving objects, this also is judged by the difference in the stopping points, a difference believed to be either approximately or strictly constant (primacy of the absolute difference over the relative difference). Stage III (prepared for by intuitive regulations in stage II) marks a liberation from this centration of the initial intuition upon the stopping points: in becoming reversible, spatio-temporal operations allow the child to see that a unit of duration may be the same the next day as the day before, hence that, at equal speeds, the distance travelled will also be the same. The conservation of speed will thus become operational. Now, this evolution from stage I to stage III is exactly parallel to that described in Chapter Seven: differences in speed are evaluated at first only in terms of the stopping points of moving objects, then distances and durations are differentiated from the spatial arrangement of these points and speed is constructed operationally, by generalization from the schema of overtaking, as a ratio between time and distance travelled. It is when this construction is completed, of course, that the conservation of uniform speed becomes possible, this conservation being simply the metrical sequel of the earlier construction which was both qualitative and metrical.

But Chapter Nine taught us that the difficulties reappear when the movements to be compared are no longer of equal durations and unequal lengths, or vice versa, but have both unequal times and unequal distances, especially when the movements are in succession and no longer simultaneous. When these new conditions appear, the ratios in question must in fact be deduced by formal operations and no longer concretely, and in particular the 'relationships of ratios' which form proportions must be constructed formally. Hence the existence of two new substages: level IIIa during which speeds of movements in succession are not even understood in the case of equal spaces with unequal durations, or vice versa, and sub-stage IIIb during which the problem is solved for movements in succession (as it was from the beginning of stage III in the case of simultaneous movements), but not so far the problem of times and distances being both unequal. Finally, stage IV, which begins towards 10 to 11 years, sees the formation of the conception of proportions of the hypothetico-deductive level, by which speeds of movements in succession may be compared, even in the case of both unequal times and unequal distances.

Now, it is noteworthy that the problem of the conservation of speeds should lead to results which are exactly parallel. In fact, in sub-stage IIIa the child with concrete operations manages not only to conceive of the conservation of two speeds, one of which is twice the other, but also to indicate the distance which the faster of the two objects will travel in half a unit of time (the car's halfday); but, curiously enough, he cannot carry out the same operation (simple halving) with the slower moving object. Now, this difference, which is at first sight surprising, is self explanatory when compared with the results of Chapter Nine. If it were only a question of forecasting the path which the slower moving object (the doll) viewed in isolation, would do in one half unit, there would naturally be no additional difficulty there, since the problem is solved for the faster object considered separately. But the question is to find out what the doll will do in half a day while the car does half its own journey in the same half day. In other words, we do in fact put the problem in terms of movements perceived in succession and defined by equal times and unequal distances: according to the results of Chapter Nine, it is therefore in sub-stage IIIb that this kind of question is solved and this is just what we find again here. As for the car's and the doll's journeys as entire units of time, the problem is easier, since for each of the two moving objects each daily journey is comparable with the one which went before, and even if it is a case of movements in succession there are from this point of view times and spaces which are respectively equal.

As for sub-stage IIIb, two final questions remain to be solved: that of the constantly increasing difference in the

distance between the stopping points of objects moving at
unequal speeds, and that of the ratio of 1 to 2 in their
respective paths. Now, in both these cases, even if the
times are equal, there are still four unequal spaces interrelated by a proportion each time. Understanding that
distance between the successive stopping points of the two
moving objects increases regularly, is in fact seeing that if
the journeys, calculated in succession from the starting
points, are in the ratio of 1 to 2; 2 to 4; 3 to 6; etc. the
distance separating these journeys increased by the difference $2-1=1$; $4-2=2$; $6-3=3$, etc. On the other hand,
to understand that the ratio of the distances traversed by
the two moving objects will always be 2 to 1, is in fact to
grasp this proportion $1/2=2/4=3/8$ etc. In short, in each of
these two questions there occur relationships between ratios, hence proportions, and these are between 4 different
lengths: a part journey and the whole journey for the doll
and the car. So it is clear that the solution of these two
problems in the form of forecasting the journeys to come,
implies a hypothetico-deductive deduction consisting of
constructing a system of formal proportions: thus there
appear new operations, very different from those which
suffice for solving these same questions by the successive
composition of particular cases. In short, the general solution of these two questions is formal because it requires an
awareness of proportionality, i.e. of secondary operations,
while the gradual construction of the journeys only requires concrete operations, because it does not presuppose
the schema of proportions. Put in yet another way, formal
solutions result from reflection on the concrete construction, and this is why there is a time-lag between the
solutions of the same questions as in stage III (a and b)
and in stage IV, although they are logically identical; so
we see once again that 'formal operations' are only 'concrete operations', which are however transposed from the
level of the organization of experience to the level of
propositions and their implications, i.e. transformed into
operations bearing upon other preliminary operations.

Thus stage IV, which is characterized by the formal
solution of the foregoing questions, marks the appearance

of operations which are new in one sense, but which in another sense directly reproduce the construction already completed in stage III on the level of concrete operations. This is a good example of a vertical time-lag (from the concrete to the formal) analogous to all those with which the child's intellectual development abounds. This time-lag extends so far that it involves not only the appearance of operational solutions, which are concrete towards 7 to 8 years, and formal towards 10 to 11 years, but even the intuitive regulations which precede them and pave the way for them in both cases. We have, in fact, seen how in stage II, the initial centration on the stopping points gives rise to a gradual decentration, which articulates the intuition into a system of regulations preparing for concrete operations. Now, in stage IIIb, in relation to the questions of formal proportion, which are still insoluble at this level, an analogous decentration in relation to the stopping points is again found, leading to the same fluctuations characteristic of intuitive regulation: while denying that the absolute distance between stopping points increases during future journeys, the child of sub-stage IIIb is in fact progressively unsettled by new experiments, hence reactions of Gil's type (§ 3) foreseeing a distance either 'just a little shorter' or 'just a little longer'. The evolution leading from level IIIa to level IV by way of IIIb thus, broadly speaking, repeats that leading from level I to level III by way of stage II and this again is parallel to what we observed in Chapters Seven and Nine regarding the actual construction of the relationships of speed.

CHAPTER ELEVEN

Uniformly Accelerated Movement

The study which we have just read on the conservation of
speed naturally implies, by way of a complement, an
analysis of acceleration. If, in fact, the progressive discovery of the uniformity of a speed, particularly conservation
of the ratios between movements of dissimilar uniform
speeds, really implies the elaboration first of concrete and
later of formal metrical operations, these operations must,
by the very fact of their existence, permit acquisition of
the concept of uniformly accelerated speeds. This is what
we are now going to investigate.

1. Technique and general results

The easiest situation to study in the child's case is that of
accelerated movement on an inclined plane. The subject is
first shown a white board, which acts as a snow-covered
road down which a ball rolls. The preliminary question (Q
1) is to find out how the ball (or sledge) comes down, and
if its speed always stays the same. Once this point is clear
(a general affirmation of acceleration is nearly universal,
which allows the interview to proceed, but by no means
implies anticipation of the spatio-temporal ratios), the
child is shown a large drawing representing a child travelling on his sledge down a uniform slope. The slope is
marked with flags at equal distances (four intervals): Q 2
then is to discover on which of these intervals the speed of
the sledge will be greatest and what the relations of speed
will be from one interval to the next (greater, less, or
equal). Returning after this to the board, we plant little

flags at equal intervals (and again four in number as on the drawing), and ask Q 3: how long will the tobogganist take to travel the first interval, then the second, the third and the last one? Finally, comes Q 4: the tobogganist again comes downhill, but with a watch in his hand, and every minute (or every three or five minutes, as the child wishes) he shouts 'hey' to the spectators placed at the side of the track; at every 'hey' a spectator plants a pennant and the question is to find out what the distances will be between the pennants. Q 3 thus concerns the decrease in the times over equal distances and Q 4 the increase in the distances covered in equal times.

Out of sixty-five children interviewed (twenty-four girls and forty-one boys, from 5 to 14 years old) it was possible to establish the following stages, in correlation with those for the conservation of speed. During stage I, the subject does not possess the concept of uniform acceleration, any more than he did that of the conservation of uniform speed in the same stage. In the course of stage II the child shows an intuitive conception of uniform acceleration, but cannot translate it into relations of time and distance travelled, i.e. into operational relations of speed. In the case of times corresponding to equal spatial intervals he either believes these times are also equal because the distances are, or else he translates the increase in speed by an increase in the time. As for distances travelled in equal times, the subject either thinks they are equal because the times are, or else, curiously enough, that they become less and less because the pace is faster. In stage III, the mistakes remain the same at first, because continuous acceleration implies comparisons between successive speeds with equal times and unequal distances or vice versa (unlike uniform movement in which case the successive journeys are equal in distance and duration), and a mechanism analogous to formal proportionality, but the solution is later discovered by progressive experimentation and intuitive regulations. Finally in stage IV (average appearance: 11 years), acceleration is conceived operationally, to the extent that it is continuous and regular, whether it is translated in the form of uniformly accelerated

speed (constant difference in the lengths from one unit of
duration to the next, or constant difference in the duration
from one unit of length to the next), or whether in the
form of a gradual increase in the differences. In spite of
the error of physics involved in this last solution, its
operational structure is, of course, on the same level as the
first.

2. The first stage: No acceleration as a function of descent.
The second stage: Intuitive acceleration

In the great majority of cases, our subjects are familiar
with acceleration from their own experience. They have
used sledges, have already cycled (on their own cycle or
sitting on the seat fixed for them on their parents' cycle),
have let balls or marbles roll down inclined planes, etc.
They express this acceleration by speaking of the burst of
speed (elan) gathered by the object in the course of the
movement. But just as in the last chapter we saw some
young children who, though they have certainly known of
the existence of practically uniform movements (a train, a
car, etc. after the positive acceleration of starting up and
before the negative acceleration of coming to a stop), are
unable to carry forward an equal distance to show this
uniformity, so here we find some young subjects who
cannot translate their experience of acceleration by saying
that the moving object goes faster and faster, or simply
'faster' in the course of its movement. Here are two examples of this initial stage:

PIE (5; 6) is shown the board: Have you ever been on a
sledge? Yes. See this lovely slide straight downhill, and this
little sledge. On a slope like that will the sledge go at the
same speed all the way, or will it be quicker at the top, or
in the middle, or at the bottom? The same speed all the
way. Why? It's coming down all the way. Is there no place
where it goes quicker, up at the top or down at the bottom?
Yes, at the top. Why? It starts off with a burst of speed
(elan). What does that mean? It's when you go slowly and

afterwards you go fast. So on a slope like that when do you have most speed? *Going down. You don't have any going up.* That's right. And why do you get up speed going downhill? *Because you get a burst of speed (elan).* How's that? *To go fast.* And when do you have most speed (elan), up at the top of the slope, near the bottom, or half-way down? *At the top.* Why? *Because at first you are not moving, then you get a burst of speed.* Yes, but where does the sledge go quickest, at the top or the bottom? *The same all the way.* But where does it have most speed? *At the top.* And where does it go hardest? *Everywhere. At the top first.*

SAM (6; 11). Have you got a sledge? *No.* A bicycle? *Yes.* Going downhill, do you go at the same speed all the way? *Faster when I start off.* Show me (from the window) a hill you know. *Over there* (points out a steep slope near the school). When you come down that on your bicycle do you go quicker at the top or near the bottom? *The same all the way.* Watch this ball (letting it roll down the board). Where does it go fastest? *At the top.* Watch again. *In the middle.*

There is no point in lingering over these cases. Clearly at the level where speed is still simply the intuition of overtaking, attached to the intuitive order of the stopping points but without correlation of the time and the distance travelled, acceleration may only be conceived in the shape of an elan or short intense effort. However, this intuition of an elan remains quite subjective or egocentric: it is made up of muscular, or kinaesthetic, or physical impressions and is by no means connected at first with the idea of an external force such as gravity acting on a descending object. It has already been seen in another work (*The Child's Conception of Physical Causality*, Chapter Four) that stream water does not run downhill by reason of its weight, but by putting on a spurt to travel towards lakes etc. and low-lying parts generally. This same idea is met again here: a burst of speed, an elan, even going downhill, seems to the young child something actively adopted by personal effort, not something passively undergone. Hence on a slope the elan is greater at first, since it indicates the intention of movement, as opposed to the previous state of

rest; as for the speed, it is either the same throughout,
which amounts to saying that the question is meaningless
for the subject, or else it depends on the *elan*, hence Sam's
judgement: 'faster when I set off'. So these subjects were
not asked Q 3 and 4.

Stage II on the other hand is characterized by a basically empirical intuition of acceleration as a function of the
incline. So this is an articulated intuition, less egocentric
than intuition of a purely personal *elan*, and connected
with experience of better differentiated actions. This intuition is normally incomplete: the acceleration is neither
continuous nor regular (the ratio of the speeds from one
interval to the next would emerge as e.g. 1=2; 2<3 and
3<4); or 1=2; 2<3 and 3=4, etc.). But it is sometimes
correct, that is to say, looked at carefully, each interval
is given a movement faster than the preceding one
(1<2; 2<3 and 3<4). But, even in this last case, there
is no correlation of time with distance travelled and the
relationships involved consist only of a translation in terms
of 'faster' or 'greater *elan*' or 'slower'. Moreover, from
stage II two types of reaction are found which reappear
in the course of stage III.

According to the first of these two types, equal distances correspond to equal times and vice versa:

BER (6; 8) Q 1: *The ball goes faster near the foot. It goes
slower at the top because it was only getting under way.*

Q 2: Does the sledge go at the same speed all the way?
*No, it goes slowly for the first bit, and faster for the last
bit. And 2 and 3? Same speed. And 1 and 2? Slower on the
first one than on the second one.*

Q 3: same times. Q 4: We'll put in a flag for every minute.
What sort of lengths will that give us? *The same length for
every minute.*

According to the second type of reaction, the equal
distances covered correspond to times becoming constantly
longer, by reason of the elementary relation (more quick-
ly=more time), but it is interesting that, corresponding to
equal times, the distances covered are smaller and smaller,
by reason of the intuition (already studied in Chapter Six)

according to which one goes faster when one has less far to go:

DAL (6; 7) Q 1 and 2: *It goes faster at the foot, because it gathers speed going down. Intervals: 4>3; 3>2; 2=1.*

Q 3: One minute, two minutes, three minutes and four minutes. Why? *Because it goes harder all the time.* Do you go faster when you run than when you walk? *Yes.* Then do you take a longer or a shorter time? *A longer time.*

Q 4: Dal draws shorter and shorter intervals: Why? *Because it goes faster.* But why do you make it a short distance if it goes faster? *Because it finishes quicker.*

MIC (6; 10) Q 1: When you're sledging is the speed the same all the way? *It's very fast in the middle.* Why? *Because I gather impetus.* Where do you go fastest, at the foot, or in the middle? *Fastest at the bottom. There is more impetus.* Q 3: How long does it take to the first flag? *Two minutes.* And from the first flag to the second one? *Three minutes.*

Q 4: We put in a flag every three minutes. Mic draws smaller and smaller intervals: Do you travel the same distance when you go fast as when you go slowly? *A shorter distance.* And when you run, how far can you go? *I do a shorter distance the more I run, the closer I get* (cf. confusion of the order of the stopping points with the distance). But when the watch shows three minutes here (third interval) does the sledge go at the same speed? *Faster. The little girl would go fast and faster. The whole time there is the same number* (of minutes) *to do.* Is the distance the same as well? *A shorter distance.*

Watch: I'm tapping on the table (index finger) for ten seconds. Now, I'll tap again for another ten seconds, but faster: will that be more or less taps? *If you tap for the same number of seconds, there will not be so many taps. If you tap quicker, there will not be so many taps.* Watch (experiment). *There are more taps.* Now I'm walking for ten seconds. If I walk faster, shall I be doing a shorter or a longer distance. *You will finish* (!) *faster.* So finishing quicker: 'get closer'='shorter distance'.

There is no point in stressing these two kinds of reaction just yet, because, curiously enough, they will reappear throughout stage III, given that the speeds to be compared with one another are successive and not simultaneous, and it is a question of equal times and unequal distances, or equal distances and unequal durations.

3. The third stage: Articulated intuition of acceleration but without accurate correlation of times and distances travelled

Sub-stage IIIa

In Q 1 and 2, the children at this level, like the foregoing, answer that the speed increases during the descent. At most this increase is conceived as more continuous and regular. As for Q 3 and 4 once again we observe the contrast between judgements bearing on simultaneous movements with those relating to movements in succession, or successive sections of a single movement: though these subjects of the third stage have in fact mastered the spatio-temporal relationships involving the first of these two situations, they are by no means able to apply these relationships to acceleration and they regard the latter in the same way as subjects of stage II (cf. in Chapter Seven and Nine the same time-lag between the reactions of stages IIb and IIIa according to whether the movements are simultaneous or in succession). In this connection the two types of answer already distinguished in § 2 are again found.

With the subjects of the first type, equal distances correspond to equal times, in spite of acceleration and equal times to equal distances:

LAN (8; 4) Q 1 to 2: *It's a little faster near the foot. Why? Because it's going downhill. But it does that all the way? Yes, but it goes a little slower up at the top because it has only just started.*

Q 3: *First interval? Five minutes. And the second? Same. Why? It's the same length. But it's going faster? Yes. And there (third)? Still faster. And how long? Five minutes as well.*

Q 4: he plants the flags at equal distances. *Because it's always one minute.*

NEL (8; 8) Q 1 to 2: At first slowly, because you've just let it go (the ball) and then fast because it's been going for quite a while. Ratios of speeds of intervals: $1<2=3<4$.

Q 3: First interval: *One minute. And the second one? The same. Why? It's the same distance.* But it goes faster? *Yes.* So does that give you the same time? . . . . . . *And the fourth? One minute again.*

Q 4: He draws four equal intervals corresponding to the partial durations which he chose to be five minutes: Are they all equal? *Yes. Why? Because five minutes is a lot.* Is it just as fast at the top as it is down below? *No, slower, because it has just pushed off.* And so it does the same distance in five minutes as it does at the foot? *Yes. Why? It's always five minutes.*

Certain other subjects, characteristic of a type II, on the other hand, accept that the times increase with acceleration while the distances diminish. Here are some examples of this topsy turvy logic, which is the more curious because in the case of simultaneous movements, these subjects use correct operations:

LIL (7; 11) Q 1: It goes faster at the end. Why? Because it's on a slope, it has gathered speed. Q 2: each interval faster than the one before. Q 3: One, two, five, six minutes. Why? Because it goes quicker all the time. Well then, if it goes quicker? It takes more time.

Q 4: The little girl looks at her watch. Every three minutes she shouts Hey! So you have to put in flags to show the distances she does in three minutes. Will the first stretch be the same as the second? No, the first one will be longer. But does it go faster on the second? Yes. So? It does a shorter distance.

ALB (8; 6) Q 1 to 2: It goes faster and faster. Q 3 (equal intervals): It will take three minutes, here, then four minutes, etc.

Q 4 (equal durations): A shorter length each time (he puts in the flags) because it goes faster. Why? You do a shorter distance when you come down faster.

AND (9; 2) Q 2: second interval same speed as the first, but third one quicker and fourth still faster. Q 3: So how long to travel the first length? *Two minutes.* And the second? *Four minutes.* And the third? *Six minutes.* And the fourth? *Eight minutes.* So where does it go hardest? *At the end.*

Q 4: We ask him to draw the distances corresponding to five minutes each time: he makes them shorter and shorter. Which one will be shortest? *At the end.* Where does the sledge go fastest? *There, at the foot.*

Before discussing these strange reactions, let us state again that the two types distinguished by no means appear to characterize two substages, for some children seem to pass indifferently from one to the other in connection with the same question, or are of the first type with Q 3 and of the second with Q 4 or vice versa. Here are some examples of these alternations:

EVE (7; 2) passes from type I to type II. She thinks that the sledge goes faster towards the end. Q 3 (equal intervals): *Ten minutes apiece.* How does it go here (last interval)? *Faster.—Fastest of all,* etc. So do you think it takes longer, or the same time to do the first stretch and the last one? *Less time for the first one, because it goes less quickly.*

Q 4: starts again with equal intervals. But at the end, is it faster or slower? *Faster.* So does it go farther or not so far in five minutes if it goes quicker? *Not so far.*

IAC (7; 5) on the contrary, passes from type II to type I. The tobogganist goes faster all the time, because he gathers speed. Hence (Q 4) with equal sections: one, two, three and four minutes. Are the lengths between the flags equal? *Yes.* Does it go faster all the time? *Yes.* Why did you say one, two three and four minutes? *I should have said one minute each time.*

In the same way, with the intervals to be given for one minute each time (Q 4) Iac starts by giving shorter and shorter distances. Why always smaller? *I made a mistake: they should be the same all the time.*

GU (7; 10) is type II for Q 3 and type I for Q 4. The sledge goes slower at the top, because it was only starting off, and faster at the foot because it had already travelled for quite a long time. Equal intervals (Q 3) are then timed one, two, two and a half, and three and a half minutes: Why longer at the foot? *Because it comes down faster.*

But the intervals each corresponding to one minute are all the same length because they are all one minute.

GIS (9; 8) is also of type II for Q 3 and type I for Q 4. The sledge goes faster and faster because it gathers speed. Hence Q 3 with equal intervals: *Three minutes, then a little more, four minutes and (the last one) a bit more than four minutes.* Where does it go fastest? *At the bottom.* And where does it take the most time? *At the bottom.*

As for equal durations (Q 4) it travels equal lengths. Why? *Because it does three minutes each time.*

MON (7; 10) conversely is type I for Q 3 and type II for Q 4. The sledge gathers more speed all the way down. But the equal intervals (Q 3) each take one minute. On the other hand the intervals corresponding to one minute (Q 4) are shorter and shorter because it goes faster all the time.

ARL (9; 5) also is type I for Q 3 and type II for Q 4. *The sledge goes faster all the way down.* Why? *Because at the top it's only just beginning: it's just starting to go.* Equal intervals (Q 3) are then each covered in five minutes. But in five minutes (Q 4) the distances travelled are shorter all the time. Show me the shortest one? *There.* Why is that the smallest one? *Because it was going faster.*

It is evident that these reactions are exactly similar to those of stage II. They differ from them in fact on only two points, one of which is given independently of these interviews and the other is to be seen only in retrospect. The first is that unlike subjects of stage II, children placed in stage III know perfectly well, when the speeds of two simultaneous movements have to be compared, how to correlate operationally the distance travelled with the time taken. It is only because the question here concerns speeds characterizing the successive parts of one movement, and bearing on equal times and unequal distances or vice versa (and not on respectively equal times and distances) that they revert to difficulties already overcome in the case of simultaneous movements. This systematic time-lag belonging to sub-stage IIIa is already familiar from Chapter Four and it is exactly the same in both cases (equal times and unequal distances or vice versa). As for seeing why these subjects of stage IIIa fail in questions of acceleration when they successfully co-ordinate the times and distance of successive trajectories in the problem of the conservation of a uniform movement, the reason is simple: in this last case, the distances and times are both equal from one section to the next. The second difference between stages II and IIIa is that, once the foregoing replies are given, subjects of level IIIa may be easily enlightened and helped to more advanced reactions: they have only to be questioned on simultaneous movements, and then brought back to the question of acceleration, for them to feel their contradictions and start to answer correctly. This will appear spontaneously in sub-stage IIIb. It is easy to elicit it in IIIa.

However bizarre these reactions may appear they are easy to understand when taken separately. Only their incoherent arrangement sets a problem, along with the persistence of this incoherence throughout stage III. Their common principle is that acceleration, even if intuitively correlated with the incline, is not yet, for the reasons just seen (partial journeys to be compared being in succession, and not simultaneous) conceived as a relation between time and distance travelled.

The reactions of type I, first of all, are self explanatory. In the absence of the ability to compare the speeds of two successive movements the simplest attitude certainly consists of supposing that equal times will correspond to equal distances and vice versa. As for type II, in almost every one of our researches on time and speed, the relation 'faster=longer' has been found, and so this need not be specially resumed here (see Origins of the Conception of Time, Chapter Three) and in the present work, Chapters Six and Seven. There remains the curious reasoning according to which the distances traversed diminish regularly with the increasing speed. But this too is already known to us: this is what makes younger children, in the case of two unequal distances with the same starting and finishing points (Chapter Four, § 2) or in the case of two concentric tracks to be compared (ibid, § 3) say that the shorter distance corresponds to the greater speed because it is completed more quickly. In stages I and II, this undifferentiated intuition is accompanied by a confusion of relations of order relating to stopping points with relations of distance, as if speed were measured in terms of the goal to be reached, i.e. of the distance still to be traversed, and not of the distance travelled: thus Mic (stage II, § 2) says that 'a greater speed corresponds to a smaller distance: the more I run the nearer I get'. But in stage III where this intuition is only residual, reasoning simply amounts to the equation: faster=stopped sooner =less distance to do.

However, even if each of these reactions is individually explicable in this way, it is still curious that indisputable cases of type II should simultaneously make a correspondence between a greater speed, and on the one hand a longer time (hence a greater distance traversed), and yet on the other hand, a shorter distance traversed. In stage II this incoherence is not surprising, for at a preoperational level it is normal for such contradictions to be produced between intuitions, which operations alone could make consistent by making them reversible. But how can such gross contradictions persist in stage III which is that of concrete operations? At this level in fact, temporal 'groupments' are completed in their dual aspect of the order of succession, and 'nesting' of durations, along with the group of metrical durations based on the idea of uniform and continuous movement. Hence this idea of the conservation of speed is itself acquired when a single movement is considered, difficulties only beginning with the comparison of two dissimilar uniform speeds: in this case their difference increases all the time, which is in fact equivalent to conceiving their relation as an acceleration. If these ideas of time, of conservation of uniform speed (and naturally of spatio-temporal relations of speed in the case of simultaneous movements) are acquired from the beginning of stage III, how, then, can the fact be explained that in the field of accelerated movement, absurd notions concerning the relations between the speed, the distance and the times can persist and even appear in a mutually contradictory form?

Let us first recall that comparison of the successive phases of a single accelerated movement cannot be likened to comparison of the phases corresponding to a single uniform movement, but may in fact be likened to the comparison of the successive phases of two uniform movements of different speeds. Indeed by the very fact of its acceleration, a single accelerated movement constitutes from one moment to the next a different movement with a new speed, so that comparison of these speeds is psychologically equivalent to comparison of different movements. In Chapter Nine the children were asked to compare two successive movements with equal times and unequal distances or vice versa, to find out which had the greater speed. The present questions on accelerated movement amount respectively to asking, if in two successive phases the same space is traversed in different speeds, what will the unequal times be: or, if these phases have equal durations and different speeds, what will be the unequal spaces: hence these are clearly the same problems. We saw in Chapter Nine that these questions are progressively solved only in the course of stages IIIb and IV. And above all, we saw that in the absence of their solution in sub-stage IIIa the subjects of this level present, exactly like our present subjects, all sorts of residual errors analogous to those of stages I and II with respect to simultaneous movements. Moreover, we have just seen in Chapter Ten that when they are reasoning on the relationship of two distinct uniform movements (a relationship which may in point of fact be likened to an acceleration since the difference in the stopping points constantly increases) these same subjects of level IIIa reason in a similarly prelogical way, even while reasoning quite logically regarding the conservation of a single uniform speed. Thus we can conclude from all these analogies that the present situation is by no means exceptional, but conforms to the general rule of a vertical time-lag.

Once again the reason for this curious time-lag is simply

that the comparison of the successive phases of an accelerated movement, as well as of two dissimilar movements in succession, involves a formal or hypothetico-deductive mechanism, whilst the comparison of simultaneous movements, or of the successive though equal phases of a single uniform movement, only requires concrete operations. Now, formal operations come into play when two systems are to be correlated which are dissimilar, i.e. cannot be simultaneously manipulated, nor, consequently, reduced to a single reversible process. And the rôle of formal operations is to make these two distinct systems simultaneous, which can only be achieved mentally, by hypothesis. Hence the hypothetico-deductive nature of these new operations which otherwise reproduce concrete operations in detail. So one can see why, in this present case, the children of stage IIIa reason differently with accelerated movements as against simultaneous and uniform movements. In this last case (cf. Chapter Seven and Nine) it is a question of a single situation, in spite of the duality of the speeds to be compared, and their reasoning then attains the logic of concrete operations. On the contrary when their thinking must hypothetically correlate two successive situations as if they were simultaneous, then, lacking a formal mechanism, logic of any kind is still absent, and there reappear at this level IIIa the prelogical procedures proper to the earlier intuitions. In fact, so long as the subject has not succeeded in forging the hypothetico-deductive tools allowing him to reason simultaneously about two distinct situations, he is left to make what use he can of intuitive procedures, from which he has only just freed himself on the concrete level; even more he will not be aware of the contradictions involved in these procedures, as in order to see them he would have to possess the formal logical mechanism which is just what he still lacks in the case of two different situations to be compared mentally.

4. The third stage: Gradual success in correlating times and distances successively traversed

Sub-stage IIIb

In the course of the second half of this same stage, the subjects react at first like the previous ones (except perhaps that type I becomes rather less common as age increases), but they go on to correct themselves spontaneously, or as an almost immediate result of the questions asked, until everything is answered correctly. Furthermore, it is to be noted that the question of equal distances (Q 3) appears to be a little easier than that of unequal distances (Q 4) so that in fact several of the following subjects answer the first of these correctly from the beginning:

RAY (8; 2) Q 1 to 2: *It goes faster in the middle than at the top, and faster at the end than in the middle, it goes faster and faster all the way down.* And so (Q 3) how long between one flag and the next? *Five, three, one, and half a second.* Why is it less all the time? *Because it's faster all the time.*
  Q 4 (equal durations): Makes smaller and smaller intervals: *Distances shorter and shorter because the sledge goes faster and faster.* You go a shorter distance when you go quicker? *Shorter. Oh, no, the same.* If you run? *Oh, yes, a longer way* (corrects the intervals) *because the sledge goes faster.* How long for each one? *One minute each.*

NA (8; 8). Same reactions with Q 1 to 3.
  Q 4 (equal durations): *They're the same distances.* When you go faster? *Oh, longer* (he makes another drawing but this time with smaller intervals each time). When you go quicker what distance do you do? *Oh, yes, it's longer each time* (alters correctly).

LEO (9; 9) Q 1 to 2: *When you go down, you go faster all the way, because you gather speed from the top.* How long, for these sections? (Q 3)? *Two, four, six minutes.* Why? *Because it's going faster all the time. Oh, no, I made a mistake, it's two minutes each time, two minutes all the way.* Are they all at the same speed? *No, faster at the foot. Oh,* yes, *then the times are shorter and shorter.* Right so now (Q 4 equal durations of five minutes), what distances? *(He makes them equal, but the last one a little bigger).* What about these? *I made a mistake at the beginning: they should be longer all the time, because it's going faster and faster.*

WIL (9; 10) Q 1 to 2: *Faster all the time, because it gathers speed all the way.* Q 3: *decreasing times.*

Q 3 (equal durations of three seconds): *He starts off by drawing increasing distances, i.e. correct.* Why? *I don't know. It goes very fast, so he has gone a longer way every time he gives a shout.* (He draws the distances again, all equal). *No, they are all the same, because he shouts out every three seconds.* When you walk faster, what sort of distance do you do? *Oh, yes* (he returns to his first idea).

DRE (10; 3) Q 1: *It starts off slowly but goes faster and faster.* (Q 2: relations of speed of intervals): 1 = 2 < 3 < 4. Why are the first two the same? *It hasn't got up much speed yet.* And the times (Q 3)? *Three seconds: two and a half, one; a half.* And if he gives a shout every three seconds (Q 4)? (He draws the distances shorter all the time). Why? *They are shorter all the time because it goes faster all the time, it takes less and less time, so the lengths are shorter and shorter.* (NB surprising logic). How long is it each time? *Three seconds . . . Oh, yes, the lengths are longer each time.*

CHRI (10; 4) Q 1 to 2: *Faster all the time.* And the times (Q 3)? *Four seconds, six, eight, and nineteen seconds.* Why? *Because it goes faster all the time.* So if it goes faster? . . . . . . Repeat. *Oh, yes, four, three, two, one seconds.*

Q 4: distances smaller all the time? *because it goes faster at the foot than at the top . . . Oh, yes, the faster it goes, the farther it goes* (he starts again correctly).

AN (10; 4) Q 1 to 2: *It goes faster at the foot, because it gathered speed from the top.* Q 3: *One second each time.* Where does it go fastest? *At the bottom, oh, yes, one, one, a little less than one, and then a little less again.*

Q 4: equal durations:? *about the same for them all.* Does it go at the same speed all the way? *No, not so fast at the top and faster at the foot.* Same times? *No, less at the foot; three, three, two, one.*

Q 4: *All the same because it does three minutes each time.* Same speeds? *Oh, no, longer distances at the foot.*

It is evident how these initial errors may last until an average age of 10 to 11 years in the absence of formal thinking. The only difference between these subjects and the previous ones is in fact that they correct themselves spontaneously, or because of the questions asked. But in both cases the correction comes from a kind of evocation of simultaneous movements, i.e. of the concrete situation of comparison of speeds: this situation which must actually be reproduced with the aim of helping the subjects of sub-stage IIIa to correct themselves, is sooner or later imagined by the subjects IIIb themselves and this allows them to translate successive journeys into simultaneous journeys. Thus there is here a commencement of formal thinking but it is only a modest beginning which is still closer to simple representational imagination than to hypothesis properly so called. One small fact is indicative of this resistance towards hypothetico-deductive thinking of every subject at about the present level: it is no use telling them that the track represented by the drawings or by the board is considered to continue beyond the last flag and only represents one section of track, the majority of subjects persist in reasoning on what is really there, and not upon this hypothesis, and begin by declaring that the last interval will have a reduced speed, 'because they put the brake on near the foot'. This is only a slight indication, but it reveals the general difficulty of children's thought in going beyond what is actually there, in order to construct solutions in a purely deductive way based simply on the given factors of the problem, considered as hypotheses to be accepted throughout the process of reasoning. Now, it is just this hypothetico-deductive thinking which is required to correlate reversibly several separate situations, while concrete operations are enough to introduce reversibility in each case considered separately.

5. The fourth stage: Immediate solution of the problems by formal operations

We shall classify in this stage IV subjects who accept without hesitation that the time taken for each new equal distance decreases and that with each new equal time the distance traversed increases. The simplest correct solution would be that giving the successive distances the values one, two, three, and four in equal durations, and the successive durations the value one, a half, a third, a quarter over equal distances. But of course the discovery of an exact physical law is not what is expected of our subjects: it is simply an operational mechanism able to express an acceleration. From this viewpoint two types of response may be distinguished. A first type (usual age of appearance: 10 to 11 years, with some early reactions from 9 years and even one at 7; 9!) allows decreasing times simply by subtraction of a nearly constant difference:

Jos (7; 9). *It goes faster all the time.* Times: five, four, three, and two minutes. Distances: addition of a constant difference.

AL (9; 6). *Each interval faster because on the second one it has already gathered some speed.* Times: four, three, two, one minutes. Distances increase rapidly.

JAC (10; 4) same reactions: *It takes less and less time going down and with equal times? the distances are bigger all the time.*

JEAN (11; 1). Four, four, three, and two minutes. Distances grow regularly.

NAC (12; 0). Times: fifty seconds, forty-five, forty and thirty-five seconds. Distances: constant difference.

A second type of reaction reveals awareness of a more complex law:

BEN (10; 5). Times: thirty seconds, twenty-eight, twenty-five, twenty and fourteen seconds, i.e. difference of two, three, five, and six seconds for five intervals *because it gathers speed all the time.* Distances: differences increasing in the same way.

HEN (12; 2). Times: one, three-quarters, half, quarter of a minute. Distances: increasing differences.

RENA (13; 2). Times: thirty seconds, twenty-seven, twenty-four, twenty, eighteen—no, sixteen seconds. Why sixteen? *Because it's always less. For the first stretch, there is perhaps twenty metres impetus, and for the second forty metres. You always have to take away lots of seconds towards the end because you have so many more metres impetus.* Distances: he measures so as to have a difference which regularly increases: approx. ten, fifteen, twenty-three, and twenty-four millimetres.

It is evident that the subjects of the first type do not notice that their simple subtraction of times does not correspond well to their addition of the differences in distances. The subjects of the second type, who are more advanced logically, do not of course find any better solution for a problem which waited for Galileo in the history of science before its solution. But they have a clear awareness of a relation between the increases in the distances and the times. Rena in particular concentrates in quite a remarkable way upon measuring the progressive differences, which is contrary to the idea of uniform acceleration but very interesting as an indication of the capacity of hypothetico-deductive reasoning immediately achieved in this fourth stage.

Thus we may conclude that the question of accelerated movement, while not finding a concise metrical solution, nonetheless gives rise to a progressively more operational spatio-temporal construction which is entirely parallel to that which appears in the comparison of two uniform but unequal speeds.

PART 5

Conclusions

CHAPTER TWELVE

The Operations Constituting
Movement and Speed

The results of the foregoing studies show that instead of being immediately apprehended, movement and speed give rise to a long elaboration of responses at first sensorimotor, then intuitive and finally operational. These operations themselves commence with a system of qualitative 'groupments' before resulting in (extensive and above all metrical) quantitative groups. The concern of these conclusions is to give a total view of this development (setting aside purely perceptual questions), and to correlate this with the other closely related evolution studied in a complementary work: that of the conception of time.

Analysing quite genetically, with no theoretical presuppositions, how the conceptions of movement and speed are elaborated, we were in fact led to distinguish six great operational systems, operating ever more closely together, of which four depend only upon qualitative logic, i.e. present a structure analogous to that of relations and classes, but applied to infra-logical or internal transformations within the construction of the object. These are:

1. Operations of 'placement' which engender the ideas of succession in space or of order and which thus constitute a first type of qualitative grouping, necessary for the construction of the idea of displacement.

2. Operations of 'displacement' (or change of position) which from the qualitative point of view, form one single grouping with the foregoing (although mathematically the group of displacements appears to

be much more restricted than topological groups), but may however be distinguished from this as follows: in placement it is the subject who moves in order to place the objects in order, while in displacement it is actually the objects which change their position.

3. Operations of 'co-displacement', i.e. correspondence between placements or displacements, operations which simultaneously engender the ideas of succession in time, or duration and of absolute speed (i.e. relative to a stationary system, or placement).

4. Operations of 'relative displacements and co-displacements' permitting composition of correlative movements and their speeds.

5. Operations which are 'extensive', i.e. mathematical and no longer qualitative, but still not metrical, which permit construction of relations of ratios, or proportions between times taken and lengths travelled.

6. Finally metrical operations permitting measurement (through the construction of repeatable units) of these distances and durations, hence of the paths traversed and the speeds.

1. Operations of placement: Order of succession in space

Let us for a moment forget every mathematical fact we know, and confine ourselves to relating the data of experience in the simplest way such as they might be construed even by a young child without any presupposition: from such a point of view, movement appears to be above all not a distance traversed—an idea which analysis has shown to be much more abstract and derived than might be imagined—but a change of position or location. A pencil was on the table a moment ago, but it is not there any longer and is lying on the ground: so it has fallen, and this displacement is not seen as a precise path, evaluated in terms of distance, but in point of fact as a 'change of position' in which the location 'on the table' is replaced by the location 'under the table'. A marble thrown by a player rolls along the ground: the important thing is not the number of decimetres of space that it covers, but that its movement started from a base line and in particular that it arrived at the goal aimed for, i.e. reached a very definite final position. It is therefore positions or placements, and alterations of these which define movements sooner than intervals or distances traversed. This is why, when young children are asked to transfer a given linear trajectory on to a second line not parallel to the first, but with the same starting and stopping points, they concern themselves only with the stopping points and not with the distances travelled (Chapter Three). This primacy of the terminal points is in any case the natural consequence of the 'finalism' inherent in the earliest conception of movement.

Now, if displacement is thus to be conceived genetically as a 'dis-placement' in the etymological sense of the word, i.e. as a change of position (A changes its position with reference to B, if at first it precedes the latter in a given direction, and later follows after it, or vice versa), it was appropriate to begin our study of movement with an analysis of 'placements' themselves: not of course by undertaking the whole geometry of order, but simply the order of succession or orientation in any sequence of moving objects. This was the more necessary because all young children conceive of speed itself in terms, not of relations of times and distances traversed, but simply of the intuition of overtaking: A travels faster than A^1 (when both move in relation to B simultaneously and in the same direction) if A, which was at first placed to the rear of A^1, or at the same point, is finally placed ahead of it. Because speed itself, as well as movement in general, is conceived at first in terms of relations of placing, then surely the whole genetical structure which follows depends upon these relationships.

Let us then take the three balls A, B and C, which

follow one another along a tube or wire rod, in such a way that their order cannot be altered any more than that of any three points in a line. The operation constituting placement will consist of arranging them in a single direction, e.g. such as 'A comes before B', and 'B comes before C', etc. The composition of these two operations engenders a new operation: e.g. 'A comes before C' is the product of the two placements AB and BC. Let us name the direction thus defined 'direct'. The inverse operation will therefore consist of arranging the elements in the inverse direction of travel, hence (from C to A) 'C comes before B' and 'B comes before A'.[1]

One point remains to be noted. From the fact that the groupment of operations of placement is constituted by asymmetrical relations ('preceding' or 'succeeding') of a transitive type, related to one another in the manner of a 'qualitative seriation'[2] another grouping may be obtained: that of the nesting of intervals comprised between the elements in series. For example, there is an interval between A and B, which is nested within the interval comprised between A and C, etc. Now, if the relationships of order or placing are asymmetrical, the intervals consist of symmetrical relations: the interval is the same between A and B as between B and A. It is this symmetry of the intervals which allows a definition of the relationship of 'between'. E.g. between A and C there is an interval, occupied by the element B: it follows that B is also between C and A, and it is just this symmetry which is expressed in the famous axiom of Hilbert 'if B is between A and C, it is also between C and A'. Regarding the acquisition of these two complementary groupings, observation furnished a decisive result: neither is present as an inborn mechanism of thought, and a construction is implied in both of these in which there is involved first perceptual activity, then intuition and its regulations, only completed by operations. These 'grouped' operations

---

[1] The equation would therefore be $(A \rightarrow C) + (C \rightarrow A) = (A = A)$.
[2] See *Origins of the Child's Conception of Number*, Chapters Five and Six.

which are thus found only at the end of this development, appear consequently as the final form of equilibrium of reasoning, this equilibrium being due to the fact that intuitive regulations have attained complete reversibility. The child is unable at the beginning of this evolution, (as we saw in Chapter One) to deduce either the inverse order of the three balls, CBA, or that the middle object B will always stay 'between' C and A as well as 'between' A and C, whatever may be the operations carried out. In the course of a second stage the questions are solved, but only empirically, while in the course of stage III (towards 7 to 8 years) all the operations are grouped on the concrete level. As for formal operations, we were able to establish a very long time ago,[8] that one must wait till the age of 10 to 11 for the child to understand that B is necessarily at the same time 'to the left of A' and 'to the right of C' or vice versa.

Let us now suppose that the series is enclosed, in the order ABCDABCDA ... etc. The same operations of order may of course be effected, in this new case, with just this difference that a cyclic order is then obtained such that the direct sequence gives the periodicity A ... DA ... DA ... etc. and the inverse sequence the periodicity D ... AD ... AD ... etc. Analysis of these operations represented concretely by the rotation of a series of colours on a cylinder, gave the same results and at the same ages (Chapter Two).

Now, to explain the development of these operations of placement, linear as well as cyclic, it must certainly be recalled that from the sensori-motor level of intelligence and the preverbal level onwards, the subject has constant opportunities of acquiring the practical schema of each of the relations involved in groupings. For example, he may sometimes watch a succession of objects first in one direction, then in the other; or he may move his own position with respect to this series of objects, first in one direction and then in the other: and he may see this series of objects changing position (or better still may move them himself),

[8] *Judgment and Reasoning of the Child*, Chapter Three, § 4.

in one direction and the other, etc. In particular, and this has even been studied in detail on an earlier occasion,[1] he sometimes learns to turn objects round and round, thus discovering a cyclic order of succession, thanks to the rotation he gives them. In all these sensori-motor experiences, depending on a uniform organization of perceptions and habits under the direction of practical understanding, the different schemas of linear and cyclic 'placement' are thus elaborated in a similar way to the experimental situations of Chapter One and Two.

However, it is quite clear that these practical schemas are not thoughts. In other words, seeing A, the subject learns to anticipate the perception of B, and seeing B after A, to anticipate the perception of C. It is moreover possible, though this is a new learning process—which, at this psychological level, is by no means included in the previous one—that, seeing C, he learns to anticipate the perception of B etc. This practical reversibility is not only accessible to the child of 10 to 12 months: it is even the necessary condition for construction of the schema of the permanent object, i.e. of the idea that it is possible for each modification of reality to return to its starting point. But this only constitutes a restoration in practice and not a deductive operation: the child of this level is by no means able to think of the series ABC, independently of the normal perceptual phases of the action under way.

The stage I envisaged in the present work, in other words that of the elementary intuitions preceding operational thought, is thus only a period of reconstruction of the relations already acquired on the purely practical level and which have to be translated into representations (i.e. into evocative, and later anticipatory and reconstructional intuitions) independently of the activity. And just as perceptual and motor anticipations and reconstructions of actions permitted construction of the schema of practical restorations, so the progress of intuitive anticipations and reconstructions explains the regulation of the initial intuitions and the passage from stage I to stage II: the simple

[1] *Construction of Reality in the Child*, Chapter Two.

and irreversible intuition of stage I still attached to perception itself, becomes more supple through articulated intuitions, the regulations of which herald reversible operations. Consequently of course these last can only constitute a final form of equilibrium, and not an *a priori* structure, prior to any development.

Without experience, in fact, no operations are possible, since operations proceed from actions, and it is activity which leads the child to discover direct and inverse orders, as well as the invariability of the symmetrical relation 'between'. But, without the activity of the subject, translated by the gradual reversibility of actions and intuitions up to complete reversibility of the operational mechanisms, actions would not be transformed into operations and these would therefore not come to be 'grouped' into mobile and coherent systems. So the relations of experience and deduction may be seen as follows. In the earliest stages the subject is concerned with actions which are not reversible or grouped, and which do not necessarily coincide with the properties of objective reality (subjective assimilation). In fact, experience, with its modifications, constantly imposes new relationships which do not necessarily coincide with the expectations of the subject (accommodation to phenomena). These two kinds of transformation are thus orientated at the same time in different, often actually contradictory, and yet partly undifferentiated directions; while the first of these remains peripheral to the subject's activity and the last is on the surface of experience, they continually interrelate, and in a chaotic and unregulated way. Conversely, as the subject becomes better able to co-ordinate his actions, he no longer only considers the actual and immediate experience, but every past experience, and possible future experiences. There then ensure two correlated developments: (i). The subject succeeds in 'composing' his actions at first by anticipating their results more fully, and reconstructing their earlier phases (intuitive decentration and regulations) with greater accuracy, then by becoming aware of the actual conditions for co-ordination of actions and visualizations, and by regulating his anticipations and reconstructions by means of operations of combination, of seriation, etc.: this is how reversible groupments are formed, the final completion of the co-ordination belonging to the subject's activity. (ii). But then modifications of reality, instead of being perceived only in the narrow field of actual experience, produce the same anticipations and reconstructions, and so exceed the limits of perception in every way, often even the limits of what may be visualized, coinciding more and more with operations. This is why mathematical operations, which mark the final stage of this dual evolution, equally well express the transformations of objective reality along with the phases of the subject's activity: at this level of co-ordination operational transformations and modifications of reality are thus at the same time differentiated, yet in permanent equilibrium with one another.

2. Operations of displacements: Movements

All that has just been reviewed in the case of operations of placement should be repeated for those of displacement, because in point of fact they are the same operations, and it is impossible to dissociate them psychologically. In order to study the order of succession of a series ABC ... the elements A, B, C ... were set in motion outwards and returning, and rotary movements imparted to the entire system in order to analyse better the invariability of the relation 'between': movements from side to side, and rotation, are thus two displacements. We certainly could, and a mathematician would doubtless have insisted on this, have left the series immobile and traversed it mentally in the order ABC ... or CBA. But what is meant by going over a sequence mentally? For the psychologist, who analyses thinking instead of taking it as given, in the fashion of the mathematician this necessarily involves movements. If it is a movement of one's gaze, or of some perceptual organ, on to each of the successive elements A, B, C ... or ... C, B, A, clearly the direction of travel of the series will be relative to a moving object, which is the eye or the hand, etc. If it is a question of a 'pure' and 'abstract' thought, such as that of the topologist who 'traverses' in his mind's eye the infinity of the successive points of some line or other, or a curve of Jordan, it is clear that the movement is still there, but internalized in the activity of the thinking subject, whose attention is centred successively upon some points A, B, C ... or ... C, B, A, and that without this internal movement, the very idea of 'direction of travel' would have no meaning. Operations of placement are therefore always relative to a subject who changes the position of objects or of himself: this is the first point.[1]

But what is a displacement if not in fact a change of position with respect to a system considered as immobile, hence a change of place with reference to a preliminary placing? A geometrical displacement is relative to a system of co-ordinates, i.e. to a previous placing of the points of reference, in the same way as the movement of a ball in a room is, even by a baby, referred to the placing of the furniture, doors and walls. The operations of displacement are thus always relative to operations of placement: this is the second point.

This is why, even if the geometrician, reasoning as he must by setting aside the activity of the thinking subject, considers the group of displacements as a very restricted sub-group in a hierarchy of groups of which the most general is the principal group of pure topology, the psychologist, who studies the operations of the mind in their genetical order, definitely ought to consider the qualitative operations of placement and of displacement as unified

---

[1] We shall subsequently study the order of stationary series, from the point of view of the child's geometry and of fundamental topological intuitions. In the present work, which bears exclusively on the child's conception of movement, we preferred to limit ourselves to ideas of order involved in movements of objects themselves.

from the start[1] which in no way prevents him from recognizing that the metrical operations of displacement are much later in appearing, and far less general. This moreover is evidently the meaning the famous doctrine of H. Poincaré, for whom space was psychologically derived from a group of displacements made experimentally by each subject in terms of movements perceived in objects and his own displacements.

This said, the problem is then as follows: how is it possible, if the organization of displacements is begun with perceptions and bodily movements from the sensori-motor level of intelligence, that operational groupment is only completed so much later on the level of imaginative thought? In fact, one recalls the questions analysed in the course of Chapters Three and Four: comparison of the paths taken on two lines with the same starting and finishing points, but one of which is a straight line and the other zigzags: or else, a moving object setting off from O, making a series of zigzags OC, CB, BA etc. between O and D, and finally reaching the starting point again did it travel farther in the direction OD or in the direction DO? Up to around 7 years the child does not manage to dissociate the equality of the paths travelled from that of the stopping points (Chapter Three); also up to 7 years he does not accept in every case the equality of a single journey OD with a single journey, DO, and one has to wait for the level of formal operations towards 10 to 11 years, for him to understand that whatever the partial journeys (OA, AB, BC, CB, etc.) there will always be an equal distance in one direction as in the other if it returns to O.

But these curious results are self explanatory if the close relation of operations of placement and displacement is recalled. In fact, the child at first conceives a displacement not in terms of the distance travelled, but only as changes

[1] Besides, the kinship of the two kinds of operations has nothing contradictory to the view of mathematicians, if, as we saw in Chapter One, 'A movement is reciprocally univocal transformation of the points of the Cartesian place, which conserves the orientation of a curve of Jordan (simple closed curve).'

of position, i.e. in essence the 'placement' of its stopping
point: it is in this way that he will judge two unequal paths
to be equal if they stop together at the same point (Chapter Three). Consequently if D is placed at a higher level
than O instead of being situated on the same horizontal
level, the journey OD will be considered as 'longer' than
the path DO because it ends in a qualitatively different
stopping point (demanding more effort, etc.). In this same
way, if O and D are on the same horizontal straight line,
and D is farther away from the child, the journey OD will
not have the same value as the journey (DO, Chapter
Four) etc. Towards 7 years on the other hand the path
traversed will be defined by the interval between the starting and stopping points, or the segment OD, following the
form of the path, when it is a wavy or zigzag line as well
as a straight line: the child will thus construct the equation
OD=DO from the point of view of the interval, since this
is symmetrical, unlike displacement viewed as a change of
position, which is asymmetrical, i.e. $(O{\rightarrow}D] = -(D{\rightarrow}O)$.
It is only at this level that displacements can be considered
as operationally 'grouped'.[1] It only remains then to learn
how to combine mentally complex journeys which cannot
be visualized simultaneously and this will be the achievement of formal thinking (10 to 11 years).

Operations of displacement may therefore be represented as follows. Let there be a series of elements
arranged in sequence, ABCDE ... according to a linear
order. Let us first withdraw all the surrounding space, i.e.
other objects and in particular the kind of empty container
in which objects are placed, which we call space. In other
words this series ABCDE will at first form a space in
itself, hence a one-dimensional space, and nothing is kept
there (distances etc.) other than the actual order. This
posited, one element will be said to be displaced if it
changes its sequence, and follows those terms which it

[1] This is why the sensori-motor 'group' of displacements is only a
groupment from the practical point of view: motor co-ordination
of means and ends in terms of the finishing point, and not co-
ordination of hypothetical displacements. An additional problem
relating to the perception of distances has not yet been begun.

formerly preceded: e.g. A will be displaced in relation to B and to C, if it comes to occupy the place situated behind C and if ABCD ... is therefore transformed into BCAD ... so that A which preceded B and C, comes after them at the end of its displacement. The operation is moreover the same as if A remained stationary and B and C move on to the point where both are in front of A after coming behind it. It is at once evident that in a series ABCDE, each of these terms in turn, starting with B have only to be moved forward in relation to all those which precede it, in order to obtain the series EDCBA, i.e. the reverse order. From this point of view, the operations of placement and displacement form the same single 'groupment': the inverse operation of the placing AB is the displacement BA and the inverse operation of this displacement, i.e. the reversal of the inversion is the replacement AB. Basically both kinds of operation therefore simply form a single operation, and this is actually what corresponds to their psychological origins.

However, instead of separating other objects foreign to the series ABCDE ... let us now reintroduce them: it can then be seen that the element A is not only 'placed' relative to B, C, D, etc., but also in relation to all kinds of other factors: if, for example, it is a question of dolls on a table, A is indeed placed 'in front' of B, C, D etc., but it is also placed on the table, 'after' a particular groove, 'beside' a particular mark, etc. In short, it occupies a 'position', clearly defined by a collection of other relations of order, and if this position is called A_0, we observe that in the case of a displacement of A, in relation to B, C, D etc. the position A_0 does not move with it, but remains in situ, i.e. continues to be situated as before relative to the objects foreign to the series ABCDE. It is the same with B, whose position B_0 is stationary in relation to the moving object B, with C, whose position C_0 is the same with respect to the moving object C etc. Corresponding to the initial series of objects ABCDE ... there is therefore a series of positions, A_0, B_0, C_0, D_0, E_0 ... defined by the relation of these objects, not with one another, but with a system of reference formed by the factors extraneous to the series

ABCDE ... and remaining stationary while the elements of the series move. It is this distinction between the moving objects and the stationary positions which permits operations of placement and displacement to be divided into two distinct sub-groupments, in spite of their being identical at first.

As regards displacements, it is enough to reproduce the operations defined above (changes in order or placing) but applying them to the relations of the elements ABCDE ... with their positions A_0, B_0, C_0, D_0, E_0 ... We shall therefore say that A moves from A_0 to C_0 that B moves from B_0 to A_0 and that C moves from C_0 to B_0 if A has replaced C, if C has replaced B, and B has replaced A. So these are still the same 'displacements' but this time relative to a system of reference defined by positions. As for the positions themselves, these will be said to be in direct order of succession if the moving object A, or the observer (the subject's gaze etc.) travels over them according to the direction of travel A_0, B_0, C_0, D_0, E_0 ... and in inverse order if the same moving elements (object or subject) travel over them according to the direction of travel ... $E_0 D_0 C_0 B_0 A_0$.

Consequently, to distinguish operations of placement from those of displacement, it will be enough to say that the arrangement of the former is relative to a movement (displacement) of a moving object or of the observer himself (the arranged or 'placed' elements thus remaining by definition stationary), and that the movements of the latter are relative to a system of reference or placement, defined by the initial positions. But it must be fully understood that, in spite of this dissociation which in both cases separates the total reality into two compartments, one mobile and the other stationary, each of the groupments involved in fact remains dual; no order or placement exists without a movement which at the very least is that of the subject or observer and no displacement exists without an ordered system of reference.

The best proof that there is nothing artificial about this construction and that it really corresponds to the actual genetical development, is that it is easily found, not only in the facts described in our Chapters One to Four but also in all the child's behaviour relating to geometry and movement in his spontaneous activities. The child does not learn to impart order or movement to objects at school or in the experiments imposed on him by the curiosity of psychologists: he does so by spontaneously handling solid and mobile objects. Now, the solid objects ABC . . . can only be moved by replacing one with another, and so the operations of placement and displacement come to life at the same time. Undoubtedly space itself is for a long time simply the system of these relations between solid objects (but it is by no means our intention to discuss this here, for the child's geometry has remained singularly unexplored . . .) However, sooner or later, the fact of displacing objects involves the arrangement of their positions as such, $A_0B_0C_0$ . . . : it is then that this system of stationary, unoccupied positions, distinct from the actual solid moving objects, begin to form a geometric space or a specifically spatial order, as opposed to the system of physical movements, which is characteristic of the moving elements or objects occupying the space. Consequently, after conceiving displacement simply as an empirical permutation, or change of place, the child will come to define it in relation to the positions alone and no longer to the other objects. This last system seems simpler to us, reasoning as we do more readily as geometricians than as physicists, than the system of correlative displacements, or if it may be expressed in this way, of permutations of positions: but it was observed (Chapter Four) that for the child the system of multiple, interrelated displacements of the objects ABC . . . is exactly equivalent in difficulty to the system of displacements of a single moving object in relation to unoccupied positions, and is not as might have been supposed any more difficult to grasp.

This being granted, if the displacement of A consists of changing its position in relation to a placement $A_0B_0C_0$ . . . (or, also of course in relation to a multidimensional placement), the idea of the 'path travelled' will be introduced as follows, in a qualitative form long before becoming metrical. As has already been seen with reference to the relations of order or placing (1), corresponding to every series of asymmetrical relations between a sequence of elements A, B, C ... there can be matched a series of symmetrical relations defining the interval comprised between these elements. When it is simply a question of relations of order, such that the placement of the elements A, B, C ... is only defined in relation to these terms without reference to any other system, the interval comprised between A and B is empty (assuming that these two terms follow each other directly), the interval between A and C includes B (B is then placed 'between' A and C) etc., but it will nevertheless be possible to say that the interval comprised between A and C is bigger than between A and B; and the interval comprised between A and D is bigger than between A and C etc., (nesting of intervals). Now, when in addition to the relations of order given between A, B, C ... one considers those relating them to their 'positions', or which interrelate these last with one another, the idea of an interval then assumes the meaning of a distance, (the totality of possible positions comprised between A and B), and the interval thus becomes the path traversed. From the qualitative point of view, it is immediately obvious by reason of their nesting that the ratios $A_0B_0 < A_0C_0 < A_0D_0$ ... etc. But it then becomes possible to pass from quality (or intensive quantity, defined by these part-whole relations alone) to extensive quality (by comparison of A_0B_0 with B_0C_0, etc. i.e. of the successive parts with one another) and thence to metrical quantity (by choice of a unit, e.g. A_0B_0, whence $A_0C_0 = nA_0B_0$, etc.).

It is quite obvious that this construction of the path traversed from the symmetrical intervals comprised between the sequence of elements by the relations of placement and displacement, corresponds exactly to the genetically given factors provided by our Chapters Three and Four. In the course of the first stages the child is only worrying about the order of the stopping points but not about the order of the starting points. He defines the path traversed by the stopping point alone and is thus constantly misled for want of being able to construct the interval. Later, (articulated intuitions), he certainly considers the interval, but still by no means dissociates it from the order of the stopping points: the interval is thus not conceived as symmetrical hence the denial of the equality of the paths traversed on the outward and return journey. The accurate operational concept is only finally constructed when the groupment of nesting of intervals is accomplished in correspondence with the groupment of seriation of relations of order (placements and displacements to the extent that these are changes of order). But it is interesting that the concept of the distances traversed, to the extent that it is a pure distance, seems to remain for a long time in the background in relation to the ideas attached to the order of the starting and finishing points: the child will say e.g. 'stops farther ahead' in preference to 'does a longer distance' etc. Now, this is self-explanatory in terms of what has just been seen of the duality of the qualitative operations of displacement: the first kind refer only to the changes of position among the elements A, B, C ... in relation to one another, and then the interval recedes to the background, while the permutations play the vital rôle: the second kind, on the contrary, bear on the changes of order in relation to the 'positions' themselves and then only are the ideas of distance and length of the intervals brought into the foreground.

3. Operations of co-displacements: Speeds and times

We have observed so far the close solidarity of the operations of physical displacement and of spatial placement which are mutually formed in terms of one another, and so simultaneously shape the stable framework of space and its mobile content, i.e. the physical object at rest or in movement. But more is involved: this same co-ordination of placements and displacements explains the construction of the ideas of speed, of succession in time and of duration, and this is because two or more displacements are arranged at the same time, i.e. in correspondence with one another. It is this act of correlation which is named operations of co-displacement.

A single displacement and consequently a chain of displacements in turn is a movement having no speed: whether A goes from A to D in one hour, one second or at an unlimited speed, it is still the same displacement. There is thus no absolute speed in the sense of the speed of a movement in isolation (there is moreover no absolute displacement either, since if A changes place in relation to B, B may equally well be considered to be the moving element and A to be stationary). On the other hand, if the successive positions of one moving object are ordered in relation to those of another object the concept of speed necessarily intervenes and this is in fact how it appears from the point of view of its psychological origins ... for young children, speed is 'overtaking' i.e. the reversal of the order of the respective positions of two moving objects in the course of a displacement. Now, however incomplete and even misleading this conception may be in its original intuitive form (which consists of judging speeds, like movements in general, according to the stopping points only), it becomes in fact the basic principle of groupment, through regulatory corrections, and the later operational corrections which it introduces, permitting interpretation of all the qualitative relations of speed (qualitative, as opposed to extensive and metrical). This is what we shall now try to show.

Let us first see how operations of co-displacement derive from earlier operations, then we shall examine the ways in which they actually correspond to genetical development.

Given a certain number of objects placed in the order $A_1B_1C_1D_1$ . . . which are then displaced in the order $B_1C_1A_1D_1$. By virtue of the operation described so far, the order $A_1B_1C_1D_1$. may, without going beyond spatial observations and without introducing durations, be considered as a system of positions given in a single spatial bloc, or lying all together, and the order $B_1C_1A_1D_1$ . . . as another analogous system (=likewise en bloc), but incompatible with the first one without a displacement. We shall call these mutually incompatible systems 'states' or 'stills' and displacement can then be said to consist of a passage from state I to another state II. Whether this passage is made at any selected speed, and implies a (temporal) duration or no duration (imaginary infinite speed), is not in question so long as only one displacement is involved, or a chain of displacements in succession, each state being simply the spatial system considered before the transformation of displacement or else the new system resulting from the displacement.

But now let us grant that corresponding to the placements $A_1 B_1 C_1 D_1 \ldots$ there are the placements $A_2 B_2 C_2 D_2 \ldots$ given in the same state I, the objects $A_2 B_2 C_2 D_2 \ldots$ being placed e.g. each in the vicinity of its corresponding partner. This is still the same state I if, by any means (alignment over one another etc.), these correspondences may be made without displacements and the two series $A_1 B_1 C_1 D_1 \ldots$ and $A_2 B_2 C_2 D_2 \ldots$ thus being compatible within a single spatial bloc which could be called simultaneous if this were not an unnecessary reference to time (figures given on a single plane are no more designated by the term of simultaneous, than a displacement as such has a speed). And let us take it that in state II we have the order $B_2 C_2 D_2 A_2 \ldots$ with each of these four elements placed opposite (but close to) the elements $B_1 C_1 A_1 D_1 \ldots$ (A_1, thus being opposite D_2 and D_1 opposite A_2): then this is equivalent to saying that the displacement of A_1 (in relation to B_1 and C_1) corresponds to a greater displacement of A_2 (since A_2 is displaced in relation to B_2; C_2 and D_2) In this case A_2 which corresponded to A_1 in state I, moves ahead of it (in the direction of the movement) in state II, i.e. there is overtaking and introduction of the ideas of speed and time.

Let us first give the name of co-displacements to the distinct displacements which occur between two equal states I and II (hence in this example, the displacements of A_1 and A_2). On the other hand let us say that two placements $A_1 B_1 C_1 D_1 \ldots$ and $A_2 B_2 C_2 D_2 \ldots$ are in one—to—one correspondence if a correspondence can be established between each element of the first and each element of the second in the same order, i.e. if one may recognize by an unambiguous criterion in the case of each term of the first placement what the term in the same order belonging to the other placement would be. And we shall say that two corresponding terms A_1 and A_2 are displaced 'without overtaking' if their new placements are also in correspondence, while one of them is greater than the other if its new placement is farther ahead than the earlier one.

When these operations are possible (and it is at once evident what they represent in the true genesis of the child's conception of speed), four consequences necessarily follow: (i) Co-displacements are no longer characterized only by changes of position (placements), in the exclusively spatial sense of the term, but by speeds: displacements without overtaking will be of equal speeds while one displacement will have a greater speed than another according to the degree of overtaking. (ii) In addition to the spatial order of succession, ensured by the comparison which defines overtaking, there then appears a temporal order of succession, i.e. the order of the states themselves: state II comes after state I. This temporal order is distinct from spatial order since placements no longer correspond in the case of overtaking. Each state thus defines a system of 'simultaneous phenomena' (= the system of placements) 'given' together in space, and the succession of two states defines a 'before' and 'after' in time. (iii) The interval in space between two successive placements of a single element (hence the interval between the points at either end of a single displacement) forms a 'path traversed': every overtaking thus marks an inequality in the paths traversed and the greatest speed on the other hand is recognized by the fact that a longer distance has been covered between two equivalent states. Regarding these spatial intervals or 'distances' we saw in connection with operations of displacement how they may be defined qualitatively—as opposed to measurement—in terms of sub-divisions drawn either from the order of the elements under consideration (the interval AB being always smaller than the interval AC, i.e. AB<AC<AD etc., independently of any system

of reference), or else from the order of the positions
($A_0 B_0 < A_0 C_0 < A_0 D_0$ . . etc) (iv) Finally, the duration forms the general interval given between two states,
hence between the limits of the time passed (see ii above)
as opposed to the spatial sequence. Thus the duration is
recognized by the path traversed related to the speed
(=logically multiplied by the inversion of the relation of
speed). For example, if a path a has been travelled at
speed v_1 while at the same time path b ($b=a+a^1$ where
a^1 is, therefore, the difference between the two paths) is
travelled at a speed v_2 ($v_2=v_1+v^1$ where v^1 is, therefore,
the difference in speeds) its duration is then equal to that
of a, because the difference in the paths traversed a^1 is
compensated by $-v^1$ (inverse of the difference in speeds).
In fact we have $a+a^1-v^1=a$ since the difference in speed
v^1 is actually defined by a^1 the increase (or difference) in
the paths traversed ($a^1=v^1$ and $a^1-v^1=O$). Let us note
with respect to this construction of duration by means
of the path traversed related (logically and not metri-
cally) to the speed, that it is just this which the psychological study of the origins of this idea led us to discover
in young children (see *Origins of Time in Children*,
Conclusion][1].

[1] Let us point out, in a general way, that the only interest of these
various operations, which are literally childish by reason of their
simplicity, is just that they do call only for arrangement in series
and qualitative articulation, with no appeal to extensive or metrical
quantity. From a philosophical point of view, the following application might be drawn from them, to a hypothetical physical world,
whose total viscosity would render all measurement impossible,
and which would know no geometry other than pure topology. We
know that in homeomorphy (topological correspondence) comparison
is according to order alone, with no conservation of distances, because curves can expand and contract, intertwine (knots) and
so on, but not become fragmented or form straight lines, angles,
circles, etc. There is however conservation of the intervals in the
sense that between two pairs of corresponding points one finds the
same corresponding figures, since topological correspondence is a
one-to-one correspondence in both directions. Let us then suppose
that a process of expansion is transmitted from A_1 to C_1 on a first
curve and from A_2 to D_2 on another curve (A_2 corresponds to A_1 but
D_2 is farther ahead in order than C_1). If there existed a physical or
psychological means (vision, etc.) of establishing this correspon-

It is very interesting to observe that each of these operations occurs in fact in the genetic development of the idea of speed. At the beginning of this evolution in fact, only visible overtaking matters (stage I Chapters Six and Seven) without the subject taking into account any comparison of the starting points, i.e. of paths traversed in the same times. In the course of the whole of stage II progress consists of generalizing the idea of overtaking by means of correlations allowing the extension of comparisons to cases where there is unseen overtaking and above all where the moving objects catch one another up without overtaking, or even do not completely catch up, travel from opposite directions etc. In all these situations, the corrective mechanism of judgement, as we saw, consists of regulatory decentration which leads to attention being drawn to the starting points as much as on the stopping points, hence to anticipating the consequence of the movements up to a potential overtaking, or to the reconstruction of their earlier phases to the point where it is possible to establish the comparisons necessary for the establishment of potential overtaking. It is in terms of a process of this kind that the interval or path traversed begins to play a part, allowing speed to be gauged when the starting and finishing points are the same, but the paths are unequal: operational comparison then gradually supersedes merely visual comparison. Finally, in stage III speed is directly judged by comparison of starting and stopping points, i.e. by overtaking which is completely generalized, together with the intervals comprehended by these, i.e. by the paths traversed correlated with the duration.

---

dence, one might say in this case that the speed of extension is greater along the second curve since 'overtaking' is present. In an entirely elastic world it is by this single criterion that one would recognize speed. On the contrary in our world of solid objects, perception gives the child the figures of straight line, parallels, angles, etc. long before the intellectual operations of a metrical order are constructed. This is why it is so difficult to reconstruct the genetical operations founding the major categories of space and time: in fact it is a question of reconstructing operations which remain qualitative even while they are being applied to perceptual figures which anticipate metrical structures.

But of course all the foregoing remains limited to the case of synchronous movements, in whole or in part, with simultaneous starting and stopping. The comparison of movements in succession on the contrary arises from extensive and metrical operations. (See Chapters Five and Six.)

4. Relative displacements and co-displacements

There remains a special case to be examined: that of the composition of relative movement (which we dealt with in Chapter Four) or relative speeds (which were considered in Chapter Eight) both as yet arising from simple qualitative operations before giving way to metrical calculation.

A movement is a change of location (displacement) with reference to a system of fixed positions (placements). But this system of positions, while being fixed in relation to the movements considered may at the same time, itself be in motion in relation to another system of fixed positions. It is then that there arises the need to 'compose' the two movements and their two speeds with one another, and we shall try, as with the foregoing, to describe how these operations of composition are genetically formed, and not just as they may be abstracted after the event.

Let there be a system of positions A_0 B_0 C_0 . . . arranged in order, such that the stationary points of reference may serve as guides for the observer to judge the movement of a moving object on a table or on the ground. Let A_1 B_1 C_1 . . . be a system of elements likewise 'placed' in a constant order and which may either be sections of the same concrete whole (e.g. the successive parts of the board in Chapter Five) or else discontinuous elements (e.g. the cyclists in Chapter Eight who follow one another in an invariable order). Finally, let there be A_2 a moving object placed upon A_1, or in front of A_1. It is then possible to conceive of two kinds of composition, distinct but complementary and reducible to the same principle, when A_2 moves in relation to the series A_1

$B_1 C_1 \ldots$: one may compose the movements of A_2 in relation to the fixed positions $A_0 B_0 C_0 \ldots$ when A_2 is carried along by $A_1 B_1 C_1 \ldots$ or else one may compose the movements of $A_1 B_1 C_1 \ldots$ in relation to A_2 and not in relation to the fixed positions $A_0 B_0 C_0 \ldots$

In the first case, A_2 is in motion, upon the series $A_1 B_1 C_1 \ldots$ which is itself in motion upon $A_0 B_0 C_0 \ldots$ Let us then suppose that the series $A_1 B_1 C_1$ moves in such a way that A_1 reaches D_0. During this time A_2 has moved and arrived at C_1; it is clear that in relation to $A_0 B_0 C_0 \ldots$ the moving object A_2 has thus travelled the path $(A_1 C_1) + (A_0 D_0)$ and that it has therefore itself gone beyond $D_0 \ldots$: if $(A_0 D_0)$ is equivalent to the paths traversed m_1 and $(A_1 C_1)$ to the path m_2 the composition will then be quite straightforward $m_1 + m_2$, if A_2 and the series $A_1 B_1 C_1 \ldots$ are going in the same direction, and $m_1 - m_2$ if they are moving in opposite directions. In theory this composition is thus nothing other than that of displacements (see 3) except that it deals with a double displacement, i.e. with an addition or subtraction either of the relations of order or of the distances travelled. Nevertheless we observed the great complication implied by the manipulation of this dual displacement: in order to understand the relation of the movement of A_2 with $A_1 B_1 C_1 \ldots$ and $A_0 B_0 C_0$ at the same time, it is necessary to think first of all of the movements of A_2 in relation to $A_1 B_1 C_1 \ldots$ and of $A_1 B_1 C_1 \ldots$ in relation to $A_0 B_0 C_0 \ldots$ as if they were in succession, then later to relate them once more in a dual relationship. Thus it is a question of hypothetically 'decomposing' them in order to recompose them deductively: which implies by definition as it were, hypothetico-deductive thinking and formal operations. This is why even while it is analogous in its structure to the composition of simple displacements, the composition of dual displacements, or relative movements, is only acquired towards 10 to 11 years instead of 7 to 8 years, because of the vertical time-lag which exists between the same operations according to whether they are concrete or formal.

As for the second problem (relative speed of $A_1 B_1$

C_1 ... in relation to the movement of A_2) it arises from exactly the same schema. Let us suppose A_2 no longer placed upon $A_1 B_1 C_1$ ... but now alongside it and located at A_0. In a time t_1 the element A_2 which is stationary will watch $A_1 B_1 C_1 D_1$ file past (but not $E_1 F_1$ ... etc) The speed of the series $A_1 B_1 C_1$ ... will thus be a function of these few as they pass (A_1 to D_1) in a time t_1 or if preferred, a distance $d(d=A$ to D) in a time t_1. Now if A_2 travels towards (=in a contrary direction to) $A_1 B_1 C_1$ ... he will meet and pass D_1 after a time t_2 shorter than t_1 (hence $t_2 < t_1$) i.e. in t_1 he will meet and pass $A_1 B_1 C_1 D_1 + E_1 F_1$ etc. In other words again, the length d will be covered in less time (t_1) than before, i.e. the speed of $A_1 B_1 C_1$ ... will be greater from the point of view of A_2 than from the point of view of A_0. If A_2 on the contrary moves forward in the same direction as $A_1 B_1 C_1$ ... after a time t_1 he will not have been overtaken by D_1 but only by $A_1 B_1$ or C_1 and he will need a time t_3 greater than t_1 in order to be overtaken by D_1. The length d will thus be travelled in a longer time $(t_3 > t_1)$ and the speed of $A_1 B_1 C_1$ will thus be less from A_2's point of view than from A_0's point of view.

This second composition appears at first sight to be much more subtle than the first. In point of fact it amounts to the same thing, from the operational point of view, except that in the first one it is question of adding or subtracting spaces travelled in the same time, while in the latter one may either add or subtract times $(t_3 > t_1$ or $t_2 < t_1)$ with the same distance, or else the reverse (number or times met and passed, or overtaken, greater or smaller than at A_0). But from the point of view of intuitive difficulties it seems much more difficult to co-ordinate two distinct points of view (that of a mobile A_2 with that of A_0 or of A_2 stationary at A_0) than to add or subtract two movements. Now, the experiment showed on the contrary (Chapter Eight) that this second composition is acquired at the same time as the first and that as soon as formal operations are acquired which bear upon multiple displacements in succession (Chapter Three) the child is capable of acting with ease and subtlety in this problem of relativity.

5. Extensive operations:
Proportionality of times and distances covered

The foregoing operations lead to purely qualitative groupments which the child masters between 7 years (concrete operations) and 11 years (formal operations) and which are accurate as far as they go, but they remain basically inadequate for the mastery of all the elementary problems of movement and speed. In the field of displacement, they lead solely to the deduction that a path traversed will be equal in both directions of travel (or that an inverse displacement cancels out the corresponding direct displacement), that two displacements added become one displacement, and finally that a partial displacement will always be smaller than an entire displacement. But they do not permit of measurement nor even of proportionality. In the field of speeds, they lead to the statement that in two synchronous durations, the moving object travelling along the longer path has a greater speed or in the case of equal distances travelled that the faster moving object is that which takes the shorter time, but in this latter case it is also necessary for the durations compared to start or finish at the same time. Finally, from these compositions may be deduced the least or greatest relative speed according to the movement of the observer. But in none of these cases do the qualitative operations described so far permit of the measurement of the speeds and they are not even capable of extending any of the relations we have just recounted to movements which are no longer simultaneous but in succession. Consequently they remain powerless to establish the concepts of uniform speed or acceleration, intuitive though these concepts are in some respects.

In other words, the operations considered until now in Sections 1 to 4, deal only with intensive quantity (comparison of the whole and the part, viz. $A < B$ if $B = A + A^1$

as in pure qualitative logic) and not with extensive quantities (comparison of the parts with one another, viz. $A < A^1$ or $A > A^1$ if $B = A + A^1$) nor, above all, with metrical quantities (repetition of a unit $A = A^1$, then $B = 2A$ if $B = A + A^1$). But as we saw in the course of Chapters Nine to Eleven, as soon as intensive operations are formed, they expand by that very fact into extensive and metrical operations.

Particular mention must be made, in this connection, of the question of proportionality, which as we saw in Chapter Nine appears in the comparison of the speeds of movements in succession. If the distance d is travelled in a time t at the same speed as the distance d^1 in a time t^1 we have in fact $d/t = d^1/t^1$, and if the speeds are unequal, the proportions are absent. Now before trying to carry out any measurement it sometimes happens that the subject evinces a definite feeling for proportions and especially for disproportions, which poses an interesting psychological problem, i.e., the correlation of qualitative metrical operations.

We know, in fact, that the idea of proportion appears in two quite distinct forms in geometry: the metrical form, which is the equality of two numerical ratios $a/b = c/d$, and the form known as qualitative, or purely geometrical.[1] From this latter point of view, after Grassman, we say that two pairs of segments a and a_1 are proportional, i.e. a: $a_1 = b$: b_1 "if, upon two intersecting straight lines, starting from the point of intersection, segments a and b are marked off on the first, and a_1 and b_1 on the second, the straight line which joins the extremities of the segments bb_1 are parallel.' (Enriques: ENCYCL. MATH III^1 p. 58).

Nevertheless, this purely geometric form is basically different from a simple logical or qualitative proportion

[1] Based on the theorem of Thales: the segments formed by two parallel straight lines intersecting the sides of an angle are proportional or upon the theorem: the areas of two triangles are equal if they have one angle in common, and the sides adjacent to this angle are inversely proportional. These two theorems are self-evident without having recourse to the metrical concept of ratio.

(the word 'qualitative' being taken in different senses in logic and in geometry) such as 'son is to father as grandson is to grandfather', or 'Paris is to France as Rome is to Italy'. These logical correlations, it is true, likewise form the equality of two ratios (inverse ratios in this first example, or the part qualifying the whole in the second) ... But two fundamental differences make them contrast with mathematical proportions: (i) Logical correlations simply affirm the identical or equivalent nature of qualitative or intensive structures (the same inverse ratio: the same relation of the part to the whole etc. in a word, the same comparison or the same 'nesting',) whereas geometrical proportions imply intensive quantity i.e. quantitative comparison of each part with each of the others. In fact, if a_1 and a^1_1 are two segments of the value $b_1 = a_1 + a^1_1$ and a_2 and a^1_2 are two segments of value $b_2 = a_2 + a^1_2$, such that $a_1/a_2 = a^1_1/a^1_2$ then we also find that $a_1/a^1_1 = a_2/a^1_2$, i.e. a quantitative ratio between each part a and the subsequent a^1. On the other hand, logical correspondence only allows a quantitative ratio between the part a (e.g. Paris) and the whole, b (e.g. France). (ii) One can always translate a geometrical proportion $a_1 : a_2 = a^1_1 ; a^1_2$ into a metrical ratio, whence one can extract $a_1 \times a^1_2 = a_2 \times a^1_1$ whereas logical ratios are not reducible to numbers. It follows that the multiplication (Paris × Italy = Rome × France) or (son × grandfather = father × grandson) has no meaning.[1]

---

[1] Nevertheless there is a system of qualitative operations ('groupment') in which it might appear at first sight that the idea of proportion finds its logical equivalent: this is the 'grouping of the multiplications of a single species or class' to which in point of fact genealogical relations do belong (father, son, brother, uncle, etc.). Starting off from a point $+A$ (= the ancestor of a male line) let us take a certain number of straight lines (of equal length) out to the points $B_1 B_2 B_3$ etc. representing his sons. From each point B extend likewise a number of straight lines to points $C_1 C_2 C_3 C_4 C_5$ etc. representing the grandsons. One may therefore represent the 'line' in the form of an isosceles triangle with A at the summit, into which are fitted a series of other triangles at each level B, C, etc. So we can imagine on one of the sides of the triangle as a whole the relationships AB_1 and $B_1 C_1$ and on the other side of the relationships AC_n and $D_n E_n$ and we can say: The relationship 'A

In short, even in its geometric form designated 'qualitative' i.e. extensive and not metrical, proportion is an equation of two quantitative ratios which are not measured, but which are still capable of measurement, since they imply the concepts of straight line, parallels and angles, whereas logical correspondence is an equation of two intensive ratios likewise not measured but in addition not capable of measurements.

How then does the child arrive at this conception? He must of course be in possession beforehand of qualitative operations, on the concrete level, but also on the formal level: on this latter level, he has mastered it as soon as he can compare movements in succession with unequal times and equal distances or with equal times and unequal distances. But now let us suppose times and spaces both unequal as in the examples in Chapter Nine: 4 cms. in two seconds compared to 5 cms. in 3 seconds, or 4 cms in two seconds compared to 7 cms in three seconds. The child compares the differences in times (here 1 cm. and 3 cms.) Then he compares these differences of 1 or 3 cms with the distance covered by the first moving object (4 cms) and the difference of one second with the time taken by the first object (two seconds). Comparing these two he then arrives at the idea that 1 cm's difference is less in relation to 4 cms, than one second in relation to two seconds, and thus he concludes that in the first example the second object moves slower than the first and that in

---

is father of B_1' is to the relationship 'B_1 is the father of C_1' as the relationship 'A is grandfather of C_n' is to the relationship 'C_n is grandfather of E_n'. And in point of fact the straight lines joining B_1 to C_n and C_1 to E_n will be parallel. One will likewise find: the relationship AB_1 is to the relationship B_1D_1 as the relationship AC_n is to the relationship C_nG_n etc. But in fact it is still a question of logical correspondence through the placing of the part within the whole and through qualitative equation between two forms of 'nesting'.

However since the partial relations correspond in this case to the generations and one can count the latter by viewing each generation as a unit, logical correspondence may be translated in this case into a mathematical proportion. However, this translation adds number, which was not contained in the original dual relationship.

the second example the reverse is true. The feeling for proportionality is thus the product of the qualitative operation sometimes called 'the education of correlates'—(Spearman) and which is only a correlation by logical multiplication of relationships (=relationships between ratios); but this operation instead of being applied (as in 3 to 4) to the relationships of the part to the whole alone, (or of the whole to the part) is extended to the comparison of the parts with one another. It is this comparison between a and a^1 within b ($b=a+a^1$), e.g. 4 cms. and the difference of 1 cm. included in 5 cms. or 4 cms. and the difference of 3 cms. in a total of 7 cms. or even one second with one second in a total of two seconds etc. which transforms logical correlation, or relation of the ratios of part to whole, into mathematical proportion or relation of the ratios of part to part.

Now, where do these comparisons come from, of the parts a and a^1 with each other, which characterize proportion? Simply from a generalization of the qualitative operations quoted earlier. The latter are restricted to nesting the parts a_1 and a^1_1 into the whole b_1, and, once it has been observed that $a_1 < b_1$ since $b_1 = a_1 + a_1$, to nesting according to the same principle=another part a_2 into another whole $b_2 = a_2 + a^1_2$. The comparison of these two 'nesting' relations leads to the two logical comparisons: a_1 is to b_1 as a_2 is to b_2 and a^1 is to b_1 as a^1_2 is to b_2. But these comparisons of course lead to finding out if there also exists a dual relationship between the parts themselves: $a_1/a_2 = a_1/a_2$?

This is how proportionality appears: it constitutes, as we saw from the examples recalled above, a comparison of the parts with one another, hence a total comparison of two nested relations, whereas logical comparison is merely a double comparison of parts with the whole. But this last comparison, although limited, prepares the way for and leads to proportionality prior to any measurement. Comparing the way in which two parts belong to two wholes sooner or later prompts the comparison of these two parts with their complementary parts. It is this last relationship which marks the passage from the intensive to the extensive or from the qualitative to the mathematical.

6. Metrical operations

As soon as the comparison of the parts with one another has been brought into action, through the generalization of qualitative operations one random part a may then be equated to another a^1 hence $b=a+a=2a$, which leads to the choice of a as unit and constitutes a measurement. We have examined elsewhere the one which develops in the field of time and we have noted in Chapters Three and Four how the measurement of displacements appears by the transfer of an equal distance.[1] Measurement of time and path traversed then pave the way from stage III onwards, for the understanding of uniform movement, and in stage IV, for understanding the relationship between two uniform movements of different speeds, and accelerated movement.

[1] But the problems of the origins of spatial measurement is far from being exhausted in these few remarks and we hope to return to this exhaustively in connection with Geometry of the Child.

Index

THE AUTHOR

Jean Piaget is currently co-director of the Institute of Educational Science in Geneva and Professor of Experimental Psychology at the University of Geneva. For more than forty years he has been in the forefront of scientific investigation into the origins and development of intellectual faculties in the early years of life.